HOW TO CREATE MO
employees and own

(RE) CONSIDERING YOUR
SERVICE
VALUE
PROPOSITION

ANDREW
MANNING

 **SELF-PUBLISHING**

CONTENTS

HOW TO CREATE MORE VALUE for the customers,
employees and owners of service organisations

(RE) CONSIDERING YOUR
SERVICE
VALUE
PROPOSITION

ABOUT
THE AUTHOR

Andrew Manning has led or advised a wide range of service organisations throughout his career, including law firms, real estate brokers & consultants, accounting and management consulting firms, building maintenance companies, cleaning companies, energy management businesses, security and catering operations, a tool & equipment brokerage, ICT teams, social health & care organisations, charities and wedding organisers.

The customers of these organisations have ranged from multinational corporations to SMEs, national and local government, health, education and other public service providers, as well as private individuals.

Andrew has been the Chairman, CEO, COO, Non-Executive Director, general manager and consultant of various service organisations. He is an alumnus of Harvard Business School, having completed its Advanced Management Program, and has also attended its "Achieving Breakthrough Service" executive education course.

He currently runs his own business, providing interim and part-time executive, non-executive and consultancy advice to service organisations, and is an educator on strategy and service at several business schools.

Andrew is also one of a handful of people who can rightfully claim to have managed a law firm, cleaning company and riding stables! These have a lot of things in common...

He is thus a proven leader and advisor to an extremely wide range of market leading service organisations – both large and small – as well as a keen student of service. Like all of us, he is also a significant consumer of services!

WHO SHOULD READ THIS BOOK AND WHY

Who should read this book?

You should read this book if you lead, manage, work at, work with, invest in, are advising, or want to start, a service organisation.

It should be of use to general managers, functional specialists, change specialists, investors, lenders, consultants, educators, and students. It should also be of assistance to all those politicians and civil servants who are faced with making decisions about public services.

Is yours a service organisation?

According to the European Central Bank, services in 2014 (including non-marketed services, such as those provided by the Government) comprised 73.9% of the economy in the Euro area, 80.4% in the US, 74.3% in Japan, and 48.2% in China. These areas generate 49.1% of the world's GDP.

Furthermore, if you think this book isn't for you because your organisation is either a manufacturer or producer of raw materials, or a technology business, etc, then consider the following:

▶ How many services that are supplied as part of a package with a car, a computer, a washing machine, or many other types of manufactured goods?

▶ How many manufacturing, raw material based or agricultural based businesses don't have internal departments, such as accounts, IT and HR, that provide services within the organisation, and how many don't have "after sales" service departments?

And then there are public services such as health, welfare, education, utilities and defence that are provided by the Public Sector, which includes central government, local government and Third Sector organisations. In fact, organisations that provide public services can represent over 40% of GDP in some Western economies.

So, some part of your organisation is almost certainly a service provider, and therefore this book is for you too!

Why should you read this book?

We are in the most competitive economic environment for many years and this, along with technological innovations, has created the most competitive environment for services in decades.

This can be competition for customers, for employees, for other resources, for budgets, for finance and/or competition for profits.

As an in-house team, you may be competing with an outsourcing alternative or an offshoring alternative.

As a public service provider, you may be competing with other public services for a share of government expenditure, and/or against the private sector or Third Sector alternatives.

As an individual or a team, you may be competing with the internet or other technology that can replace people.

As an individual, you may be competing to get promoted or retain your job, or for more attention from your peers and superiors.

If you are a student, your aim is to pass exams. If you are an advisor, it is to provide the best advice.

If you are an investor, then you will want to better understand the service organisations you are investing in and spot opportunities before others do.

If you are a politician and/or a civil servant, you will be seeking ways to provide public services that are affordable, fit for purpose, and of sufficient quality that voters will support you.

Do service organisations have enough in common to permit analysis?

But you may ask, if services do represent such a broad range of activities, do they really have enough in common to identify some common learning points?

My experience of both working with and studying all sorts of service businesses, and as a consumer of all sorts of service, strongly suggests that they do.

Moreover, I will demonstrate that gaining an effective understanding of these common points is fundamental if we are to meet customer, employee, and shareholder/owners expectations, and to achieve a competitive advantage.

How will you benefit from reading this book?

This book will help you, and your colleagues, to ask yourselves the following questions:

▶   "Is our service good enough in an increasingly competitive environment?"

▶   "How can we improve our service to become and/or remain good enough?"

▶   "How do we avoid costly mistakes when we are looking to make changes to our service and service organisation that will enable it to remain competitive?"

The book will help you to think about these three questions in a structured, informative manner. To achieve this, it is designed to provide you with:

▶   A robust foundation for thinking about service in a holistic manner, and an understanding of the key interrelationships and trade-offs in any service and service organisation.

▶   A framework through which to consider the potential impact of changes to your organisation's strategy and business model and the value it delivers to its customers.

By sharing this book with your colleagues, you can create a common level of understanding upon which to build a better service organisation that is more able to survive and thrive. In addition, by providing you with a greater insight into service organisations, it should help you to both protect and advance your own career.

"You don't have to be a genius or a visionary or even a college graduate to be a success. You just need a framework and a dream."

Michael Dell

This book provides a framework to understand and improve service organisations. It doesn't provide a dream.

Will you think differently or more about service after reading this book?

This book is designed to provoke thinking, as it is a book of questions and a few answers. You may not agree with some or most of it, or the framework on which it is based. That doesn't matter to me, and shouldn't to you if it succeeds in sparking additional understanding and thinking that will help you to see your service organisation more clearly.

Without asking the right questions, you won't find the right answers for your service organisation.

And the right answers for each service organisation are different: you will be serving different types of customers with different services in different localities.

Furthermore, you will be competing with other service providers and if your answers are the same as theirs, you will have no competitive advantage, and so surviving and thriving will be that much harder.

"It's not what you look at that matters, it is what you see."
Henry David Thoreau

This book aims to help you see.

ACKNOWLEDGEMENTS AND THANKS

I would like to thank the following people who have directly or indirectly assisted with the writing of this book.

Ward Johnson, Dr Markus Moeller, Sheridan Broadbent, Ian MacDonald, Supun Weerasinghe, Ilias Assimakopoulos, Shiv Kumar, Neil Daws, General R. Swami, and Pavel Petrov, who were all fellow students on Advanced Management Program 182 at Harvard Business School, and were kind enough to read and comment on various drafts or parts of this book.

Dr. Andrew Green, of the University College of Estate Management, and Dr Ashley Dabson, of Henley Business School at the University of Reading, who both were also kind enough to read and comment on early drafts.

Professor Ananth Raman, of Harvard Business School, who gave me some encouragement to write the book. He also made me realise that theories and models in business literature are just tools that help you to think, not the answers to every business question that arises!

Professor Frances Frei of Harvard Business School, whose lectures, articles and book have made me think a lot about service.

Professor Das Narayandas, also of Harvard Business School, for helping me think more deeply about customer value, markets and marketing, and for generally being inspirational.

The writings of the following have also been instrumental in my learning and how I think about service, and will no doubt shine through: James L. Heskett, W.Earl Sasser Jr, Leonard A Schlesinger, Christopher Lovelock, Christian Gronroos, David Maister, Richard B. Chase, Jane Kingman-Brundage, Valerie A. Zeithaml, A.Parasuraman, Leonard L. Berry, Christine Hope, Alan Muhlemann, Jim Holden, Bradley T. Gale, Frederick F. Reichheld, Don Pepper, Martha Rogers, Abraham H. Maslow and many others. Thank you for your thoughts and ideas, and apologies if I have misunderstood or misinterpreted your views in forming my own.

Colleagues and clients throughout my career who helped, one way or another, to shape my thinking. In particular, Barry Ostle, Chris Geaves, Peter Shearman, Mike Fowler, Laurie Soden, Mike Harvey, and the development department at Edward Erdman. Eugene Bannon, Peter R. Jenkins, Bob Tee, Steve Hockaday, Rob Oldham, Stephen Harrison, Nigel Hamilton, Alan Bloom, Cedric Clapp at EY, and via EY, George Iacobescu, Gerald Rothman and Ralph Williams at Olympia & York. Leo Quinn, Colin Millar, Bob Baker, Andy Brierley, David. L. Baker, Alan Jordan, Vic Olner, Ian Stroud, Dave Gibney, Martyn Hayward, James Monteith, Phil Catlin, and Jon Bourlet at Honeywell. Mark Tincknell, Andy Darkin, David Pike, Mike Roberts, Derek Quinn, Jeff Alden, Paul Brown, Darren Frost, Dominic Holland, Stuart Pearce, Gillian French, and the GasForce team at Connaught plc. The Partners and staff at Bevan Brittan LLP, Red Kite Law and Osborne Clarke. The employees, volunteers and customers at the Avon Riding Centre for the Disabled. All at Silcoa Ltd, and Howard Piper and all at Nationwide Hire Ltd. My fellow judges of the PwC West Country Business of the Year Award. I have learned a lot about service and about business – good and bad – from you!

My great-grandparents, grandparents, parents, brother, great uncles and aunts, uncles and aunts, cousins, in-laws, nephews, nieces and friends. I have learnt a lot about life, values and service, from you.

And thanks to my wife Val (as you will see, serving Val is a theme in my life!), son Ben and daughter Sophie for allowing me the time to write and being (mostly!) supportive. Love you all.

And to the one time England Test cricketer Mike Smith, of Gloucestershire CC and Bevan Brittan LLP. Sports stars often generate books, usually about themselves or their sport. The genesis of this book came from a throwaway remark from Mike, which he has no doubt forgotten, at the end of a customer service program I was running... "You should write a book about it."

WHAT IS
A SERVICE?

INTRODUCTION

I have found that the most profound understanding of what service customers want and need – how to be good, bad or indifferent at delivering that service, how to differentiate the service from those offered by competitors, and how to make it financially sustainable – comes from going back to first principles and undertaking a close examination of what is actually meant by a service.

Such an analysis has led me to conclude that all services comprise three core common elements.

The first two chapters of this workbook focus on leading the reader to a similar conclusion. The remaining chapters then examine the implications of this for the creation of value for the customers and the service provider. I have termed these core common elements a Service Value Proposition, or SerVAL Proposition.

KEY QUESTIONS

To assist this process, I will explore the following questions in this chapter:

▶ How does the "average person" typically define a service?

▶ How do academic textbooks typically define a service?

▶ How do dictionaries define a service?

▶ What can be gleaned from these definitions?

▶ What is the Service Benefit?

▶ What is the Service Experience?

▶ What is the third element?

▶ What are the three core elements of a service?

▶ How important is each core element?

- ▶ What is a SerVAL Proposition?
- ▶ Why are the core elements of a service the principal basis of competitive advantage?
- ▶ How can you apply this to your service organisation?

HOW DO PEOPLE TYPICALLY DEFINE A SERVICE?

Whenever I run a workshop about service, I start by asking the delegates to identify as many different types of service that they can think of in two minutes. This list tends to be quite long and the typical services include:

accountancy, law, real estate broking, consultancy, banking, medicine, care, welfare, education, plumbing, landscaping, cleaning, building maintenance, retailing, logistics, hairdressing, catering, car maintenance, gardening, travel agents, advertising, IT services, hotel and spa, fitness training, refuse collection, utilities, construction, retail, airlines and government...

This is a long, broad and eclectic list that usually reflects the services they have recently purchased and their own jobs. But do these services have anything in common that can help define what is meant by a service?

When I ask this further question, delegates frequently observe that services have some common ingredients, such as people, systems and processes, tools and equipment, IT and real estate. Some will mention that there is an "output", others an "experience". They also frequently come up with a number of common characteristics of services, such as that services are "intangible" and involve some form of "activity".

HOW DO ACADEMIC TEXTBOOKS TYPICALLY DEFINE A SERVICE?

Academic textbooks on service typically adopt a similar approach in seeking to define a "service" and tend to focus on describing the characteristics of services compared to "goods".

However, these descriptive characteristics and ingredients can be so varied and so variable between different services, they are almost meaningless in terms of producing a robust definition of a service that is useful to service providers. So, when searching for such a definition, what other sources can be considered?

HOW DO DICTIONARIES DEFINE A SERVICE?

According to The Oxford English Dictionary, a service is:

"The action of helping or doing work for someone."

This doesn't provide great insight, other than mention that a service is an activity, rather than an object, and it has a customer ("someone").

In 2013, a service was defined on Wikipedia (itself a relatively new service!) as follows:

"A service is a set of singular and perishable benefits delivered from the service provider, mostly in close co-action with his service suppliers, generated by functions of technical systems and/or by distinct activities of individuals, respectively, commissioned according to the his/her needs by the service customer from the service provider, rendered individually to the service consumer at his/her dedicated trigger, and, finally, consumed and utilised by the triggering service consumer for executing his/her upcoming business or private activity."

This is a bit of mouthful, to say the least, but it gives a few more pointers, which I have highlighted in bold.

These definitions and descriptions suggest that a service is something relatively intangible that creates an output to meet a need and thus provide a benefit. They also suggest that a service involves an activity that we can experience, either by seeing it and/or by participating in it.

WHAT CAN BE GLEANED FROM THESE DEFINITIONS?

Synthesising these various perspectives and definitions, a service might therefore be summarised as follows:

A SERVICE = OUTPUT/BENEFIT + EXPERIENCE

If we consider a number of the services in the list above in these terms, then we might assess them as follows:

Service	Output/Benefit	Experience
Accountancy	Audit report/ independently verified Annual Report & Accounts and compliance with legislation	Team of auditors working with accounts departments, meetings between Directors and senior Auditors, Audit committee meetings
Medicine	Diagnosis and prescription for medication/feeling better	Phone call to doctors' surgery, waiting at the surgery, meeting and examination with the doctor, visit to the pharmacy, consumption of tablets
Refuse collection	Rubbish bins collected/waste removed, lack of smell, lack of vermin, lack of health hazards	Putting waste bins out for collection, putting waste bins away after collection (in the weather conditions prevalent), waste collection lorry making noise very early in morning, waste collection lorry blocking roads and creating traffic jams

WHAT IS THE SERVICE BENEFIT?

This analysis indicates that the output and the benefit are not necessarily the same thing. The output of refuse collection is the rubbish being collected and the benefits are the lack of smell, health hazards etc.

The output of a lawn mowing service, for example, is shorter grass.

The benefit of shorter grass may depend on the customer. The customer may be doing this to feed animals in the winter, to use a field to play sports on, to make the lawn of their house look smarter or to help them sell their house.

If the customer has sheep in his field, then he may receive no benefit, particularly if he has no plans to keep them during the winter or doesn't feed them with mown grass during the winter.

The simple example above highlights that the service output can produce different benefits in differing circumstances for different customers. Therefore, the output in some cases can produce very little benefit to the customer. This strongly suggests that the service output and the service benefit need to be considered separately.

This changes the relationship described above, as follows:

A SERVICE = OUTPUT + BENEFIT + EXPERIENCE

However, these examples also suggest that the service output itself has no intrinsic value. The fundamental value of the service is the benefit that is received, and the benefit depends on the needs of the customer. The output is something obtained as part of the service experience: you experience the audit meeting and report, you experience the prescription and the medication, you experience your waste bins being collected, or your lawn being mowed etc.

The core elements of a service can thus be reduced to the simple equation of:

A SERVICE = BENEFIT + EXPERIENCE

This is where the Service Benefit means meeting a customer's need.

WHAT IS THE SERVICE EXPERIENCE?

The "Service Experience" element of a service is what the customer experiences whilst being served by the service provider.

The Service Experience is principally derived from how customers interact with the service provider. The factors shaping that experience will include:

▸   The method of interaction, for example, via the internet, over the telephone or face to face

▸   Where they have this interaction.

▸   Which employees of the service providers they interact with, and how that person(s) looks and behaves.

▸   The frequency, depth, breadth and length of the interaction.

I explore this in more detail when I consider the Service Delivery Mix and the Service Delivery Model in later chapters.

The experience of having your hair cut will depend on how the hairdresser behaves, the condition and design of the hairdressing salon, whether the scissors are sharp and clean, whether there are magazines to read whilst you wait, how long you have to wait, whether you are offered a drink, how easy it is to book an appointment etc.

The experience of shopping in a store will depend on the location of the store, its surroundings, whether it has parking close by, the external appearance of the store, the internal layout of the store, the location of the goods in the store, the number, availability, appearance, knowledge and attitude of staff in the shop, the amount of time they spend with you, the time it takes to pay, the technology used to take payment, etc.

The experience of going for a meal in a restaurant will have similar influences as retailing, including the location, surroundings, parking, appearance, layout, number, availability, behaviour of staff, the ambience, the lighting, the music, the degree of privacy, how long it takes to be served, and of course, the appearance, taste, temperature etc of the food.

The experience of buying legal advice will vary, depending on the nature of the lawyer you engage, how they behave, how much time you spend with them, how often and how they communicate with you, whether you visit their offices or not, and if so, the location, surroundings, appearance, layout, decoration and furniture in their offices. It will depend on the length of the relationship you have with them and how often you use them. For example, is this a one-off transaction or do they carry out a lot of work for you on a regular basis?

The above examples show that the Service Experience for the same service can be quite varied, because it involves a range of ingredients and the nature and behaviour of those ingredients.

WHAT IS THE THIRD ELEMENT?

Is that it then? Is a Service something that provides a Benefit and an Experience of some kind to a customer?

Whilst that might suffice as a high-level definition, I believe that there is one further element that is fundamental to understanding what customers want from a service and how they evaluate it. This other element also impacts the financial viability of delivering the service.

This other element is the cost to the customer who receives that Benefit and Experience, which includes, but is not limited to, its price. I will expand on this in Chapter 2. The importance of the cost to the customer can be considered as follows. For any service, if a customer pays a high price then they are likely to expect a significant Service Benefit and excellent Service Experience, and will be disappointed if they do not receive it. However, they may be prepared to accept a lower (but adequate) Service Benefit and an average (but adequate) Service Experience for a lower price.

Low cost/low price airlines are a great example of this equation at work. The Service Benefit is the same as a "standard" airline, as you are transported to the same destination (and as someone quipped in a workshop I ran, you don't want your airline to "go the extra mile"), but the Service Experience is poor compared to premium airlines and the price low. This is an acceptable trade-off for many people, particularly with short flights.

However, without the price element of the equation, you would think that the service was poor, as the experience is noticeably worse than that provided by standard and premium airlines.

It is important to remember that all services involve a price, whether the service is sold commercially, delivered as an in-house department, or is a public service. The price for an in-house service is their budget, which is allocated as an overhead to other departments. The price for public services is national and/or local taxes.

WHAT ARE THE THREE CORE ELEMENTS OF ANY SERVICE?

For the purpose of this book, and to aid your thinking about service, a service will be defined as:

*An activity performed by an individual or an organisation ("the service provider") for an individual or an organisation ("the service receiver"- more commonly called "the customer" or "the client") that provides that customer with some form of **benefit** and an **experience**, typically for a **price**.*

A service thus can be considered as containing three core elements that are involved in a "trade-off" relationship, as follows:

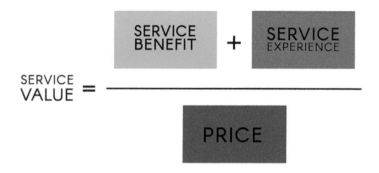

This is a value equation, which I have termed the SerVAL Equation.

Note: A SerVAL Equation with a "value" of less than one means the customer is paying too high a price relative to the service they are receiving. That isn't sustainable. A SerVAL Equation with a value of greater than one means the service provider is providing a better service than is necessary for the price they are receiving. That may not be sustainable and is certainly not optimal from the service provider's perspective.

HOW IMPORTANT IS EACH CORE ELEMENT?

Are any of the three core elements of the Service Value Equation more important than the others? How about the Service Benefit compared to the Service Experience?

At the most basic level, this question is best answered by a quote from Michael Hammer of the Massachusetts Institute of Technology:

"A smile on the face of a smartly dressed limousine driver is no substitute for a Car."

No matter how good the service in a restaurant is, if the food is poor you will not go back. No matter how friendly, smart and reliable your cleaner is, if he does not clean the floor well, then you won't be happy. No matter how prestigious and experienced your lawyer is, if she does not complete your transaction then you may sue her.

So service organisations must deliver the required Service Benefit. The key element of a service for a customer is the benefit that he or she receives from the service.

The value of this Service Benefit must also be reflected in the price paid for it. If the price is too high, then the Service Benefit is not worth having.

The Service Benefit is thus the most important element of the Service Value Equation. It is the core reason for procuring the service, but it cannot be considered in isolation from the Service Price.

Nor can it be considered in isolation from the Service Experience. Given the choice between two service providers that generate the same Service Benefit for the same Price, the customer will choose the good Service Experience over the poor one.

Furthermore, unless the Service Benefit is binary, i.e. the customer either receives the benefit or doesn't, it is likely there will be a degree of trade-off between the Service Benefit and Service Experience.

I recently went into my bank, whose premises were a bit small and cramped, and it felt that the other customers were too close when I was discussing my business.

The male staff in the branch had silly haircuts and poorly done up ties. Whilst they were friendly and helpful, did I really want to trust my money with the staff who were so poorly dressed?

However, the Service Benefit was good, as they gave me some cash very quickly. So this was a poor Service Experience with a good Service Benefit.

The same day, I went to my local car dealership to get a potential fault checked. The showroom was spotless, modern and gleaming, and I was given a great cappuccino, newspapers to read, a TV to watch, and was attended to by very smart staff.

When they finished looking at the car and decided that there was no fault, they mentioned that one of the light bulbs had failed but they hadn't replaced it.

Did I want to book in to get it fixed? Great Service Experience, poor Service Benefit, as they could easily have changed the bulb whilst checking the car.

I did get some benefit, however – the peace of mind gained from knowing that the car had nothing fundamentally wrong with it.

This trade-off might be considered thus:

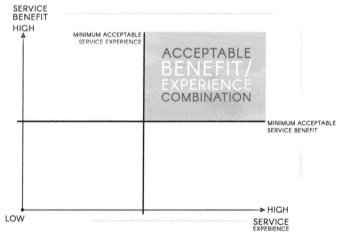

SERVICE BENEFIT v SERVICE EXPERIENCE
TRADE OFF

So, whilst the Service Benefit is the most important of the three core elements of a service, it should not be considered in isolation, as if forms part of a holistic relationship.

I discuss this trade-off in more detail in Chapter 9, where I consider how customers evaluate the quality of service they receive.

WHAT IS A SerVAL PROPOSITION?

The Service Value Equation that a specific service organisation offers to the market and its customers is that organisation's particular value proposition. I term this its SerVAL Proposition.

IT IS THESE CORE ELEMENTS THAT FORM THE PRINCIPAL BASIS OF A COMPETITIVE ADVANTAGE. BUT WHY IS THIS THE CASE?

Fundamentally, a competitive advantage results in:

▶ Customers choosing an organisation's SerVAL Proposition in preference to its competitors' propositions (or because they have no choice).

▶ The service organisation making equivalent or superior financial returns to its competitors, as a result.

The latter is clearly important because any fool can benefit its customers by selling products or services cheaper than its competitors. But, as a result, it will make less profit than its competitors.

By using the model of a service developed above, a competitive advantage comes from having a SerVAL Proposition that is different from competitors and valued by its targeted customers (which might be a particular market segment) more highly than the SerVAL Propositions provided by its competitors.

This differentiation and customer value creation can occur in a range of combinations. For any service, in simple terms, these combinations are:

Service Benefit	Service Experience	Service Price
Higher	Same	Higher
Same	Different	Same
Lower		Lower

The difference in potential Service Benefits sits on a scale from zero upwards, as does the potential difference of Service Price. The opportunities to offer a different Service Experience are very wide too. This provides enormous scope for differentiation!

These combinations may suit the needs of the whole market or just those of a niche market. This can be considered as follows:

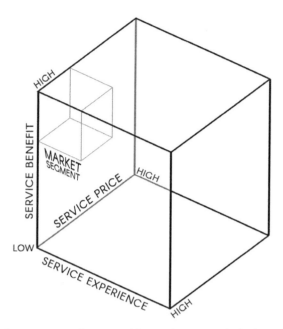

The other aspect of competitive advantage is being able to deliver the chosen SerVAL Proposition in a manner that generates superior financial returns to the service provider. This also reflects the chosen Service Delivery Mix and Service Delivery Model, which I will examine in Chapters 3 and 5.

SUMMARY

There are no universally accepted definitions of a service. However, commonly used descriptors, various academic sources, and the application of a customer-focused mindset suggests that all services can be fundamentally considered as containing two core elements.

▶ A Service Benefit – why people want the service.

▶ A Service Experience – what people go through and feel when they receive the service.

However, to assess whether the Service is good, bad or indifferent, and to compare it to others, and whether or not they can afford the service, it is also important to consider the Price they pay to receive the Service Benefit and Service Experience.

A service can therefore be very usefully defined as a value proposition containing three elements:

These three core elements form the basis from which a competitive

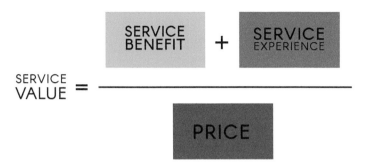

advantage can be developed and are the underlying basis that customers use to compare services and service providers. To help you to start considering your organisation's service (s) in this manner, I have set out some questions below for you to consider regarding your service organisation. You should also consider the same questions for your key competitors.

CHAPTER ONE:
KEY QUESTIONS TO CONSIDER

▶ What Benefit does your service provide to your customers?

▶ What does your Service Experience involve?

▶ What Price do you charge for your service?

▶ How does the Price compare to the levels of Benefit and the Service Experience that is received by your customers?

▶ Is this good value?

▶ Is your SerVAL Proposition attractive to the whole market or just to certain segments?

A CORE MODEL OF A SERVICE

INTRODUCTION

In Chapter 1, we identified that a service can usefully be defined as a Value Proposition, containing three core elements, namely a Service Benefit, a Service Experience and a Service Price. These core elements are the principal sources of competitive advantage for any service organisation.

In this chapter, I am going to consider these three core elements in more detail, through addressing the following key questions.

KEY QUESTIONS

▶ Can additional Service Benefits be included in a Service?

▶ Are all the Service Benefits tangible?

▶ What are the different elements of the Service Experience?

▶ Does the Service Price just involve the price paid to the Service Provider by the customer?

▶ Is there a fourth core element in a Service?

▶ What does the detailed SerVAL Equation look like?

▶ What are the benefits that service organisations can gain from applying this model?

▶ How can you apply this to your service organisation?

CAN ADDITIONAL BENEFITS ALSO BE PROVIDED AS PART OF A SERVICE?

In my experience, and I am sure in yours too, the benefit that a customer can receive from a service is not necessarily limited to a single core benefit. Services can also include "add-on" benefits for the customer. These might be considered as "enhancing" benefits. This can be best demonstrated by way of some simple examples.

The output of a haircut is shorter hair. The actual benefits of shorter hair can include increased safety as it will not get caught in things or it is easier to wash and comb etc. The haircut can also involve a "free" hair wash, shampoo and dry. These are enhancing benefits, as the customer didn't buy the service to get their hair washed, but to get a haircut.

I used to manage a gas appliance maintenance business that provided maintenance and repair services for central heating boilers, the core benefit of which was warm buildings and, for commercial buildings, compliance with UK legislation. But it would also test, for a small additional price, the level of corroded materials (rust) in the sealed water system, and drain and replace the water if there were high levels of corrosive. The benefits of this were greater heat output and better water circulation (and hence, heat circulation) and lower heating costs, i.e. improved system efficiency. This was not a service that customers would generally buy separately because the cost/benefits were too low, but the marginal cost/benefits to them as part of another service were good.

The opportunity to provide enhanced benefits creates an opportunity for a service provider to add more value to its customers and differentiate itself from its competitors.

ARE ALL THE BENEFITS TANGIBLE?

Services don't just involve tangible benefits, and indeed these tangible benefits may be quite limited. Again, a simple example demonstrates this point.

There are minimal health and safety or personal grooming time benefits from getting your hair cut a couple of inches if you are an office worker, so why get a haircut at all? The reason is the psychological benefit. The customer may also be looking for a hair style that makes him feel good about himself and is fashionable. It, therefore, addresses the individual's need for social acceptance, to belong to a group, and be admired.

In the above example, the psychological benefit of the haircut (being fashionable) is more important than the physical benefits of shorter hair and, therefore, actually becomes the core benefit.

Another way of considering the existence of psychological benefits is to assess whether the hairdresser who provides the service is also important to the customer. For example, the customer may want to use a hairdresser he knows will deliver the haircut he expects (his "usual" hairdresser), or one who has a fashionable reputation. There can ,thus, be a psychological benefit from the hairdresser who actually provides the service.

The Service Benefit element of the Service Value Equation might, therefore, be more fully represented as follows:

For some services, the core benefit may be psychological.

WHAT ARE THE DIFFERENT ELEMENTS OF THE SERVICE EXPERIENCE?

The Service Experience is also comprised of a number of different sub-elements.

Firstly, there is an "enabling" experience, by which I mean the activities and customer interactions that are necessary to deliver the core Service Benefit.

Secondly, there can also be an "enhancing" experience. These are those activities or "add-ons" that make the overall experience a little better. Consider the following example.

The enabling experience in the hairdressers is based around the location of the salon, a receptionist to take bookings, a waiting area and basic hairdressing equipment.

The enhancing experience is the salon's provision of magazines, coffee, local gossip, friendly staff, parking etc.

There are also two other key sub-elements to the Service Experience. And, importantly, these may be outside of the control of the service provider, and yet will have a huge impact on the overall service experience!

The first of these is the pre-service experience – what the customer experiences in order to receive the service.

If the pre-service experience before a haircut involves a long drive, the risk of being stuck in a traffic and potentially struggling to find a parking space, then the customer may consider the overall potential service experience to be poor, and so could decide against purchasing.

Some of this pre-service experience is clearly outside the service provider's control (although they could move location), whilst other elements of it could be controlled by the service provider; for example, being able to order a service over the telephone or online.

The second key sub-element is the post-service experience, e.g. the journey home and other factors mainly outside the service provider's control.

The service provider can control some of the post-service experience, however; for example, sending their customers marketing communication, customer satisfaction material and additional information.

The pre and post-service experiences are likely to vary from customer to customer, and will also differ from time to time. This may assist with market segmentation. For example, customers with a long way to travel that choose to travel by car to the hairdressers may not be a good target market.

Therefore, the Service Experience contains four elements, as follows:

The Service Experience itself can confer both actual and psychological benefits in support of the core Service Benefit.

Does a hairdresser make people feel "extra good" about themselves and want to pay a premium charge for a "better experience" if he's located in the smartest part of town, gives customers a lot of attention, the best coffee, the latest magazines to read, and a seat in the window, where everyone can see them getting their hair cut by a "noted" hairdresser?

The Enhancing Benefit and Enhancing Experience can be very closely related, but I have kept them separate for the purpose of clarity of thinking in the Model.

DOES THE PRICE FOR A SERVICE JUST INVOLVE THE PRICE PAID TO THE SERVICE PROVIDER?

Price is the third key element of the Service Value Equation, as it provides the context to the levels of Service Benefit and nature of Service Experience that is received, i.e. whether or not it is worth the customer buying the service. It also has an impact on whether people can afford to buy the service. In summary, whether customers are willing and able to purchase the service. However, is the price element of the Service Value Equation simply the direct price that is paid by the customer to the service provider for the service, e.g. the actual cost of the haircut or a holiday? The answer is "no, it is not". Again, this is well illustrated by an example.

In order to book my summer holiday, I used to take my whole family (wife, two teenage children, two dogs) in my car to our local town. Having parked, we walked between several travel agents, joined the queue to see a sales representative, reviewed a number of options, made a selection and paid the price of the selected option by using my credit card. The only day we could do this was on a Saturday, and as a consequence, I missed watching my favourite soccer team play. I also developed a great relationship with the travel agent that we normally used – she is a friend of the family, and she has organised great holidays for us for many years.

There was a direct cost for this holiday – the price I paid. However, there was also an enabling price that I paid – the direct cost of fuel for the car to travel to the local town, the wear and tear on the car, and the direct cost of parking. There was also the time involved with travelling to the travel agents, waiting there, the inconvenience involved in trying to find a parking space etc, as well as missing the soccer match.

These days, I purchase my holidays from home via the internet, at any time of the day or night. I may pay the same direct price for the holiday, but my enabling costs, however, are much lower – the cost of using my computer and the internet, compared to the cost of fuel and parking the car. The amount of time and inconvenience involved is much less (unless the website crashes!). I get to see the soccer match, but I am worried about the impact on my relationship with the travel agent, and the impact on her business as a friend. Moving to the internet has cost me a degree of worry and guilt, which is another price I have paid.

The price element of the Service Value Equation should, therefore, be considered in terms of the total price to the customer, that is the:

▶ Direct price paid for the service

▶ Enabling cost to purchase the service

▶ Opportunity cost of time and resources utilised to purchase the service

▶ Amount of inconvenience involved with purchasing the service ("the convenience factor")

▶ The psychological price paid.

In addition, there can sometimes be a real cost of changing service provider. For example, the fee a bank or mobile phone provider may charge if you seek to change to another service provider. These are known as "switching costs". These don't just apply in business to consumer services. The time, cost and inconvenience of re-procuring a service can be considerable in business-to-business situations as well.

The "Service Price" is, thus, a "bundle" of six components.

DIRECT PRICE

DIRECT ENABLING COST

TIME OPPORTUNITY COST

(in)CONVENIENCE FACTOR

PSYCHOLOGICAL COST

SWITCHING COST

The "Service Price" is, thus, best considered as the **Total Cost to Customer**.

In the internet holiday purchasing example above, the actual Service Benefit has not changed, as I have bought the same holiday. But potentially the psychological Service Benefit has changed, as I have lost the reassurance I would have gained from my trusted travel agent that I am heading to a great destination. However, the Service Experience has changed significantly, not just from a face-to-face purchase to a computer screen-based purchase with a lack of human contact, but also in terms of the pre and post- purchase experience, and the enabling experience. The direct price hasn't changed, but the enabling and psychological costs have, along with the opportunity cost and the inconvenience factor. So this is a totally different value proposition.

Different Service Benefit, Service Experience elements and Total Cost to Customer bundle elements can be found in lots of examples, and not just by comparing internet-based services with more traditional services. The simple example below illustrates some basic potential differences between two common forms of food retailing.

If a food retailer offers low prices, a wide range of foods and a great service experience, but is located in an out of town shopping mall, their customers may face significant travel costs and a long journey fraught with problems, thus generating a high inconvenience cost. How do they compete with a more local convenience store? Traditionally, the solution has been lots of free parking. But traffic volumes have increased significantly since the store was built, and so the car park is now often full, and now there is the choice of web-based food retailers that provide home deliveries...

IS THERE A FOURTH CORE ELEMENT IN A SERVICE?

I believe there is one further key element of a service – the brand of the service delivery organisation. It might be considered as the "wrapper" for the service.

In particular, the brand can be a key provider of psychological benefits / costs to customers.

I can accept that the Brand might be considered as part of the

Service Delivery Mix, and indeed it should be. However, to support our thinking about services, I believe it is also beneficial to consider it as part of the SerVAL Proposition.

Think of the importance of Brand for the service benefit and service experience that customers expect from service providers, such as McKinsey, Goldman Sachs, Virgin, Google, Microsoft, McDonald's, AT&T, Visa, Facebook, Amazon, Disney, MasterCard, Walmart, Starbucks, etc.

WHAT DOES THE DETAILED SERVICE VALUE EQUATION LOOK LIKE?

The detailed Service Value Equation can, therefore, be considered as follows:

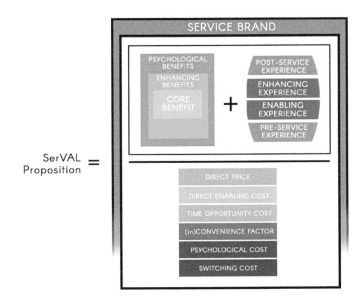

WHAT ARE THE BENEFITS THAT SERVICE ORGANISATIONS CAN GAIN FROM APPLYING THIS MODEL?

I have found that the SerVAL Model provides considerable insight into the following fundamental issues for service organisations. These are all explored in more detail in later chapters.

Understanding and meeting customer needs

All service organisations' individual SerVAL Propositions to their existing and potential customers are core to their survival and ability to thrive. Failure to consider the detail of their SerVAL Proposition is likely to mean that service organisations do not have a true understanding of why customers buy, or don't buy, their services or those of their competitors, and why their customers may be satisfied/dissatisfied with the service they receive.

Furthermore, service organisations must deliver a SerVAL Proposition that meets the needs and budgets of their customers or no one will buy their service. The consequences of just focusing on direct price and not considering the Total Cost to Customer for the Service can be significant. It can be the difference between winning, losing and retaining customers. For example, the rapid growth of internet-based and related home delivery retail services is having an enormous impact on the relative Total Costs to Customers between different retail service providers.

Understanding local market implications

The SerVAL Proposition model can also facilitate analysis of why some services may be successful in some markets and not in others, or the changes that need to be made for them to be successful in different markets.

In different markets, people may require different Service Benefits, levels of Service Benefit or different Service Experiences. This may be for a range of reasons, such as the Benefit is not as great in a particular area for a particular reason.

I have direct experience of a service being successful in one market, but not in another. Energy saving services can generate high benefits in markets that consume a lot of energy; for example, where buildings utilise high levels of air conditioning or heating due to local climatic conditions, but low benefits when this isn't the case.

The level of benefits also fluctuates when the energy prices change.

This may reflect local culture, as cultural variances can have an impact on the Service Benefit and Service Experience required by customers. These can be significant from a number of different perspectives, including national and regional, as well as the language, religious, values, ethnic and ethical perspectives. This can be very important for multi-regional and multinational services, as well as in large urban areas with a diverse population base.

Demand and supply conditions may also be different in different local markets, and hence direct price can vary. Furthermore, all the other parts of the Total Cost to Customer may vary too. The inconvenience factor and direct enabling cost, and the time opportunity cost for a service may change due to, say, the availability of, and cost of, local public transport networks.

The attractiveness of any SerVAL Proposition can, therefore, vary considerably from market to market, location to location and culture to culture. Analysis in this manner can facilitate market segmentation and market entry/exit and/or service development and delivery decisions.

Obtaining and retaining a competitive advantage

Service organisations must also seek to deliver a SerVAL Proposition that is different from their competitors, so that their selected group of customers chooses to procure their service, rather than their competitors'. Service organisations can compete on each, all, or a combination of the three core elements and sub-elements of the Service Value Equation.

Creating a sustainable economic model

Service organisations must be able to provide their SerVAL Proposition in a sustainable economic manner. This is key, as anyone can provide lots of Service Benefit, a great Service experience, a low price and hence, huge customer value until they run out of cash.

Understanding the costs associated with creating and delivering the SerVAL Proposition, and the impact of cost savings on the SerVAL Proposition is of fundamental importance to the survival and success of service organisations. For example, I will show in later chapters how cost savings can actually lead to margin reductions, rather than increases, due to the impact on the SerVAL Proposition.

It is also very important to understand that the way that the SerVAL Proposition is delivered can impact the longevity of customer relationships, and hence, in combination with margins, the long-term value of customers.

Understanding the implications of change

Whilst most service organisations have achieved a Service Value Equation equilibrium over time – or they would not have survived – in an increasingly dynamic, competitive market, this equilibrium is under constant pressure to change: with customers wanting more for less, and competitors giving them this.

This competitive pressure means that service organisations must change their SerVAL Proposition to deliver more value to their customers, i.e. provide a better combination of Service Benefit, Service Experience and Total Cost to Customer, whilst retaining their economically sustainability.

When making such changes to their SerVAL Proposition, or making changes that will enable their current SerVAL Proposition to become more profitable, the Service Value Equation allows service organisations to consider the impact of the proposed changes for their customers and their own competitive position in a holistic manner.

In practice, this doesn't often seem to occur and, in a quest for lower costs to enable lower prices or to boost their margins, service organisations seem to change their Service Experience (inadvertently or deliberately) without considering the impact on their SerVAL Proposition in the round.

This is a particularly risky approach because, in my experience, the Service Experience and the Price are typically the elements of the Service Value Equation that customers comment most frequently on.

I explore this significant issue in some detail in Chapter 12.

"The shop assistant was so rude", "your receptionist is so friendly", "the plumber arrived exactly when he said he would", "my lawyer really understands my business", "your offices are so nice", "it is really difficult to park at that shop", "he is so unreliable – sometimes he never turns up at all", "my real estate agent is so poorly dressed", "she really knows what she is talking about – did you know she went to Harvard?" "my accountant almost didn't get my accounts in on time as his computer system kept crashing, and the reports he sends me are so badly presented I can hardly read them", "my bank is brilliant; their website is really easy to use and I can transfer money whenever I want."

It was expensive, cheap, good value for money...

The SerVAL model allows service organisations to understand the potential consequences for their SerVAL proposition of any organisational changes they plan.

Understanding the Public Services challenge

The Service Value Equation also allows a greater understanding of the challenge the government faces in delivering public service – whether directly, or through an outsourced service provider.

I have discussed in Chapter 1 how the Price element of the Service Value Equation acts as a key part of the customer's evaluation of the value they receive: it provides an economic perspective to the Service Benefit and Service Experience. However, with many public services, the price is not a direct price. Instead, it is an indirect price (taxation).

Therefore, customers do not directly connect the price and the service, and assume they are "free" to consume as much as they can or think they deserve. They may expect Service Benefits and a Service Experience that are far higher than the actual, indirect price they are paying. This can (and does!) lead to huge dissatisfaction with public services. Taxpayers want better health services, better schools, better roads, higher pensions, stronger military etc without necessarily wanting to pay for them.

Furthermore, we may all have a perception of the overall price of public services – the overall level of tax we pay – and then apply this to a particular public service. For example, we may think taxes are high and that we should get better library services, without understanding that the vast majority of the taxes pay for, say, health and defence. This separation of price from the Service Value Equation is a huge challenge for Public Service providers.

This challenge is exacerbated when public services are being partially funded through budget deficits, as the level of Service Benefit and/or Service Experience may need to be reduced without any impact on the price, i.e. taxes remain the same, or even rise, in cases where such budget deficits are unsustainable.

Understanding the in-house team challenge

A similar challenge (as identified above for public services) is faced by in-house service organisations. Typically, they are funded as part of an overall overhead allocation, rather than specifically for their service. There is often no ready price comparison either, which can give in-house customers the impression of a "high cost"/"low benefit"/"poor experience" from in-house service providers.

Cost benchmarking is often used to address this in-house team challenge, but such an approach only looks at one element of the Total Cost to Customer – the price (overhead allocation to their budget) and ignores the Service Benefit and Service Experience element of the SerVAL Equation.

WHAT ABOUT YOUR SERVICE ORGANISATION?

To help you to start considering your organisation's service (s) in this manner, I have set out some questions (below) for you to consider regarding your service organisation.

You should also consider the same questions for your key competitors.

CHAPTER TWO:
KEY QUESTIONS TO CONSIDER

▶ What is the core Benefit that you provide for your customers?

▶ What enhanced Benefits do you provide for your customers?

▶ What enhanced Benefits could you provide for your customers?

▶ What does your Service enabling Experience involve?

▶ What Service enhancing Experiences do you offer?

▶ What Service enhancing Experiences could you offer?

▶ What is the pre-service Experience of your customers?

▶ Does this apply to all customers or clearly identifiable groups?

▶ Can you improve this pre-service Experience?

▶ What is the post-service Experience of your customers?

▶ Does this apply to all customers or clearly identifiable groups?

▶ Can you improve this post-service Experience?

▶ What Price do you charge for your service?

▶ What enabling costs do your customers experience?

▶ Does this apply to all customers or clearly identifiable groups?

▶ What time opportunity costs are experienced by your customers?

▶ Does this apply to all customers or clearly identifiable groups?

▶ What inconvenience factors might your customers experience?

▶ Does this apply to all customers or clearly identifiable groups?

- What psychological costs might your customers experience using your service?

- Does this apply to all customers or clearly identifiable groups?

- What switching costs might your customers experience in moving to use your services?

- Does this apply to all customers or clearly identifiable groups?

- How does the Total Cost to Customer compare to the levels of Benefit and the Service Experience received by your customers?

- Is this good value?

WHAT ARE THE VITAL CHARACTERISTICS OF A SERVICE?

INTRODUCTION

In Chapter 1, I mentioned that leading textbooks typically identify five key common characteristics of services. These are:

- Intangibility
- Perishability
- Simultaneity
- Variability
- Inseparability.

In this context:

"Intangible" means services do not have "solid substance" and therefore cannot be touched, gripped or handled.

"Perishable" means that things don't last andor cannot be stored.

"Variability" means that each service received tends to be different from previous ones.

"Simultaneity" means that the service tends to be provided and consumed at the same time.

"Inseparability" means that the service cannot be separated from the person that delivers it, and thus refers to the customer/service provider interaction.

I will express these characteristics in a manner that is easier to remember, namely:

V ariable

I nvolvement (inseparability)

T angible

A ttainment period (simultaneity, or otherwise, of service consumption and benefits)

L asting (perishable)

In this chapter, I will consider how these characteristics can significantly impact the SerVAL Proposition. I will also demonstrate how gaining an understanding of these characteristics – and seeking to address them – can help service organisations to create value for their customers and their shareholders and, therefore, gain a competitive advantage.

SOME KEY QUESTIONS

To assist with this, I will examine the following key questions:

▶ What are the implications of services being "intangible"?

▶ Are services really perishable, and, if so, does it matter?

▶ Why are services so variable?

▶ Are services always produced and consumed simultaneously?

▶ Is the customer / service provider interaction important?

▶ How can you apply this to your service organisation?

WHAT ARE THE IMPLICATIONS OF SERVICES BEING "INTANGIBLE"?

The academic argument tends to be that "goods" are tangible and services are "intangible". However, as shown below, "Intangibility" is not a robust definition of a good versus a service, as services can vary enormously in intangibility (and goods can often come "wrapped up" in a service).

There are clear variations in degrees of intangibility. The diagram below (taken from 'Service Operations Management-Strategy, Design and Delivery', Hope and Muhleman, Prentice Hall, 1997) illustrates this.

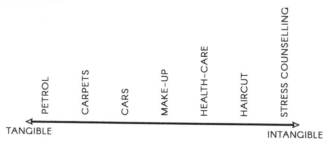

DEGREES OF INTANGIBILITY

So, some services are more intangible than others. It is also important to consider which element of the service is more or less tangible. Is it the Service Benefit that is intangible, the Service Experience or both? For some services, both Service Experience and the Service Benefit can be quite intangible and/or difficult to prove. For others, the Service Experience can be quite tangible, but the Service Benefit much less so. The most important question of all is whether this matters or not! It does! This is because the intangibility of services has some very important implications for service organisations and their customers.

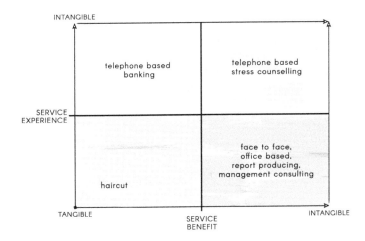

Why intangibility matters

Firstly, customers more readily purchase, or more readily value, something that is tangible, as they can "kick the tyres" and know what they are getting. This means, with all other things being equal, the more tangible a service provider can make the Service Benefit and the Service Experience, the easier it should be to persuade people to purchase it. Tangibility provides customers with a greater degree of assurance about exactly what they are purchasing.

Once, while bidding for a large building services maintenance contract, at the final selection presentation, we were up against a strong competitor whose CEO was an excellent presenter of visions, concepts, values and partnerships. He was bound to "wow" and excite the panel he was presenting to.

We decided to counter this by taking along the building services engineer, complete with his overalls and toolbox, to present. Here was the actual person who would undertake the tangible actions to maintain the equipment. We won the bid, and whilst taking Neil wasn't the only reason we won, he made a difference and it made our service offering less nebulous.

Secondly, when something is more tangible, it is easier to remember and may even act as a permanent reminder of the purchase. Customers more readily remember the value they obtained from the purchase if they also have a tangible record of it. This is particularly important because services can also be "perishable", as discussed in the next section below.

A tangible record of previous service delivery success can be very important in a business-to-business service environment, where the service provider's individual customer contacts are likely to change over time.

This means that they won't necessarily know what has been achieved for their organisation in the past, nor the nature of the experience received. This also applies to services bought by consumers on an infrequent basis.

One of the challenges for internet-based service businesses (particularly internet-based retailers) is:

▶ How to make what they are offering tangible in advance of purchase, so that people know what they are going to get.

This can be achieved in a number of ways, including:

▶ A guaranteed returns policies, so that it can be sent back if the purchaser doesn't like the goods received. This makes the upfront lack of tangibility less of a risk.

▶ Selling trusted brands, so that the purchasers can have confidence in the product.

▶ A high-quality website with strong images, sounds, etc. that create "virtual" tangibility.

▶ A trusted web-based retailer brand, so that purchasers have confidence in what they will receive.

▶ "Bricks and Mortar" outlets so people can actually see and touch the goods prior to purchase.

Therefore, an important objective for a service organisation should be to make its SerVAL Proposition as tangible as possible in order to make it easier to sell and more memorable post-service.

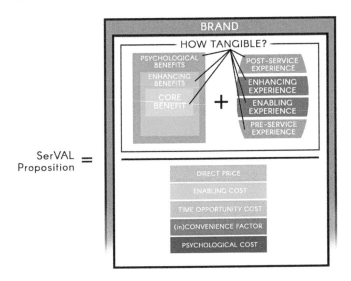

One slight note of caution, however. Some services trade on a degree of "mystery". In the past, many professional services, such as the law, have done this. Service organisations may want to consider whether making their service more tangible and making its processes more visible to its customers, as discussed below, may make it easier to sell its service, but also reduce the price people will pay for it as the mystery is reduced! Maybe they won't want to buy it at all! This is a potential risk in knowledge-based services, as knowledge becomes more and more readily available through the internet and social media.

ARE SERVICES REALLY PERISHABLE AND DOES IT MATTER IF THEY ARE?

It appears to be the accepted orthodoxy that services cannot be stored, that services are delivered and consumed during the same period of time and are generally perishable, i.e. they cannot be stored on a shelf, unlike a tin of beans, a spare part for a car or a computer.

Is this really the case? And stored by whom – the service provider or customer? The SerVAL Model suggests that it depends! For example, unless the Service Benefit is an instantaneous "one off", it is likely to continue to be received over some time period by the customer. It will have a life cycle, in much the same way as a "goods" do. The Service Benefit life cycle may well continue long after the Service Experience has finished and not just instantly end or perish.

Cleaning is a good, simple example of perishability. Items and buildings start to get dirty again immediately afterwards, but this will happen over a period of time.

Having a tooth filled at the dentist may take 30 minutes, but the Service Benefit will last considerably longer than the time spent in the dentist's surgery.

The Service Benefit life cycle is an important concept, because it reflects the total value of the Service Benefit delivered to the customer.

Why perishability matters

The perishability of a Service Benefit means it can be difficult to prove that the service has been delivered, particularly if it is very intangible. In such circumstances, it is very important to ask the customer to acknowledge that the service has been received, and to the appropriate standard. Failure to do so can lead to customer dissatisfaction and disputes over payment.

It is not uncommon for cleaning companies to insist that their customer sign-off a cleaning inspection sheet to prove that the building has been cleaned to their satisfaction and the Service Benefit has been delivered.

Cleaners are also often required to sign a work log to show that they have been there and cleaned. Check the walls of your company's lavatories and I will be surprised if there isn't a cleaners' work log displayed there. It makes the Service Experience more tangible.

The perishability of the service also means it can be difficult for service providers to prove they have delivered the required SerVAL Proposition in the past, or for customers to remember they have received that value in the past. That can be a major issue in business-to-business service organisations. If the customer representative or service provider representative has changed – which in most organisations happens every few years – how does the customer know the service provider gave a good service in the past?

One of the best relationship managers I have come across in professional services presents his clients with a hard copy report several times a year, which sets out everything his firm has done for them, including who did the work for whom, the results and the cost. He thereby creates both a tangible demonstration of value added, humanises the work and creates a permanent record of the firm's achievements for the client.

The perishability of the Service Benefit is thus a highly important factor in shaping customer value, and the customer's perception of whether that value has been received. The perishability of the Service Experience brings other challenges and opportunities. Once the Service Experience is over, it is over. It is then consigned to the customer's memory. This might be termed the customer's "Service Memory". But when the Service Memory is in someone's memory, then how reliable is it and what is actually remembered? The Service Benefit, the Service Experience or both? Does that matter? If the service provider wants to sell the customer additional services in the future and/or wants the customer to advocate its services to other potential customers, then the longer the (positive) Service Memory lasts the better. Like the perishability of the Service Benefit, the level of perishability of the Service Experience can also vary, and can be reduced, for some services, by producing an "aide memoire".

In Professional Services, for example, advice can be given verbally and therefore the only record is in the collective memory of the person(s) who received the advice and the person(s) who gave it. However, the advice can be written in a report, letter or email, and thus become a permanent, imperishable record. For the avoidance of doubt, remember that the Service Benefit is the result of the advice. The Service Experience includes when, where and how the advice was delivered and by whom.

Adopting a similar "spectrum" as Hope and Muhleman's spectrum
of tangibility, (as set out above), would show the relative degrees
of perishability of professional advice as follows:

VERBAL   WRITTEN
ADVICE   ADVICE

NO RECORD   MEMORY   PERMANENT RECORD

DEGREES OF PERISHABILITY

One of my clients is an organisation that arranges and hosts
weddings at its own venues. A tangible record of the Service
Experience can be provided, which includes photographs, framed
copies of invitations, a dried and framed wedding flower bouquet
(we still have ours from 20 years ago), etc.

The implication of service perishability suggests that service
organisations need to think how they can create more permanent
Service Memories for their services. For example, some form of
tangible record of customer satisfaction can be an important way
of making the service memory less perishable. Therefore, a key
service objective for service organisations should be to make their
SerVAL Proposition as memorable and imperishable as possible.

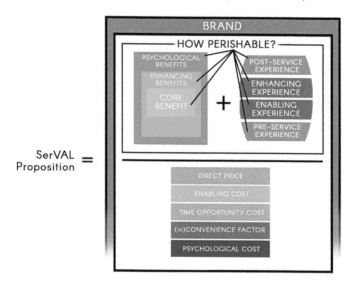

There is another key issue resulting from perishability, and this is pre-service, rather than post service perishability.

Service Benefits and Service Experiences cannot be stored and then sold. They cannot just be kept on the shelf. The Benefits and Experience are created as part of the service delivery process, so all that can be stored are the resources and systems & processes that created the Service Benefit and Service Experience. Furthermore, the necessary resources to produce the service are allocated for a definite period of time, and are either used or not used in that period. This can create significant operational challenges in terms of the efficient use of resources, as well as capacity planning and management.

Think of a dental appointment. If you miss it, then the service allocated for that time period has gone. The dentist has a 15-minute free slot during which she will not earn any income, unless she can charge you for missing the appointment. However, the service can still be received at a later time or date.

Unused capacity and capability cannot be stored or recovered. That moment in time has gone forever and the unused capacity has been wasted. To seek to minimise wasted costs, the service provider's logical operational strategy might be to try and operate at full capacity at all times, as far as possible.

However, this is not always possible if demand is not predictable and / or has pronounced cycles.

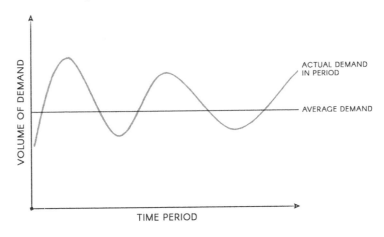

This issue is also true, of course, for unused capacity in a factory and the fluctuating demand for goods.

The only, but highly significant, difference being that keeping an inventory of Service Benefits is not possible, whereas keeping a warehouse or shop full of washing machines ready to be sold is possible, albeit this might prove expensive!

The inability to keep a service inventory can have significant implications for customers. It may mean that the service provider hasn't the capacity to start to deliver the Service Benefits and Service Experience when the customer wants it. However, for the service provider to retain sufficient capacity to meet "peak demand" at all times will create waste and negatively impact the financial position of the service provider.

The Service Delivery Model adopted by the service provider to deal with service perishability & lack of inventory, and balance the competing needs between meeting customer demand, as and when it arises, and operational efficiency has a very significant influence on customer service and service provider financial returns. This balancing act is covered in more detail in Chapter 5.

WHY ARE SERVICES SO VARIABLE?

We all consume services on a regular basis. We are, therefore, familiar with how variable the "same" service can be each time that we consume it. I have set out a simple retailing example below to highlight this.

Every time I go to my local shop, the experience is different. There may be different people serving in it, and they may serve me in a different way each time, and have more or less time to serve me or talk to me, according to how busy they are.

They may be in a good or bad mood, smiling or scowling, and I might be in a hurry or have more time. The till might be broken, they may not have enough change or the online/debit card payment system might not be working. The goods I want to buy may be easy to find, hidden away or out of stock.

There may be other customers there, who are also likely to be different each time, and there may be a parking space free outside or I might need to park further away. The weather may be different and the temperature warm or cold in the shop.

Or I may go to a different shop or go on the internet to purchase something...

So all kinds of things can vary. The basic ingredients of the service, including the people, process, real estate, ICT etc (which will be discussed in detail in Chapter 4) and the functionality of these ingredients can vary from location to location and from time to time. Compliance with processes can vary. Peoples' behaviour, customer requirements and the pre-service Experience and post-service Experience can also vary.

Therefore, the factors that drive service variability will include:

▶ The range of "ingredients" involved in delivering the service.

▶ The type of ingredients involved, with humans being particularly variable!

▶ The number of people involved.

▶ The number of different locations from where the service is delivered.

▶ The number of tasks involved in delivering the service.

▸ The number of steps in each task.

▸ The number of different ways in which each task and step might be performed.

▸ The number of multiple choices required within the tasks.

▸ The number of service options available to customers.

▸ The range of different pre and post-service experiences that may occur.

It can be seen, therefore, how and why each Service Experience is likely to be unique and varied, even without considering the human element of service delivery. And it is important to remember that the human element is not just the service provider, it is also the customers.

When I go to have my hair cut I can get a different hairdresser and sit in a different chair, drink a different cup of coffee, read a different magazine and have a different conversation about a different subject. The weather on the way there and way back will generally be different, as will the traffic and where I park.

Every time you go to the supermarket, you are likely to get a different checkout person, or the same one in a different mood. The people in the queue will be different (although I always seem to get in the slow moving queue behind someone who either wants to change one of their items, has credit card problems or cannot pack their bags quickly).

When you go online for an internet-based service, the speed of your internet connection may vary, you may be in a bad or good mood, you may get timed out or be disturbed by a member of your family or pet, and the retailer may not have the item that you want. The experience will not be exactly the same each time.

There may be a new Maitre D' at your favourite restaurant, your "usual" table may not be available and the people on the adjoining tables will be different.

The person delivering the service may be different each time, which can be expected to create a different Service Experience each time, as no person is the same as another. Even if it is the same person, their circumstances, mood or expectations may be different. People also tend not to perform tasks in exactly the same way each time, and where they are forced to, tend not to like it, which affects their mood!

The examples above also illustrate the point that the mood, etc. of the customer varies too. When he is late, with a headache, having just had an argument over a parking space, he may appreciate his normal service provider's usual jokes that bit less.

This human driven variability of a service is magnified depending on:

▶   The number of different people involved in delivering the service.

▶   The level of human judgment required and exercised to deliver the service.

The least variable/most standardised forms of service now tend to be ICT and/or process based services, where the Service Experience is much less variable each time because contact with people is relatively low and/or much more structured.

Why service variability matters

Does service variability matter? My view is that, from a customer perspective, Service Benefit variability can be more significant than Service Experience variability. This is partly because we recognise and expect, within reason, the Service Experience to vary. This potential difference in tolerance between Service Benefit and Service Experience variances goes back to Chapter 1 and the relative importance of the Service Benefit and the Service Experience. It will also vary from service to service and the consistency of the Service Experience is extremely important for some services.

Are you going to keep going to a hairdresser where you sometimes get a good haircut and sometimes a bad one, irrespective of how the experience varies?

Service organisations, therefore, need to understand if their customers want the same or a very similar Service Experience each time, and how tolerant they are of any variability.

Another consideration, that links to another service characteristic, is that it is very difficult to make a tangible SerVAL Proposition if one or more of the key elements varies significantly from time to time.

Therefore, an important objective for service organisations is to reduce the variability in their SerVAL Proposition to a level that is acceptable to their targeted customers and is financially viable.

However, it is vitally important to note that giving each customer the same SerVAL Proposition each time is not the same as giving every customer the same SerVAL Proposition.

Service providers also need to understand whether their customers want the same experience as every other customer. In short, whether customers are demanding bespoke or standardised services. The possible combinations that can be offered are set out in the diagram below.

Whichever SerVAL Proposition combination a service organisation chooses to bring to the market, the variability there is within that Proposition each time the customer buys the service will create doubt in their mind about what to expect. As a result, this may reduce their propensity to buy the service and how much they are willing to pay for it, or even persuade them to buy it from another service provider.

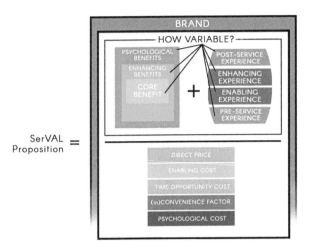

ARE SERVICES ALWAYS DELIVERED AND CONSUMED SIMULTANEOUSLY?

It is claimed that another key characteristic of services is "simultaneity", which means that the service is delivered at the same time it is received, and both its benefits and service experience are instantaneous. In short, the Service Benefit, Service Experience and payment of the Total Cost to Customer accompany the production of the service. This hypothesis can be readily contrasted with the typical time lapse between the production of a good and its use by a customer, which may range from minutes to years. However, is this a reasonable hypothesis?

The benefits received from a service are not necessarily instantaneous. For example, the benefits may be instant, such as First Aid, or long term, such as a knee replacement. The Service Experience is not necessarily instantaneous either, as it may also be received over an extended period. However, as the Service Experience is created by the service delivery process and ingredients, it is experienced as it is delivered, so it is simultaneous. The price element of the SerVAL Proposition is also necessarily simultaneous either. Payment can be in advance, in arrears, and/or during the Service Experience, and/or based on the achievement of Service Benefits.

The accompaniment of production & delivery also varies significantly between services. What this is really about is when the Service Benefit, Service Experience and Total Cost to Customer are attained. So service simultaneity can vary in scope too!

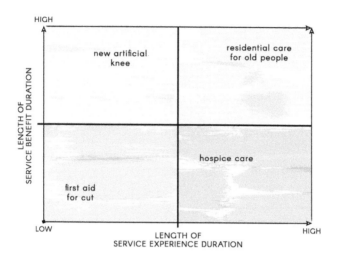

Why simultaneity matters

It is important to understand the degree to which delivery / receipt of the Service Benefits, Service Experience and the Total Cost to Customer of a service accompany its production for the following reasons:

▸ All things being equal, it is easier to sell people things with immediate benefits, rather than delayed benefits. They will tend to pay more – or more upfront – for instant benefits.

▸ How many young people will readily buy a pension plan or health plan?

▸ Simultaneous delivery and receipt can reduce the customer's perception of the risk of not receiving what they expect. This perceived risk is higher, the less tangible the service is. This provides challenges for organisations that provide intangible services with long-term, delayed or uncertain benefits.

▸ Would you rather purchase an investment plan with guaranteed returns or uncertain returns? Or how much higher would the returns need to be to cover that uncertainty?

Service organisations may, therefore, benefit from considering whether they can change the timings of the Benefits in their service offering in order to make it easier to sell or to price.

Instantaneous services with immediate or short-term benefits do, however, have some potential disadvantages for service organisations. Where the delivery of the service takes place over a long(er) period of time the service provider will tend to have much greater and/or longer-term interaction with the customer. This can impact the strength of the relationship with the customer, and potentially allow the service provider to deliver more value to the customer and generate more value from the customer.

However, it also means that the service provider needs to deliver a consistently good enough service over an extended period of time in an economic manner. The service provider also needs to ensure that short-term issues that arise during an extended / long-term Service Experience do not overshadow long-term satisfaction. The Service Memory can be very important in such instances.

It might be argued that, all things being equal, the strength of customer relationships and the value of that relationship will be a function, not just of the value of Service Benefits delivered, Quality of Service Experience and Total Cost to Customer, i.e. the basic SerVAL Proposition, but also the Timing of those Service Benefits, Length of Service Experience and Payment period.

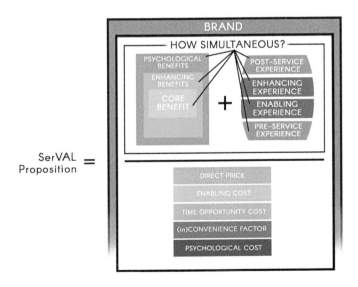

IS THE CUSTOMER / SERVICE PROVIDER INTERACTION IMPORTANT?

It has been claimed that the customer and the service provider are "inseparable", and this is a unique feature of services.

In practice, it is much more nuanced than that, because the customer and provider are also inseparable when procuring goods! (Although I have been known to be quite inseparable from my wallet when someone is trying to sell me something.)

The customer must place an order and pay for it, and the provider must deliver it and potentially manufacturer it. I order my new car at the dealers and then I drive it. What I don't have is close involvement in the manufacture of it, although I can choose its colour, the fabric of the seats, the interior trim etc.

The difference between goods and services in terms of "inseparability" is that customers of some services can be very closely involved with the production or delivery of the service, whether that be the Service Benefit or the Service Experience.

The level of separation between customer and service organisation will vary between services, as well as between service organisations, for the production of the Service Benefit. For some services, the Service Benefit is highly personal and thus the customer is totally inseparable from the service. For other services, the Service Benefit may be something that the customer needs, or may need, but doesn't directly involve their person.

A dental service will closely involve the customer in most of the service delivery process, but a financial investment service, such as a pension, may involve the customer much less. Of course, it can be equally painful!

The degree of "inseparability" of the Service Benefit will reflect, amongst other things, whether the service is being "done to" the customer or "on behalf of" the customer.

There can be a high degree of interaction between the service provider and the customer during the service creation process, which can impact the Service Benefit and the Service Experience, as well as the Total Cost to Customer and the service provider's service delivery costs. This interaction may range from the customer providing information to the service provider, or the service provider seeking the customer's opinion throughout the process, through to the customer undertaking some of the tasks involved in generating the service. Customers actively undertaking service production tasks has increased noticeably in some services, largely due to the development of improved or new technology, and reduced in others, typically due to competitive pressures.

Who generally dispenses fuel at a filling station? The customer. That didn't use to be the case.

How do most people obtain cash from a bank? The customer uses an ATM. That didn't use to be the case.

Who picks the goods from a supermarket shelf for a home delivery service. Not the customer.

The level of customer separation/involvement with service delivery will also significantly shape the customer's Service Experience. This also includes the involvement of other customers.

If you check-in online for a flight before you get to the airport, you won't have to queue for so long.

The person in front of you in the baggage queue can slow down the service because their bags are too heavy and their hand luggage too big.

The noisy person in the seat in front of you on your overnight flight may stop you from sleeping.

Separation does not just refer to the customer's direct involvement with the service production process, it also refers to how much of the service delivery process is visible to the customer. The degree of visibility in the service production process varies between services and service providers, which can have a significant impact on the service experience.

Here is a personal example of how different levels of interaction can affect the service experience, with exactly the same level of interaction and output. I generally don't mind queuing for a short time to place my order at a fast food outlet or waiting for a short time for the burger, as I can see the smiling, welcoming staff are working very hard to produce it.

However, when I go to the drive through part, I place my order into a "machine" and so can't see anyone doing anything. I get really cross and think I am waiting for a long time because they are inefficient and/or dealing with the walk-in customers in preference to me; just because there is no human interaction and I can't see how busy everyone is. If I was designing it as a customer, I would replace brick walls with glass and have a person taking the order, so it becomes much more visible.

Therefore, inseparability in service terms refers to both the involvement of the customer and the service provider in the service delivery process, and the visibility of the service production process to the customer.

This might be termed the "customer/service provider interface". Arguably, the customer/service provider interface has more influence on the Service Experience than any other service characteristic.

It has also been shown that the degree of inseparability can vary enormously between services, and between service providers, like the other service characteristics.

Why inseparability matters

The customer/service provider is very important for the following reasons:

▸ The higher the degree of interaction between the service provider and customer, the more tangible the Service Experience is likely to be.

▸ The more visible the service production process is to the customer, the more tangible the Service Experience is likely to be.

▸ The longer the degree of interaction, the longer the Service Experience will be.

▸ The more tangible and longer the Service Experience, the greater its potential impact on the SerVAL Proposition.

▸ The higher the level of interaction involving people, the greater the impact of the appearance/behaviour of the service delivery personnel will be on the Service Experience.

Do you want to employ introverted, rude or miserable people in "frontline" service delivery roles where there are high levels of customer interaction? How important is it that your customers like your employees during the service experience?

▶   The more interaction there is involving people, the more variable the Service Experience may be.

▶   The more direct physical interaction there is, the greater the importance of the physical characteristics of the service.

If customers buy all your goods over the internet, then the appearance and location of your shop will not matter to them, and if they never enter your office, then its appearance doesn't matter to them.

▶   The more interaction there is, the more important it is that your processes and systems are effective and efficient. The customer must also find them easy to use.

How frustrating it is to use first generation "self-checkout" equipment in supermarkets. It doesn't appear to work very well and you cannot work out how to use it.

▶   All things being equal, the more physically separate the customer is from service delivery, the more efficient it can be. Imagine how inefficient (and dangerous!) a factory would be if its customers were constantly involved in the production line. However, a customer's virtual involvement, through the use of ICT and the internet can increase efficiency, by structuring customer's input into the creation and/or ordering of bespoke products.

Think how the train commuter at rush hour reduces the speed of the ticket buying service if they don't know the exact route, when they want to go or return, or whether they want to travel First or Standard class. And then, to make matters worse, have a long chat about the weather to the ticket clerk (of course it is never you!). Think what this also does to the Service Experience of those waiting behind them. However, also think of their Service Experience if the ticket clerk doesn't chat or help them choose the best ticket etc.

So moving to automated / internet-based ticket machines is faster, but are they easy to use?

▶ Low levels of customer / service provider interaction generally lead to weaker relationships between the service provider and customer, however likeable the service employee is. Certainly, the relationships will be different.

What type of relationships do people have with websites? How strong is it and how long will it last?

▶ The level, nature and frequency of customer/service provider interaction will shape the perception of the brand.

SUMMARY

The range of characteristics commonly attributed to services – namely Intangibility, Perishability, Simultaneity, Variability and Inseparability – are insufficient in themselves to define a service, and they all vary considerably between different types of service. However, that isn't important.

Importantly, they all exert a strong influence on the Service Benefit and Service Experience, and how easy it is to price and sell the service. In short, they have a fundamental impact on all three elements of the SerVAL Proposition.

The more tangible the Service Benefit, and to a slightly lesser extent, the Service Experience, the easier it will be to sell a service, as long as the Benefit provides a return on the price and the customer has a budget. The SerVAL Proposition becomes more tangible and thus easier to assess.

The less perishable the Service Benefit and the Service Experience, the easier it is to demonstrate the value that has been delivered and received by a customer. The SerVAL Proposition becomes more tangible and previously delivered value is recorded.

The inability to store services, however, presents significant service delivery and operational capacity management challenges to service providers. These can, and do, impact the level of value delivered to the customer and the level of value generated by the service provider.

The more simultaneous the Service Benefit and the Service Experience is with service delivery, the easier it is to price and to sell. The SerVAL Proposition becomes more immediate. However, the longer the period over which the benefit is delivered the experience occurs and payment is made, the longer and stronger the customer relationship.

The higher the level of inseparability there is between the customer and service provider, the more important the Service Experience will be to the SerVAL Proposition. The more this interaction involves people, the more important the Service Provider's employees are to the Service Experience and the greater the potential to build strong interpersonal relationships with the customer. However, this may be offset by reduced efficiency in the service delivery process, which may impact the financial returns and potential sustainability of the service organisation.

The more people there are involved with the service delivery process and the higher the level of inseparability, the greater the level of variability that can be expected in the Service Experience, and potentially the Service Benefit. High levels of variability in the Service Benefit, Service Experience and the Price between each service event for a customer will create uncertainty in the SerVAL Proposition, thus weakening it.

Finally, the different characteristics impact each other and addressing them may involve some trade-offs. For example, increasing the involvement of customers with the production of the service in order to make the service experience more tangible is also likely to make the service more variable.

Spreading the period over which the Service Benefit and Experience will accompany production of the service may lengthen and strengthen customer relationships, but may also make it harder to sell the service and make the service more variable.

Deliberate or emergent choices about these trade-offs can lead to material differentiation between services and can thus be the source of competitive advantage.

The importance of these characteristics of a service means that they might, therefore, be considered the VITAL characteristics of a Service.

- V ariability of the service
- I nvolvement of customer with production of the service
- T angibility of the service
- A ttainment period for Service Benefit, Service Experience and Total Cost to Customer
- L asting service benefit or experience or price?

CHAPTER THREE:
KEY QUESTIONS TO CONSIDER

▸ How **Variable** is your organisation's:
  o Service Benefit?
  o Service Experience?
  o Total Cost to Customer?

▸ How **Involved** are your organisation's customers in creating:
  o Service Benefit?
  o Service Experience?
  o Total Cost to Customer?

▸ How **Tangible** are your organisation's:
  o Service Benefit?
  o Service Experience?
  o Total Cost to Customer?

▸ When does your Customer Attain the Service Benefit?

▸ When does your Customer Attain the Service Experience?

▸ When does your Customer Attain its Total Cost to Customer?

▸ How **Lasting** are your organisation's:
  o Service Benefit?
  o Service Experience?
  o Total Cost to Customer?

CHAPTER 4

THE CORE INGREDIENTS FOR SERVICE SUCCESS

INTRODUCTION

In Chapter 1, I suggested that services comprise of three core components; *a Service Benefit, a Service Experience* and *a Total Cost to Customer.* The combination of these components creates a Service Value Equation. In Chapter 2, I added a brand to the Service Value Equation as a "service wrapper". I have termed the specific Service Value Equation provided by a service provider to its customers its SerVAL Proposition.

In that chapter, I also set out a list of common inputs or "ingredients" that are typically combined in a service in order to create the Service Benefit and Service Experience, and which impact the Total Cost to Customer. I am now going to consider these ingredients in more detail, as they are integral to service success and competitive advantage. There are a lot of ingredients requiring some consideration, so I have divided my commentary into a series of short chapters for ease of reading and thought. I have grouped these ingredients together where they are closely related in characteristic or impact.

- ▶   Chapter 5 - People and Service Success
- ▶   Chapter 6 - Process, ICT Systems, the Internet and Knowledge
- ▶   Chapter 7 - Property, Tools & Equipment
- ▶   Chapter 8 - Marketing and Brand

In each short chapter, I will illustrate how these ingredients have a significant impact on the SerVAL Proposition. In Chapter 15, I will show how they impact the cost base of a service organisation.

In Chapter 6, I will highlight how the core ingredients of services have changed significantly since the Millennium, and why 21st century services can be considerably different from those that have gone before. These changes are based on the emergence of the internet as a key ingredient of many services, and the ongoing rapid evolution of other ICT systems. In combination, they have brought about the greatest changes to service organisations in decades, arguably since the introduction of electricity, the telephone and the internal combustion engine more than a century ago.

KEY QUESTIONS

The key questions I will consider in this overview chapter are:

▶   What are the basic ingredients of a service?

▶   What is the Service Delivery Mix?

▶   How important is the Service Delivery Mix to the SerVAL Proposition?

▶   How does the Service Delivery Mix provide a source of competitive advantage?

▶   How to evaluate the impact of the Service Delivery Mix on your SerVAL Proposition?

WHAT ARE THE BASIC INGREDIENTS OF A SERVICE?

The basic ingredients of a service can be identified through common sense, practical consideration and brainstorming, as mentioned in Chapter 1. For ease of description and consideration, I have categorised them as follows:

▶   **People**

▶   **Process**

▶   **ICT Systems**

▶   **Internet**

▶   **Knowledge & Intellectual Property**

▶   **Real Estate & Facilities**

▶   **Tools & Equipment**

▶   **Marketing Communication materials & other tangibles**

▶   **Brand**

These may be the Service Provider's own people, tools and equipment etc, or those of its supply chain and service delivery partners.

A number of service providers outsource elements of their service, such as a customer call centre, which forms a key part of their service experience. Others have outsourced reception services in their offices.

Think of the delivery driver and truck dropping goods off at your local convenience store. If the truck is parked in customer parking spaces, or if the driver is not smart looking or rude, then that will shape the customer experience.

And if the delivery driver is late, then the benefit being sought from the retailer, say fresh bread, is not available.

And there is one more ingredient that can have a major impact on the SerVAL Proposition – the Customer!

One of the VITAL characteristics of a service is that the customer is frequently involved with its production!

This means the customer can influence the Service Benefit and the Service Experience, and also influence them for other customers.

Think how a customer's lack of preparation or knowledge can influence how long it takes for you to get served when you queue up at your local post office, or how other customers at a restaurant can influence the service experience you receive.

On my daughter's 16th birthday, I took my family out for a meal to celebrate at a well-known restaurant and bar. In the bar area one of a group of young men, who was very drunk, decided to take his clothes off.

This had a very negative effect on the atmosphere, especially when he approached me after I had made a complaint to the management.

WHAT IS THE SERVICE DELIVERY MIX?

These items are the raw ingredients that go into a service. Just like when making food, these ingredients can be used in varying quantities and combinations to form the service "recipe" or what might be termed the *Service Delivery Mix.*

HOW IMPORTANT IS THE SERVICE DELIVERY MIX TO THE SERVAL PROPOSITION?

Major impact on the Service Benefit

It is relatively obvious that the Service Delivery Mix adopted by the service provider will have a major impact on the Service Benefit. If the processes don't work, the people are untrained, the ICT systems fail or the real estate is in the wrong place, the Service Benefit may not be delivered or prove to be less than that expected by the customer. The psychological benefits provided by a service can be closely tied up with the brand of the service organisation.

"You never get fired for buying IBM."

That is a big psychological benefit to a risk averse purchaser of a high cost IT system.

Major impact on the Service Experience

The Service Delivery Mix adopted by any service organisation will also have a major impact on the Service Experience; for example, the number of people providing the service, where the service is provided and the environment in which it is provided. Think of the different Service Experience received in a 5★ hotel in a fashionable part of a major city, compared to a cheap motel in the middle of nowhere!

Major impact on the Total Cost to Customer

The Service Delivery Mix will be the principal influence on the cost base of the service organisation, and hence its long-term sustainability, with regard to the prices it can charge for its services.

People costs can be more than 70% of the costs of some service organisations, such as cleaning or security companies. Clearly, firms in such service organisations may seek cost advantage, or profit improvement, through focusing on reducing the number and/or individual cost of people in the organisation. This may reduce the service benefit of course, e.g. a building that isn't as clean.

Firms in the retail service industry tend to have property as a high percentage of their costs. Cost advantage may be sought by having fewer properties, or in less expensive locations, but there are follow-on consequences, e.g. lower revenues as shopper footfall is typically lower in lower rent locations (hence, the lower rent!). Internet-based retailers can have very low property costs, but again there are trade-offs made, such as much less personal customer contact, which changes the service experience.

The Direct Price it is able to charge may reflect the scarcity, or otherwise, of the ingredients in its Service Delivery Mix, and their contribution to delivering the Service Benefit and Service Experience.

The Service Delivery Mix will also influence the customer's direct enabling cost (e.g. travel cost), time, opportunity cost (e.g. travel time), convenience factor (e.g. how easy it is to get there), psychological costs and switching costs. I will cover all of the above for each ingredient in the following chapters.

HOW DOES THE SERVICE DELIVERY MIX PROVIDE A SOURCE OF COMPETITIVE ADVANTAGE?

Again, it is readily apparent that the Service Delivery Mix provides one of the main sources of competitive advantage, as service organisations can use different combinations of ingredients in their recipes to produce a different SerVAL Proposition to the one offered by their competitors.

HOW TO EVALUATE THE IMPACT OF THE SERVICE DELIVERY MIX ON YOUR SERVAL PROPOSITION?

The impact of the Service Delivery Mix on the SerVAL Proposition will vary from service to service, and also from service provider to service provider, depending on the nature and mix of ingredients used, as well as their individual impact on the Service Benefit and Service Experience. It is, thus, important to gain an understanding of this when either creating a new service or new service operation, or changing an existing one.

The diagram below might represent how the different elements of a Service Delivery Mix of an office cleaning company impacts the Service Benefit and Service Experience elements of the SerVAL Proposition.

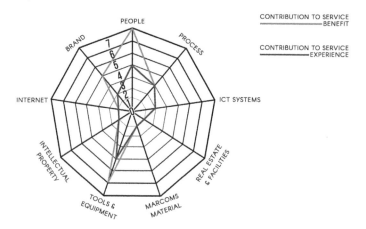

The diagram below might represent the impact of the different ingredients on the SerVAL Proposition of a professional services firm. The costs of Real Estate and Facilities, ICT and Marcoms care are likely to contribute a far higher percentage of the firm's cost base than they do in the cleaning business above.

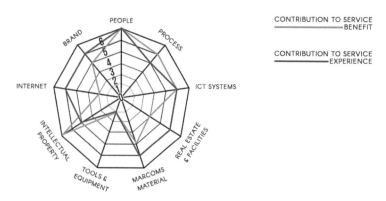

The diagram below might represent how the Service Delivery Mix impacts the SerVAL Proposition of a traditional retailer. Of course, the missing element from this is the goods they sell!

Real estate costs are likely to represent a high percentage of their cost base (other than the cost of their goods!).

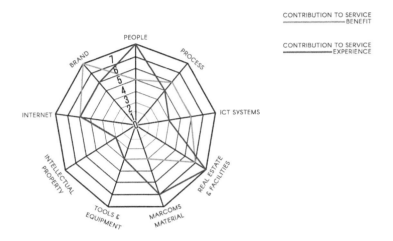

The Service Delivery Mix's impact on the total cost to customer might also be assessed in a similar manner. The example below is a hypothetical internet service-based business.

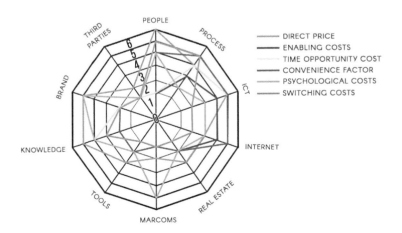

Obtaining a robust understanding of this impact is fundamental to identifying:

▶ How your SerVAL Proposition can be made more attractive to your customers and potential customers.

▶ How the ingredients drive your organisation's cost base.

▶ Whether there is a mismatch between costs and value creation.

▶ How changes to the Service Delivery Mix might change the SerVAL Proposition.

▶ How your competitors deliver their SerVAL Proposition.

HOW TO APPLY THIS THOUGHT PROCESS TO YOUR ORGANISATION?

The table below is a simple tool that is designed to enable you to start thinking about how your Service Delivery Mix impacts your SerVAL Proposition and cost base.

Once you have read the following chapters, the table can be completed for your current SerVAL Proposition, your competitors' current SerVAL Propositions, and then your potential future SerVAL Propositions, your competitors' future SerVAL Propositions, as well as those of potential market entrants. I suggest that you complete this both before and after reading the following chapters.

The following scoring system below can be applied:

1 = No impact on Service Benefit / Service Experience

2 = Minor impact on Service Benefit / Experience

3 = Moderate impact on Service Benefit / Experience

4 = Good contributor to Service Benefit / Experience

5 = Important creator of Service Benefit / Experience

6 = Very important creator of Service Benefit / Experience

7 = Principal creator of Service Benefit / Experience

Service Ingredient	Used in your service? (Yes / No)	Importance to delivering your Service Benefit	Importance to your Service Experience	% of your total service delivery costs
People				
Process				
ICT Systems				
Real Estate & Facilities				
Marcoms material				
Tools & Equipment				
Intellectual Property				
Internet				
Brand				

HOW IMPORTANT ARE PEOPLE IN THE SERVICE DELIVERY MIX?

INTRODUCTION

All service organisations, indeed all organisations by definition, have people at their core, and thus they are a critical and common part of the Service Delivery Mix. People design and deliver the service; they find, win, keep and grow customers; they lead and manage the organisation; they "hire and fire", reward, recognise and develop other people. People also design, procure and operate processes, systems, tools and real estate, and they ensure that the organisation complies with the law and regulations.

The success of any service organisation will, therefore, depend on having capable and motivated employees who perform to the required level and in the required manner to deliver the Service Benefit and Service Experience that the customer expects, in an economically sustainable, legal manner. In short, service success depends on having the "right people".

KEY QUESTIONS

The key questions that I consider below are:

▶ What is the Service-Profit Chain?

▶ How do people affect the Service Benefit?

▶ How do people affect the Service Experience?

▶ What about "back office" people?

▶ How do people affect the Total Cost to Customer?

▶ How do people affect the Brand?

▶ How do people affect customer relationships?

▶ How do people affect the VITAL characteristics of services?

▶   How do people affect the cost of service delivery?

▶   What about leadership and management?

▶   What about other people?

▶   How can you apply this to your service organisation?

WHAT IS THE SERVICE-PROFIT CHAIN?

The importance of the relationship between employing the right people and ensuring they are satisfied with their roles, in order to enable the delivery of the service expected by the customer, has been identified in various articles and books by Harvard Professors Heskett, Sasser and Schlessinger. These are set out in their well-known "Service-Profit Chain model", which is represented in the diagram below.

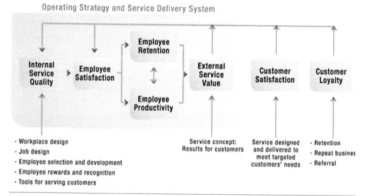

Reprinted by permission of Harvard Business Review.
From "Putting the Service-Profit Chain to work" by James.L.Heskett, Thomas O. Jones, Gary.W.Loveman, W.Earl Sasser Jr., issue July-August 2008.

In my terms, the "External Service Value", identified in the Service-Profit chain model, is created by the SerVAL Proposition.

How do people affect the Service Benefit?

The Service Benefit element of the SerVAL Proposition will clearly be influenced by the performance (of which productivity is but a part) of the people who are involved in delivering the service.

Their performance, in terms of generating the Service Benefit, will depend on their skills, knowledge and experience, as well as their general intellectual capacity, physical capacity and physical prowess, and how they are able to combine with others, in creating the benefit. This is set out in the diagram below.

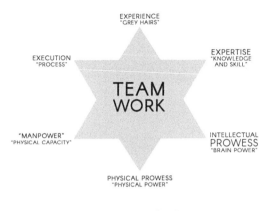

with acknowledgement to Daivd Maister

Using this framework to analyse people's contribution to customer value creation indicates that the Service Benefit creation process involves a combination of seven factors. These will vary and can be compared across different service types and service organisations. The diagrams below involves such a comparison. The first one compares service types, and the second compares the service organisations that provide the same service.

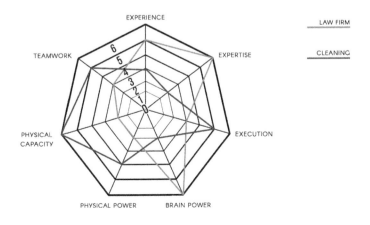

Cleaning firm 1 uses a labour intensive model, while cleaning firm 2 uses more specialist cleaning equipment.

The performance of the employees will also reflect the processes, ICT systems, tools & equipment, etc, they have been provided with to enable them to create the benefit.

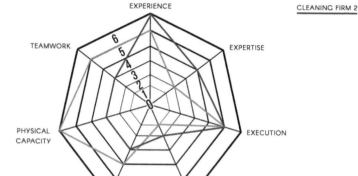

It will also reflect their motivation and desire to perform, rather than their ability to perform, and is expressed in the Service/Profit chain model as Employee Satisfaction.

The actual identity of the person carrying out the task (e.g. Dr. X, the world famous brain surgeon) or the qualifications and experience of a person more generally, may also provide some psychological benefit to the customer.

It is important to recognise that the overall impact of people on the Service Benefit will depend on how important the people element of the Service Delivery Mix is in creating the Service Benefit, as highlighted in Chapter 4 above.

The impact of a brain surgeon on the benefits expected from a brain surgery service is likely to be relatively very high.

The impact of a server on the benefits expected from the food in a fast food restaurant is likely to be relatively low.

How do people affect the Service Experience?

The direct impact of people on the Service Experience will depend on the level, frequency and nature of customer/service provider interaction. We will explore this further in Chapter 9 when we consider the Service Delivery Model.

The impact of a brain surgeon on the experience expected from a brain surgery service is likely to be relatively low, if the patient is totally sedated and never meets the brain surgeon.

The impact of a server on the service experience received in a fast food restaurant is likely to be relatively high.

It is extremely important to recognise that when the service provider's employees interact with customers, their appearance and how they behave will shape the Service Experience significantly.

This is common sense, but so often forgotten.

In fast growth service organisations, it can be relegated in importance when organisations just seek to fill vacancies in order to deliver the growing demand for the Service Benefit. It can also occur where large numbers of employees are acquired in groups, such as through mergers, acquisitions and – in the EU and UK – through labour transfers under employment legislation ("TUPE" transfers in the UK). This can have a very detrimental impact on the Service Experience and the service organisation's brand, and thus change the whole SerVAL Proposition.

Furthermore, whilst the people in a service organisation create the Service Experience, they must also reflect the expected Service Experience. The critical people factor in the Service Experience is not their performance, but their behaviour and appearance.

What about "back office" people?

If customers never see, meet or speak to the employees of the service provider, which is increasingly the case with internet-based services, then their direct impact on the Service Experience will be relatively low, even if they have a huge impact behind the scenes in the "back office" in creating the Service Benefit and the rest of the Service Experience.

However, it is important to remember that "back office" people also need to perform and be motivated, or else the Service Benefit may not be delivered!

Furthermore, "back office" people are also often service providers to "front office" people. So they, in turn, impact on the Service Experience and Service Benefit received by these "front office" people, which will impact the way they are able to interact with the organisation's customers. The Service-Profit Chain runs right through an organisation.

How do people affect the Total Cost to Customer?

What impact do people have on the price of a service? High labour costs, whether in aggregate or in unit cost terms, don't necessarily translate into a similar Direct Price premium, as the price premium will be much greater in some cases, and in other cases there will not be one at all. That is true for all ingredients in the Service Delivery Mix: a price premium will be driven by the wider SerVAL Proposition, as well as demand for the service and the level and nature of competition.

However, labour is likely to translate into a price premium when it constitutes a high percentage of the Service Delivery Mix, there is a scarcity of it, and it is a key generator of the Service Benefit and/or Experience. Furthermore, in some cases the actual identity of the person delivering the service can drive the price even higher in some cases, such as a leading lawyer , surgeon, entertainer or sports star. A service organisation's employees can also influence other elements of the Total Cost to Customer in a significant way. For example, they can create a degree of convenience or inconvenience for the customer above and beyond the standard Service Experience offered. Their availability and responsiveness can also have an impact on the customer's opportunity cost.

The mobile hairdresser that will change an appointment time to enable a customer to visit the dentist will reduce his customer's opportunity cost.

They can also influence the psychological costs that are associated with using, or not using, the Service. If the customer doesn't particularly like one of the service provider's employees then there will be a psychological cost of procuring the service from them. Equally, if the customer has a strong relationship with the service provider's people, then there will be a high psychological cost if they switch to another service provider

How do people affect the Brand?

The type of people employed, and the way they present themselves and behave, will also have a great bearing on the service organisation's brand. The more important people are in terms of delivering the Service Benefit and/or Service Experience, and the more they interact with the customer, then the greater their influence on the service organisation's brand.

Many Professional Service firms employ a certain "type" of person, with a certain background that matches well with the customer group they are targeting. This can often be clearly seen in the offices of real estate agents that sell expensive residential properties. Abercrombie & Fitch are an example of how a retail service organisation's employees are used to project an "aspirational" brand for a target market segment.

Service people are all "brand ambassadors".

How do people affect customer relationships?

People have relationships with other people, not with ICT systems, processes, real estate, tools & equipment, etc, and so are central to customer relationships. The exception to this is when people have relationships to the service provider's organisation, which is best considered as a relationship with its brand.

The greater the degree of customer interface with a service provider's people, the more that the service provider's relationship will depend on the relationship between its people and the customer. In such cases, where the service provider's employee is integral to delivering the Service Benefit and/or Experience, relationships can develop where the customer "follows" the employee, and the service organisation only has that relationship with the customer whilst their employee remains with them.

It is not unusual for lawyers to have a "following" of clients, and for their clients to come with them when they move to a different firm of lawyers.

Similarly, executives in the corporate world have strong (legitimate!) relationships with companies in their supply chain who often remain as their suppliers when they move to a different role.

From a service provider's perspective, the more of its employees have relationships with individual customers, the stronger the relationship will be with with the firm, rather than the individual.

How do people affect the VITAL characteristics of a service?

People will have a significant influence on the VITAL characteristics of a service. All things being equal, the more different people are involved with delivering a service, then the more variable it is likely to be. That is because each person is different and will generate the Benefit with varying degrees of competence, efficiency, speed and consistency, and bring their own appearance and behaviour to the Service Experience. How big an impact this will have on the Service Experience will be dependent on the degree of involvement of the customer – who are also people! – in producing the service. And people are one of the main tangible elements of any service.

How do people affect the cost of service provision?

It is relatively obvious that the people cost base of a service organisation will be driven by the number, type and location of the people it employs. However, it is not just the absolute raw-cost that is important. The unit cost of service production, and the volume of output they produce, is driven by the productivity of these people. So it is important to understand the factors driving productivity. I cover this in more detail in Chapter 14. Productivity is a key factor within the Service-Profit Chain.

In the UK, the salary/bonus premium for employees in professional service organisations in London, compared to the rest of the UK, is typically well above 20%, and can be more than 100% for senior professionals. Productivity per person (not necessarily per hour) may also be higher, with professionals typically working longer hours in London than elsewhere in the UK. (This may mean unit costs are quite similar in some cases.)

What about Leadership and Management?

Furthermore, delivery of the Service Benefit and the Service Experience will also be affected by those who lead and manage the organisation, and seek to ensure it has the right resources available at the right place and at the right time to deliver the service. This is done by utilising the right tools and processes, and following the best strategy that generates the appropriate financial returns that will enable it to remain sustainable. Leadership and management will also have a very significant influence on the motivation of employees in the organisation.

WHAT ABOUT OTHER PEOPLE?

Another often forgotten, or overlooked, element of the Service Delivery Mix are "other people". These are the third parties who are neither the service organisation's customers nor employees. They might include:

▶   The customer's advisors and influencers

▶   The service provider's supply chain, including outsourced elements of the service

- Third parties involved with a transaction
- Other customers
- Visitors to the service organisation's real estate
- People in the vicinity of where the service organisation is delivering the service
- Criminals

The customer's advisors and influencers can shape the SerVAL Proposition that is required and the customer's perception of whether they have received it. I explore this in more detail in Chapter 12. They may also interfere with the way that the service organisation delivers the service, for example, requesting additional information from professional advisors, or delaying the customer's response to its professional advisors.

If the service provider has outsourced an element of its service provision, then the performance and behaviours of the employees, systems and processes, and rest of the service delivery mix of that organisation will shape the Service Benefit and Service Experience provided by the primary service provider. Even where the supply chain is not in the frontline of service delivery, its performance can have an impact on the delivery of the SerVAL Proposition, even if it's only in very simple ways. For example, a food delivery driver to a supermarket who turns up in scruffy clothes with a filthy truck and blocks the customer car park with her truck.

The involvement of third parties in a service can also have a significant impact on the SerVAL Proposition.

An investigation I did for a law firm suggested that the principal cause of budget over runs and time delays on some large projects was not their inefficiency, or the delays and variations requested by the client. Instead, it was the involvement of third parties, such as investors, banks and their advisors.

The third party examples considered so far involve other parties that have some form of connection to the service being delivered. However, unconnected third parties can also have a significant influence on the SerVAL Proposition. In particular, they can shape the Service Experience and the Total Cost to Customer.

I have already provided examples of how other customer's behaviours in queues, etc. can impact the Service Experience.

Visitors to the service provider's premises can also affect the experience. What would you think if there were a lot of children running round in the reception of your service provider's premises, or a lot of police outside? What if the area surrounding the service provider's premises contained a slum or visible criminal elements?

Finally, there is the impact of criminals. The increased use of ICT and the internet in service provision has been accompanied by a rise in cyber crime that ranges from stealing customers' details to stealing their money or intellectual property.

SUMMARY

People are thus central to service organisations, as they are in all organisations. However, the additional importance of people in service organisations, compared to other types of organisation, is in two areas:

▶ The value they create in producing the Service Benefit

▶ Their impact on the Service Experience through the customer/ service provider interface.

The way that people perform and behave once they have been selected will be influenced by employee satisfaction and the wider "Employee Experience". Namely, what it is like to work for that organisation and perform that particular role, as well as how they are rewarded and recognised for performing that role; in short, their motivation. That is a key message in the Service-Profit chain.

Based on these observations, and by linking the Service-Profit chain model for the Service Benefit and Service Experience elements of the SerVAL Proposition concept, the original Service-Profit chain model might be expanded upon, as follows:

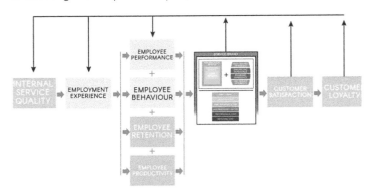

The questions below will help you to consider the current and potential impact of the modified Service Profit Chain on both your service organisation and your competitors'.

CHAPTER FIVE:
KEY QUESTIONS TO CONSIDER:
PEOPLE

▶ How important are people to your Service Delivery Mix – see questions in Chapter 4.

What type of person do you need?

▶ Have you clearly specified the type of people that you need in terms of performance and behaviours to deliver your Service Benefit?

▶ Have your clearly specified the type of people you need in terms of performance and behaviours to deliver your Service Experience?

Recruiting, replacing, developing, rewarding, recognising, retaining

▶ Do you have an effective recruitment process that delivers such people to the organisation?

▶ Do you have an effective exit process that removes those that don't perform or behave as required?

▶ Are you providing your people with the right learning and development to deliver your SerVAL Proposition?

▶ Are you rewarding your people appropriately to support sustainable, economic delivery of your SerVAL Proposition?

▶ Do you have problems retaining people?

The working environment and tools to do the job

▶ Are you providing your people with the right working environment?

▶ Are you providing your people with the right tools & equipment?

- Are you providing your people with the right ICT systems?

- Are you providing your people with the right other resources, such as suppliers, advisors, materials, good etc, in the right place, at the right time and in the right form?

- Do they have the right team supporting them?

- Does your organisation develop and deploy the right processes for your people to deliver your SerVAL Proposition?

Leadership, Management and Motivation

- Are you leading your people well?

- Are you managing your people well?

- Are they sufficiently and appropriately motivated?

Capacity and utilisation

- Do you have enough of them, in the right place, at the right time, sufficiently prepared?

- Are they under or over utilised?

Customer relationships & Brands

- What impact do your People have on your longer-term relationships with customers?

- Are relationships concentrated in a small group of people or across the organisation?

- What impact do your People have on your Brand?

Your organisation's costs of service delivery

- What impact do your People have on your total cost base?

▶ What impact do your People have on your unit costs of service delivery?

Performance and behaviours

▶ Are they performing as required and expected?

▶ Are they behaving as required and expected?

Impact on VITAL characteristics

▶ How do your people impact the V ariability of your SerVAL Proposition?

▶ How do your people impact the I nteraction with customers?

▶ How do your people impact the T angibility of your SerVAL Proposition?

▶ How do your people impact whether the Benefit, Experience or Total Cost to Customer A ccompany each other, or are delayed?

▶ How do your people impact whether the Benefit, Experience or Total Cost to Customer is L asting?

PROCESS, ICT SYSTEMS, THE INTERNET AND KNOWLEDGE

INTRODUCTION

Before beginning to consider the impact of processes and systems, etc, on the SerVAL Proposition, it is worth remembering that these processes are created by people, for people. So service organisations must get the people element of their Service Delivery Mix right in order to achieve long-term, sustained success.

In this chapter, I am going to consider how people (the service deliverer and their customers) perform tasks (processes), and how ICT and the internet have radically changed how these processes can be performed with a consequential transformational impact on services. I will then consider how ICT and the internet have significantly changed the generation, management and deployment of knowledge within service organisations. I will consider the impact on the Service Benefit, Service, Experience, Total Cost to Customer, Brand and People for each.

KEY QUESTIONS

I will address the following key questions:

▶   Does process matter in service organisations?

▶   What about IT?

▶   Is service tangled in a Web?

▶   Are service organisations knowledgeable?

DOES PROCESS MATTER IN SERVICE ORGANISATIONS?

A service organisation's processes, the way it does things (or its methodologies), are a key service ingredient. They may have either been well thought through or just evolved over time. They may be standardised across a service organisation or there may be lots of local processes.

A study I did of 25 people in one Professional Services firm found that there were 60 different processes for opening a new client file!

Processes can be enabled or driven by ICT systems, or they can simply be people-based activities.

A service organisation's processes are extremely important because they will determine:

▶ The degree to which a service organisation delivers the expected Service Benefit and Service Experience. If its processes do not work, then no Service Benefit will be delivered and an unplanned and/or unexpected Service Experience will occur.

▶ How the customer interacts with the service organisation and, thus, the Service Experience.

I will look at the impact of customer interaction processes in more detail in the chapter by considering the Service Delivery Model, and it is safe to say they are instrumental in shaping the Service Experience.

Processes will also significantly shape the VITAL characteristics of the service, such as the:

▶ **Variability** of the Service Benefit and Service Experience

▶ **Involvement** of the customer with service production

▶ **Tangibility** of the Service Experience

▶ **Attainment** period for the Service Benefits, Service Experience and Total Cost to Customer

▶ **Length** of time that the Service Benefit and Service Experience and Total Cost to Customer will last.

If an organisation doesn't have standardised processes for often repeated tasks, then it is highly likely that the service experience will be variable and not as reliable as it could be. The service benefit may also be variable, as a result.

If the processes are such that only certain people in the organisation can deal with customers, then it may not be easy for customers to receive the service they require when they need it, if the designated people aren't available.

If the processes never involve providing tangible outputs, such as reports or signed-off maintenance task sheets, then the service may be seen as being ephemeral and not having been performed, and the benefits received may fade into memory (perish) if they are not recorded.

If customers are not closely involved with the service delivery processes, and can't see them, then there is a risk that the customers will perceive that the organisation is not doing anything if the service takes some time to complete.

The service delivery processes adopted by an organisation will not just have an impact on their customers, they will also significantly impact the working lives of the organisation's employees.

Processes and People

Service delivery processes dictate and shape the level of customer interaction employees have, the variety of tasks they undertake, the amount of discretion they are permitted to exercise in undertaking their role, the level of judgment they are required to exercise, how they interact with colleagues, how they interact with their supply chain, including the efficiency of that interaction and the amount of time that they "waste".

The importance of these factors on employees' morale, motivation and performance, and hence their ability to deliver the SerVAL Proposition, was discussed in Chapter 5 when we considered the Service-Profit Chain. They must not be overlooked.

Thus, processes, directly, or indirectly, impact the Service Benefit, the Service Experience and the efficacy, effectiveness and efficiency, and hence the cost base of the service organisation. They also impact the Employment Experience.

But remember, processes are designed and used by people, and sometimes ignored by people; so it's a case of People first, process second.

WHAT ABOUT IT?

The use of ICT* systems is common in most services, even if they are as basic as a telephone. Furthermore, the increased adoption of smartphones and smart tablets and other mobile communication devices will make the use of ICT systems within services increasingly common across the whole world, even in very poor economies.

In this section, I am not going to discuss particular ICT systems, but I want to illustrate how they can directly and (via employee satisfaction) indirectly affect the Service Experience, and how they can change the availability of the Service Benefit. Additionally, I will highlight how ICT systems can fundamentally change the basis of the relationship between a service organisation and its customers. They can also impact organisational efficacy, efficiency and effectiveness, and the overall cost of delivering the service. This is covered in Chapter 12.

> ▶ * For the purposes of this section, I have excluded websites from the definition of ICT systems and I will instead cover websites separately in a later section. In this section, ICT systems mean communication systems, such as email, telephone systems, video conferencing systems, social media systems, support systems, such as the organisation's finance system, its payroll system etc, frontline workflow systems and "standard" software systems, such as provided by Microsoft , Apple etc.

What does IT do?

In simple terms, ICT systems are just ways of creating, supporting, enabling and enacting the processes described in the previous section. However, ICT's impact on the SerVAL Proposition and Employee Experience is far more than just providing process improvement or automation. It delivers profound changes to the Service Value Equation, as well as the economics and working life of service organisations.

What does ICT do to the SerVAL Proposition?

ICT systems shape when, how and where the customer interacts with the service organisation, including with whom, how often, how fast and how consistently it carries out this interaction, which can have a major impact on the Service Experience. ICT can change the availability and method of producing the Service Benefit, as well as the time it taken to attain it. ICT can also potentially change the Total Cost to Customer and significantly change the cost base of service organisations. In addition, it can have a significant impact on a service organisation's employees, both positive and negative.

Most of us see bank ATMs as a major step forward in the service of obtaining cash because they are much quicker than bank tellers, are available 24/7 365, and are found in more locations than the banks themselves. They are also much cheaper for banks than having lots of small bank branches everywhere, that are open for long hours.

However, it does mean that the relationship between the bank and its customers can change. When coupled with the telephone, email and internet banking, how many of us actually go into a bank branch anymore, and so miss out on the opportunity to build relationships with bank personnel? The relationship is with the "brand".

Think of the way that car mechanics now diagnose the fault with your vehicle. They no longer spend hours wallowing in oil before telling you they don't know what the problem is and will have to strip the engine down. They plug in a laptop instead.

This has changed both the nature of their job and the amount of time (and potentially money) you have to spend at the garage to get a diagnosis.

ICT and the Service Benefit

ICT can enhance the Service Benefit. It might increase the benefit, make it available faster, or for longer. It may even enable the development of new services with new Service Benefits.

The use of technology to enable the internet to be searched can enhance the benefits that are provided by information and/or deal brokers, as their ability to obtain current and more market information means they provide a higher level of certainty to clients that they have the best deal or have obtained a better deal.

Of course, if their clients can obtain the technology required to access the information, it could make the information broker a redundant role. Think of domestic insurance brokers, for example. Who uses them now? We increasingly buy house, household and vehicle insurance directly from the insurer, having used a price website on our PC to identify the best deal.

ICT and the Service Experience

The use of technology, such as the telephone, fax, email, social media, audio, video, social media, photocopier, to name just a few, has changed the way that customers interact with service providers, as well as the nature of that interaction. ICT has been truly transformational to the Service Experience for many, if not all, services and is likely to continue to be.

ICT's impact on the speed and availability of service

The widespread adoption of ICT also means that service providers need to be far more available and instantly responsive to their customers. Service Benefits need to be available more quickly and for longer periods during a day, week or year. An unexpected delay or lack of access will negatively impact the Service Experience. I think customer expectations about service providers' responsiveness and availability have risen more than any other service expectation over the past few years.

ICT's impact on the Total Cost to Customer

ICT can also have a significant impact on the Total Cost to Customer. If ICT enables a service organisation to reduce its costs to deliver a given SerVAL Proposition, then this provides it with the opportunity to increase value to its customers by lowering its Direct Price.

Many services have seen new Service Delivery Models emerge, with lower cost bases, as a result of the development and deployment of better and/or new ICT. Increased competition has seen lower prices being offered, as a result.

It can also have a substantial impact on the other elements of the Total Cost to Customer, namely:

▶   Direct Enabling Cost

▶   Time Opportunity Cost

▶   Convenience factor

▶   Psychological cost

▶   Switching costs

This can be seen through a simple example.

A few years ago, I had to drive into my local town to change my bank account from one bank to another. This meant I incurred travel costs (fuel, parking and vehicle depreciation). It also meant that I spent quite a lot of time walking from bank to bank, talking with bank managers, gathering brochures, analysing the deals on offer etc. I could only do this during working hours on a weekday, which was inconvenient. It directly cost me lost earnings or holiday, or stopped me from doing something else, such as watching sport, mowing the lawn or seeing friends. It, therefore, had a significant time opportunity cost, as well as a direct enabling cost and an inconvenience factor. I also had the psychological pressure of meeting my existing bank manager, and all these other nice bank managers, and having to say "no" to some of them. The switching costs were also quite high.

Now I can identify the best bank and set up a new account by using technology – my PC, phone or tablet, and phonelines, WIFI and the internet. I can do this 24/7, 365 days a year, from home, whilst watching the sport on TV. I don't have to say "no" to anyone face to face and the switching costs are low.

My Total Costs are much lower and my Pre and Post-Service Experience is much better. I can also be more confident that I have got the best deal. Therefore, you can see I have received a much better SerVAL Proposition.

ICT and bespoke SerVAL Propositions

Technology means that service organisations with large numbers of customers can obtain, manage and utilise far more information about their customers than ever before. Simple database systems, let alone high powered Customer Relationship Management systems, mean it is much easier to store and analyse basic or detailed information about customers. And the internet means that it is also easier to obtain a lot of publicly available knowledge about a customer's business, individual customers or potential customers. Overall, this means it is should be much easier for service organisations to develop and provide services for existing and potential customers, based on improved knowledge about their customers' needs. This can enable the creation and delivery of bespoke/niche Service Benefits and/or bespoke/niche Service Experiences.

ICT can also support more targeted marketing of services (and goods). The effective use of enhanced customer data management can change the Service Experience for the customer, by making the Experience feel – or actually be – more personalised.

The quality of ICT in the Service Delivery Mix

A very important consideration for all service businesses, in terms of the ICT ingredient in their Service Delivery Mix, is that their customers and employees are becoming more and more ICT literate. This means that customers have high expectations of a service provider's ICT ingredient, based on their experience of using it elsewhere in their lives. The implication of this is that the best provider of that particular ingredient sets the benchmark standard for all other service businesses, not just their direct competitors.

The level of customer expectation of the Service Experience and the availability of the Service Benefit is, thus, being increased because the ICT ingredient of a service is being benchmarked against best in class. Therefore, the competitive bar has been raised and will continue rising. The World Wide Web also makes these benchmarks worldwide (sic).

ICT and customer relationships

In addition to making the customer/service provider interface much more varied in scope, the increasingly wide range of communication media can support the building and strengthening of relationships between service organisations and their customers, which is another part of the Service Experience, and a key basis for creating value for the service organisation from their customers, as I will discuss in Chapters 12 and 16. Other than face-to-face contact, ICT systems typically form the principal communication links between the customer and service provider, and new technology provides new media for this form of communication. The use of mobile phones, email, tweets, video conferencing, etc, makes it far easier to communicate with customers than ever before.

However, the use of ICT may also change the basis of the relationship with the customer if new media are used to replace, rather than complement, historic forms of communication. After all, how strong are customer relationships that are based mostly on email or texts, compared to those based on phone calls or face-to-face meetings?

ICT and (dis)satisfied customers

The increasing use of social media for communication is expected to have an enormous impact on marketing communications, customer referrals and the brand. It means that the importance of meeting customer expectations and customer word of mouth have both been raised to a level never seen before. Satisfied and loyal customers are being asked to publicly endorse the service provider to potentially millions of people via "liking" them on-line, and many do. Equally, dissatisfied customers have an enormous ability to create damage to a service organisation through, for example, tweeting their dissatisfaction or using other social media to vent their displeasure. A single perceived failure – setting aside "brand terrorists" – can now inflict major damage, with the dissatisfied customer not just telling a few friends and acquaintances, but potentially millions of people.

So deliver the expected SerVAL Proposition to your customer or beware!

ICT and the Employee Experience

ICT, in the form of workflow software of various types, is increasingly being used to support service delivery processes. Examples range from "prompts to do something" in diary systems, through planned activity systems, such as Planned Maintenance systems. These are basically "reminder/activity planning/resource allocation" systems of various degrees of complication and sophistication. Other forms of workflow system effectively pull and push work through the service delivery process. These can make services more reliable, more responsive, less variable, faster and more effective. Workflow software also helps to manage capacity and productivity.

However, such systems are likely to change the nature of the work being undertaken by the service deliverer's employees. They may eliminate or speed up "boring" tasks or eliminate routine paperwork and administration, and most employees are likely to welcome that.

ICT systems can also increase productivity by speeding up workflow. Employees may or may not appreciate that, depending on, amongst other things, the basis of their remuneration, the volume of work they need to deal with, and their performance motivation, among other things.

They may also reduce the level of discretion and judgment that is exercised by employees and their degree of self-determination. This is often considered to be a case of "dumbing down" the work and may make employees feel they are performing never-ending, meaningless tasks at ever-increasing speeds. This is likely to have a negative impact on employee satisfaction, due to them having less variety in their work, and could mean that a different level and/or type of employee is required.

Such systems can also lead to greater levels of specialisation, such as the help desk operative, which is likely to increase the organisation's effectiveness and efficiency, and so may increase job satisfaction for some, as they develop a particular, valued specialisation. One person's "dumbing down" can be another's "upskilling".

The increased demands to always be available for customers, via mobile communication devices, may make employees feel more valued and more integral to the service, and increase motivation and productivity. However, it may also make employees feel that they can "never escape" their customers and have no down time, and so make them demotivated.

The increased use of emails and similar types of electronic communication to interface with customers also can significantly change the nature of a service organisation's employees' work experience if it radically reduces the level of face-to-face contact with customers. Some employees like that, others don't.

ICT can have a big impact on the very nature of some service work.

For example, knowledge workers in the Professions. As information is increasingly codified, and both readily and cheaply accessible, the premium put on having and selling that information as a key part of the service will diminish.

As a result, the job will become much more about interpreting, contextualising and applying the information, so the balance of the service and the job is changing.

Once again, service organisations need to consider this in terms of the type and numbers of people they employ, their skill sets and how they motivate them.

The use of technology, in terms of how a service organisation delivers services to its customers, is expected to significantly change the employees' employment experience.

Thus, ICT systems have a major effect on the Employment Experience, and due to their impact on employees (which I will expand on in Chapter 6), the Service Benefit and the Service Experience.

ICT and new Service Delivery Models

Technology allows new business models to be developed, whereas ICT replaces other ingredients, or becomes the dominant, rather than a minor ingredient, in the Service Delivery Mix.

It is generally being used to replace higher cost elements of the Service Delivery Mix – typically real estate and people – as this can have a radical impact on the cost base and pricing options of the service provider. This is very important in highly competitive, low margin markets.

Such Service Delivery Mix innovation is occurring all over the world and can also be driven by the lack of some elements of the service delivery mix in some places, such as mobile phone-based banking in Africa and Asia.

So, technology is having the most profound influence on how services are delivered, marketed and assessed by customers, and how service quality is appraised, and is becoming an increasingly dominant part of the Service Delivery Mix, which will change the whole Service Value Equation.

The example below sets out some potential questions to consider in terms of how ICT might impact the SerVAL Proposition that is delivered to an organisation's customers.

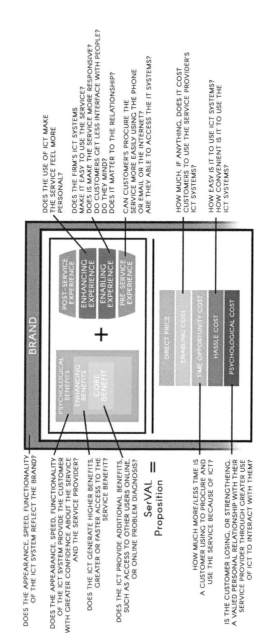

BRAND

SerVAL =
Proposition

PSYCHOLOGICAL BENEFITS
ENHANCING BENEFITS
CORE BENEFIT

+

POST-SERVICE EXPERIENCE
ENHANCING EXPERIENCE
ENABLING EXPERIENCE
PRE-SERVICE EXPERIENCE

DIRECT PRICE
ENABLING COST
TIME OPPORTUNITY COST
HASSLE COST
PSYCHOLOGICAL COST

DOES THE APPEARANCE, SPEED, FUNCTIONALITY OF THE ICT SYSTEM REFLECT THE BRAND?

DOES THE APPEARANCE, SPEED, FUNCTIONALITY OF THE ICT SYSTEM PROVIDE THE CUSTOMER WITH GREATER CONFIDENCE ABOUT THE SERVICE AND THE SERVICE PROVIDER?

DOES THE ICT GENERATE HIGHER BENEFITS. GREATER OR FASTER ACCESS TO THE SERVICE BENEFIT?

DOES THE ICT PROVIDE ADDITIONAL BENEFITS, SUCH AS ACCESS TO OTHER USERS ONLINE, OR ONLINE PROBLEM DIAGNOSIS?

HOW MUCH MORE/LESS TIME IS A CUSTOMER USING TO PROCURE AND USE THE SERVICE BECAUSE OF ICT?

IS THE CUSTOMER LOSING, OR STRENGTHENING, A VALIED PERSONAL RELATIONSHIP WITH THEIR SERVICE PROVIDER THROUGH GREATER USE OF ICT TO INTERACT WITH THEM?

DOES THE USE OF ICT MAKE THE SERVICE FEEL MORE PERSONAL?

DOES THE FIRM'S ICT SYSTEMS MAKE IT EASY TO USE THE SERVICE? DOES IS MAKE THE SERVICE MORE RESPONSIVE? DO CUSTOMERS GET LESS INTERFACE WITH PEOPLE? DO THEY MIND? DOES IT MATTER TO THE RELATIONSHIP?

CAN CUSTOMER'S PROCURE THE SERVICE MORE EASILY USING THE PHONE OR EMAIL OR THE INTERNET? ARE THEY ABLE TO ACCESS THE IT SYSTEMS?

HOW MUCH, IF ANYTHING, DOES IT COST CUSTOMERS TO USE THE SERVICE PROVIDER'S ICT SYSTEMS?

HOW EASY IS IT TO USE ICT SYSTEMS? HOW CONVENIENT IS IT TO USE THE ICT SYSTEMS?

IS SERVICE TANGLED IN A WEB?

The internet is becoming increasingly central to the delivery of many services. In fact, it has formed a totally new service delivery model for some services. We now have internet banks, internet-based retailers, internet-based ticket agents and travel agents, internet-based real estate agents, internet-based dating agencies, internet-based social media businesses, such as Facebook, and the list goes on. The creation of websites for other organisations has also become a new service in itself.

It has also become a key part of the way established service businesses deliver their services, as well as being a channel to market, and this isn't just in cutting edge businesses either.

The huge impact of the internet on service businesses merits a book in its own right, and this isn't it. What I want to achieve in this section is to just highlight the following issues that the internet raises for service businesses.

The internet and Service Benefits

The internet can create new or better services by creating new or better forms of Service Benefit. For example, price comparison websites or better market information, as covered by the example in the ICT section above.

The internet and the Service Experience

One of the most significant impacts of the internet on the Service Experience is that, combined with ICT hardware and software, it totally changes the potential basis of the customer / service provider interface. The quantity, level, basis and nature of human contact can change radically which can, in turn, change the direct Service Experience.

The internet and the Total Cost to Customer

The internet can replace people, tools and real estate in the service delivery mix. So a lower cost business model, which has fewer people, less real estate, etc, can enable service organisations to deliver the service at a lower cost, and hence offer a lower Direct Price to the customer. I have shown in an example above how internet-based service delivery models can also radically reduce the other elements of the Total Cost to Customer.

The internet and customer relationships

Internet-based services also change the form of the relationship between service providers and their customers by greatly reducing the personal relationships between the service provider's employees and its customers, and in the most extreme scenario, eliminating them altogether. Over time, this could have an impact on customer retention, as it is not clear how loyal people are to "faceless" organisations. It is also likely to make the customer relationship more dependent on the "personality" of the organisation, i.e. its brand, rather than the customer relationship skills of individuals in the organisation.

Customers will also use the internet to seek out the opinions of other customers about the service provider, which can have a long history on the web, whether they are positive or negative. This makes the long-term, consistent delivery of the organisation's SerVAL Proposition even more important.

The internet and employees

The change in the level, nature and frequency of contact between employees and customers that has been enabled by the internet will also have a major impact on the number and type of employees required by a service organisation and where they are located. It can also significantly change the employees' employment experience, whether it be positive or negative, and impact the performance and behaviour of existing employees. This will have a knock-on effect on the Service Benefit and Service Experience and could require the recruitment of alternative employees. The internet can, thus, have a major influence on the HR strategy of service organisations.

The internet and competition

Another "game changer" brought about by the internet is the way customers and competitors use the web to find out information about potential suppliers, prices etc. It has made competitive information much more accessible and comparisons of the Direct

Price element of the SerVAL Proposition much easier. In turn, this has made it even more important that service providers make a clear and obvious differentiation between their Service Benefit and Service Experience, and those of their competitors.

Failure to do so will lead to direct competition on price and an expected downward pressure on margins.

The internet has thus changed the level and nature of competition, as greater market information tends to lead to a downward pressure on prices and margins and a more rapid erosion of competitive advantage, as competitors are able to copy more quickly. New internet-based service delivery models have also increased the scope for new market entrants without legacy service delivery mixes and legacy cost bases, which potentially increases the number of competitors too, at least in the short-to-medium term, until other competitors may leave the market.

The diagram below illustrates the potential impact of the internet on the Service Value Equation.

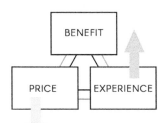

ARE SERVICE ORGANISATIONS KNOWLEDGEABLE?

All service organisations contain some form of knowledge.

Where knowledge enables the creation of both the Service Benefit and the Service Experience

The majority of service organisations, however, don't sell access to knowledge or interpret knowledge. They do, however, obtain and / or develop and apply knowledge.

The development, management and sharing of such knowledge is fundamental to:

▸   Developing SerVAL Propositions that customers want and are willing to pay for

▸ Recruiting, training, managing, motivating, developing and rewarding its employees

▸ Developing and implementing the service organisation's processes

▸ Developing and deploying the appropriate ICT

▸ Designing, procuring and operating from the right real estate and facilities

▸ Procuring the appropriate tools

▸ Producing and distributing the appropriate marketing communications

▸ Using the internet and social media

▸ Developing and maintaining an appropriate brand.

Stakeholder knowledge

Furthermore, service organisations possess some degree of knowledge about their customers (as discussed in the section on ICT above), their employees, their suppliers, their regulators, their owners and other stakeholders, which can be key to service success.

Knowledge is, thus, a core ingredient of all services, and knowledge management a core activity.

Where knowledge is the Service Benefit

Obtaining knowledge and information may be the core Service Benefit that is received by a customer from a service. Examples of this might be expert knowledge about a subject, as would be the case with a law firm or university, or market knowledge, such as with a stockbroker or real estate broker.

Typically, the core benefit is enhanced by accompanying advice that indicates how such knowledge or information applies to the customer's particular circumstances.

The service provider is able to provide the service because they either have, or can get access to, the knowledge and the customer cannot. They sell that access, and potentially their interpretation of it, to the customers. The more widely available that knowledge is, the lower the value of possessing it is, and the more important both the interpretation and application of it becomes.

The increased availability of knowledge through ICT and the internet is one of the core challenges facing the "Professions" and other services that traditionally provide a service based on a "monopoly" of specific knowledge.

Increased importance of Service Experience

The widespread availability of information means that the core benefit of services that historically sold it, will be based much more on the interpretation of that knowledge in future.

Arguably, it will also mean that the Service Experience will become the relatively more important part of the SerVAL Proposition of professionals.

It also means the Price that customers are willing to pay for the knowledge can be expected to decline, and will become much more dependent on the value that is generated from the interpretation of the knowledge and the quality of the Service Experience.

SUMMARY

It can be seen that Processes, ICT systems, the internet and knowledge are absolutely fundamental ingredients in the Service Delivery Mix, and have a significant direct impact on all elements of the SerVAL Proposition. They can also have a significant indirect impact, via the Service-Profit Chain, because of their impact on the service organisation's employees. Failure to consider this impact holistically is likely to create longer-term issues for service organisations.

And, in my experience, many organisations seem to have failed to do so.

CHAPTER SIX:
KEY QUESTIONS TO CONSIDER:
PROCESS, ICT SYSTEMS, INTERNET, KNOWLEDGE

PROCESS

▸ How important is Process to your Service Delivery Mix – see the questions in Chapter 4.

▸ Do you have clear, standardised processes for all key activities that are understood?

▸ Are they complied with?

▸ Are they effective in supporting the delivery of the Service Benefit?

▸ Are they efficient in supporting the delivery of the Service Benefit?

▸ Are they effective in supporting the delivery of the Service Experience?

▸ Are they efficient in supporting the delivery of the Service Experience?

▸ What is their impact on the Total Cost to Customer?

▸ Do they make the service more or less tangible?

▸ How do they impact service variability?

▸ Do they involve high or low levels of customer interaction?

▸ Are they visible or hidden from customer sight?

▸ How do they impact the speed at which the service is attained?

▸ How do they impact the length of time the Service Benefit is received for?

▸ How do they impact the length of time of the Service Experience?

▸ How do they impact the period over which the Total Cost to Customer is incurred?

▸ How do they impact the Employee Experience?

▸ What is their impact on your brand?

ICT SYSTEMS AND THE INTERNET

▶ How well do they enhance and accelerate the organisation's processes?

▶ How important is IT to the delivery of the expected Service Benefit?

▶ How well does IT support the delivery of the expected Service Benefit?

▶ How important is IT to the delivery of the expected Service Experience ?

▶ How well does IT support the delivery of the expected Service Experience?

▶ How does IT impact on the availability of the Service Benefit?

▶ How does IT impact on the availability of the Service Experience?

▶ How does IT impact on the speed at which the Service Benefit is received?

▶ How does IT impact on the speed at which the Service Experience is received?

▶ How does IT impact on the Total Cost to Customer?

▶ Does IT enable the delivery of more bespoke SerVAL Propositions?

▶ Does IT enable the delivery of this in a cost effective manner?

▶ Is there an attractive market for more bespoke SerVAL Propositions?

▶ How does IT impact customer relationships?

▶ Is IT being used to replace or complement levels of interpersonal contact in the customer relationship process?

▶ Is IT being used to measure Customer Satisfaction?

▶ Is IT being used to communicate Customer Satisfaction by the service organisation?

▶ Is IT being used to communicate Customer Satisfaction by customers?

- What is IT's impact on the current Employee Experience?

- What is IT's impact on the proposed future Employee Experience?

- Could IT be deployed to deliver the same SerVAL Proposition by using a different Service Delivery Model?

- Could IT be deployed to create and deliver a different SerVAL Proposition?

KNOWLEDGE

Knowledge as a general ingredient in the Service Delivery Mix

- How is knowledge managed within your service organisation to support the creation and delivery of the Service Benefit?

- How is knowledge managed within your service organisation to support the creation and delivery of the Service Experience?

- How is knowledge managed within your service organisation to influence the Total Cost to Customer?

- How is knowledge managed within your service organisation to support customer relationships?

- How is knowledge managed within your service organisation to support and enhance the Employee Experience?

- How effective is this knowledge management?

- How efficient is this knowledge management?

Knowledge as the service

- Does the provision of knowledge form the core Service Benefit offered by your service organisation?

▶   Is this knowledge becoming more readily available due to increased competition and/or via the internet and ICT?

▶   Does application of this knowledge for an enhancing Service Benefit offered by your service organisation?

▶   Could it viably become such?

▶   Could application of this knowledge viably become the core Service Benefit offered by your service organisation?

▶   How important is the Service Experience element of your knowledge provision and/or interpretation to your service organisation?

▶   Can the Service Experience viably become a more important part of your SerVAL Proposition?

▶   Would that provide competitive advantage?

REAL ESTATE
& FACILITIES, TOOLS
& EQUIPMENT

INTRODUCTION

All service organisations, from logistics companies through retailers, cleaning companies and hairdressers to lawyers and accountants, occupy real estate. Even internet-based service businesses have real estate, albeit just someone's garage, bedroom or a giant "server farm" somewhere else in the world! This can be real estate where the employees are based or customers visit, or both.

Most service organisations, if not all, utilise some form of tools and equipment. This can range from the humble pencil to a high-tech satellite. The real estate is sometimes the "tool", as is the case with a traditional retailer or distribution depot within a logistics service.

Real Estate & Facilities and Tools & Equipment are the tangible, fixed assets of service organisations. In this chapter, I am going to discuss how they can also have a significant impact on the SerVAL Proposition, as well as the cost base of the organisation.

KEY QUESTIONS

I will examine the following key questions:

▶   Are service organisations in a real (e)state?

▶   Are service organisations tooled up?

ARE SERVICE ORGANISATIONS IN A REAL (E)STATE?

Real estate and costs

For most service organisations, real estate has a very significant impact on the cost-base of the organisation, and the cost is fundamentally driven by the location, size, nature, quality and quantity of the real estate occupied. It can often be the second or third highest cost of service organisations, after people costs.

Furthermore, real estate tends to be a long-term fixed cost.

This can mean that established service organisations have a significant cost disadvantage compared to market entrants that use a different Service Delivery Mix based around ICT, the internet and a different Service Delivery Model. It can be both expensive and time consuming to lose this cost disadvantage. This means that some service organisations can be in a real state (sic) in terms of their competitive position. Think of the number of "bricks and mortar" retailers who have ceased trading due to competition from internet-based retailers. The significance of real estate as a cost can mean there is a great temptation just to see it as a cost.

However, real estate can have a huge impact on the Service Benefit delivered to a service organisation's customers, and the Service Experience received by them. This should not be forgotten when considering the costs of real estate. Therefore, a proper cost-benefit exercise is required.

Real estate and the Service Benefit

Real estate can be integral to delivering the core Service Benefit. Retailing is a good example of this. The core benefit is typically to provide customers easy and rapid access to a wide variety of choice of particular items of merchandise, competitive prices and an easy price comparison. Traditional "bricks and mortar" retailers achieve such by having a well located, suitably sized, suitably fitted out, suitably arranged retail unit that is supported by a supply chain, including suitably sized, located and fitted out storage & distribution depots. New internet-based retailing models may substitute the physical retail unit with a virtual online outlet, but still tend to be highly dependent on either their own storage & distribution depots, or those of their suppliers, in order to have the required goods available, as and when required.

Real estate can provide enhancing benefits. For example, retail department stores and large supermarkets typically also include a café or a coffee shop. Some professional service organisations, such as accountants and lawyers, provide workspace within their offices where clients can catch up with phone calls or emails etc, pre and post-service. Some railway stations offer showers and changing rooms for people who have cycled to the station.

Real estate can also provide psychological benefits to customers. For example, banks were historically banks located in buildings that appeared to be long established and impregnable (see some of the photos below). This made customers feel that their money was safe, even if it was not actually kept in that branch.

Real estate and the Service Experience

The layout of a service organisation's real estate will have an impact on how easy it is for customers to interact with the organisation and their employees. The internal and external appearance, temperature, noise and smell – within and without – will also impact the Service Experience. Its location and supporting facilities, such as the parking available and surrounding environment will impact both the pre and post-service experience.

Real estate and the Total Cost to Customer

The location of the real estate will dictate how easy it is for customers to visit the service provider, how long it will take

and how expensive it will be. It, thus, has a major impact on many of the elements of the Total Cost to Customer.

This can be important when the Direct Price is low, or even nil, such as with public services. The significance of the travel time and travel costs to customers can become more obvious to them.

Real estate and customer relationships

The time it takes for customers to travel to the real estate, and the cost of doing so, will not only have an impact on whether or not the organisation wins or retains customers, and how much it costs to serve them, but will also have an impact on how easy it is to build relationships with them. In my experience, organisations tend to have weaker relationships with customers who live a long way from where they are based, compared to those closer by. This is typically because the interactions with them are less frequent, or the SerVAL Proposition less compelling because of a higher TCC.

However, the use of technology, such as video conferencing and social media may change this.

Real estate and employees

The location of the organisation's real estate will also dictate how easy and expensive it is for their staff and potential employees to travel to work, and thus the size and nature of their potential employee pool. The working environment will also enable the organisation to attract, retain and motivate employees and their behaviours.

The layout will also affect how easy it is for employees to interact with each other and how they work. For example, open plan offices can make 'thinking'/'quiet time' work more difficult, and thus affect the motivation of employees and the organisational culture.

A combination of these factors will, in turn, impact both the type of service and nature of the Service Experience that the organisation can offer its customers.

Real estate and brand

The "character" of the real estate occupied by the service organisation is also likely to signify something to customers.

When a customer says "nice offices," what is she really thinking? Is she just making small talk, thinking, "they must be successful, that is why I am using them," or "no wonder they are so expensive / I can see where my fee goes" and so resenting the cost? It is also important what type of real estate the firm's competitors and potential future competitors are in, and how this reflects the service provider's brand.

I could go on, but the focus of this book is not facility management or real estate strategy. Suffice it to say that real estate has a major impact on service organisations of most kinds, not just in terms of the cost and how accessible it is to customers and employees. It also has a significant direct impact on the Service Experience through the employees' performances, behaviours and the culture of the organisation.

Service organisations should, therefore, only take real estate decisions when there is a full understanding of the wider impact on the SerVAL Proposition, rather than just focusing on the impact on cost. Some basic questions for a retail service are set out below.

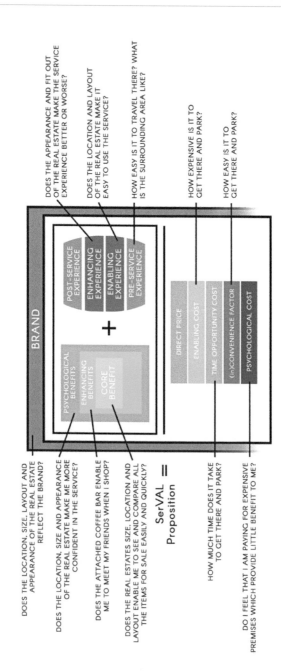

DOES THE APPEARANCE AND FIT OUT OF THE REAL ESTATE MAKE THE SERVICE EXPERIENCE BETTER OR WORSE?

DOES THE LOCATION AND LAYOUT OF THE REAL ESTATE MAKE IT EASY TO USE THE SERVICE?

HOW EASY IS IT TO TRAVEL THERE? WHAT IS THE SURROUNDING AREA LIKE?

HOW EXPENSIVE IS IT TO GET THERE AND PARK?

HOW EASY IS IT TO GET THERE AND PARK?

BRAND

POST-SERVICE EXPERIENCE

ENHANCING EXPERIENCE

ENABLING EXPERIENCE

PRE-SERVICE EXPERIENCE

PSYCHOLOGICAL BENEFITS

ENHANCING BENEFITS

CORE BENEFIT

DIRECT PRICE

ENABLING COST

TIME OPPORTUNITY COST

(In)CONVENIENCE FACTOR

PSYCHOLOGICAL COST

SerVAL = Proposition

DOES THE LOCATION, SIZE, LAYOUT AND APPEARANCE OF THE REAL ESTATE REFLECT THE BRAND?

DOES THE LOCATION, SIZE AND APPEARANCE OF THE REAL ESTATE MAKE ME MORE CONFIDENT IN THE SERVICE?

DOES THE ATTACHED COFFEE BAR ENABLE ME TO MEET MY FRIENDS WHEN I SHOP?

DOES THE REAL ESTATES SIZE, LOCATION AND LAYOUT ENABLE ME TO SEE AND COMPARE ALL THE ITEMS FOR SALE EASILY AND QUICKLY?

HOW MUCH TIME DOES IT TAKE TO GET THERE AND PARK?

DO I FEEL THAT I AM PAYING FOR EXPENSIVE PREMISES WHICH PROVIDE LITTLE BENEFIT TO ME?

IS THE ORGANISATION TOOLED UP?

Many types of service businesses utilise tools and equipment of varying kinds, from the aircraft used by airlines, the trucks by logistics companies, through to the scissors and clippers of hairdressers, the vacuum cleaners of cleaning companies, and the books and online information systems of lawyers.

Tools and the Service Benefit

It is relatively self-evident that tools and equipment will impact the Service Benefit because if a service organisation has the wrong tools, delivering the expected benefits will be difficult. Try digging a hole with a spoon!

Tools and the Service Experience

What might be less obvious is that the tools used by service organisations can also have a major impact on the customer's Service Experience. For example, is the service provider using tools that the customer expects them to? See the digger and spoon example above! In reality, the choice may be between a digger and a spade. If the firm arrives with one person and a spade to dig a very big hole, then the customer may experience the service for much longer and feel that he has hired the wrong firm.

The condition and appearance of the tools can also be important, and changing these tools may change the Service Experience too.

Tools and the Total Cost to Customer

It is also fairly obvious that the tools and equipment that an organisation uses can have an impact on its efficiency, and hence the unit cost of providing a service (see the spoon example above!) They also have an impact on the absolute cost of providing a service, and the overall cost base of the service organisation. Hiring a mechanical digger to dig the hole may well cost more than the cost of hiring the driver for a day, and these costs will influence the sustainable Direct Price that service organisations are willing and able to charge for a service.

They can also influence other elements of the Total Cost to Customer. For example, using a mechanical digger may significantly reduce the time that the customer is not able to access their land or buildings, and thus reduce their opportunity cost. However, the noise of the digger may increase the inconvenience factor for them and also the psychological cost to them if they worry that the noise will upset their neighbours.

Tools and customer relationships

Tools and equipment can also influence the strength and length of customer relationships. It is not uncommon, for example, for service organisations to be given long contracts by their customers when the service requires significant use of expensive capital equipment. Examples include passenger rail franchises, road sweeping services and municipal waste management contracts. Without long contracts, the service provider would not be able to finance the purchase or leasing of the equipment in a commercially attractive manner.

Tools and employees

Not only can tools and equipment directly impact the Service Benefit and Service Experience, tools can also have a major impact on a service organisation's employees. It can change the way they do the work, how fast they do it, and even make some elements of the work (or parts of the workforce) redundant. They, therefore, influence the Employee Experience, and further influence the Service Experience, via the Service-Profit chain, in a positive or negative manner.

A change in equipment may speed up the work by making it more responsive to customers' needs, and also increase the workforce's operational capacity. This may be good for some of your employees and bad for others. What could be the consequences of this?

Any change in key tools and equipment used by a service organisation should be considered holistically in terms of their impact on the SerVAL Proposition, and not just in terms of the efficiencies and cost.

SUMMARY

Real Estate & Facilities and Tools & Equipment are often the only tangible assets of a service organisation. They can form a high percentage of the organisation's cost base, and these costs can be quite inflexible, which is not conducive to achieving a sustainable competitive advantage in a dynamic market where new Service Delivery Models using different Service Delivery Mixes are emerging.

However, they can also have a significant impact on the Service Benefit of some services, and the Service Experience of most. They are the drivers of the Total Cost to Customer and their impact on the Employee experience can be profound. Thus, they indirectly shape the Service Benefit and Service Experience via the Service-Profit Chain as well.

Again, it is important to consider these ingredients, both in terms of their contribution to the SerVAL Proposition, as well as their contribution to costs.

CHAPTER SEVEN:
KEY QUESTIONS TO CONSIDER:
PROPERTY & FACILITIES, TOOLS & EQUIPMENT

PROPERTY & FACILITIES

How important is Property & Facilities to your service organisation in terms of:

CHARACTERISTIC	ELEMENT OF SERVAL PROPOSITION			
	Service Benefit	Service Experience	Total Cost to Customer	Brand
Location				
Quantity				
Quality				
Appearance				
Layout				
Ancillary facilities, such as parking				

CHARACTERISTIC	OTHER KEY FACTORS		
	Strength of customer relationship	Employee Experience	VITAL Characteristic
Location			
Quantity			
Quality			
Appearance			
Layout			
Ancillary facilities, such as parking			

▶   Total organisational costs?

▶   How fixed/flexible are these costs?

TOOLS & EQUIPMENT

▸ What tools & equipment are used within your service organisation?

▸ Which tools & equipment have most impact on the Service Benefit?

▸ Which tools & equipment have most impact on the Service Experience?

▸ Which tools & equipment have most impact on the Total Cost to Customer?

▸ Which tools & equipment have most impact on the VITAL characteristics?

▸ Which tools & equipment have most impact on customer relationships?

▸ Which tools & equipment have most impact on the Employee Experience?

▸ Are these positive or negative impacts?

▸ Is the impact due to the:

   o Availability of the tools & equipment?

   o Method for using the tools & equipment?

   o Time when the tools & equipment can be used?

   o Functionality of the tools & equipment?

   o Fitness for purpose?

   o Appearance and condition?

   o Noise?

   o Smell?

   o Motion?

▸ How can these impacts be improved?

BRAND, MARKETING & OTHER MATERIALS

INTRODUCTION

The two ingredients covered in this chapter are quite different in nature – marketing materials are very tangible, whilst a brand is intangible – but they are also symbiotically interrelated. Marketing material, in this context, however, doesn't only mean brochures, websites etc, used in explicit marketing communications, but also every other tangible ingredient in the Service Delivery Mix, other than the real estate & facilities, tools & equipment, hard ICT systems and people which we have already considered. These other items can all be expected to have an influence on the Service Experience, if not on the Service Benefit.

KEY QUESTIONS

To assess the impact of these factors on the SerVAL Proposition, I will look at the following questions:

▶   What does the service organisation show people?

▶   What does the service organisation explicitly tell people?

▶   Has the service been branded?

▶   How does the brand impact the Service Benefit?

▶   How does the brand shape the VITAL characteristics?

▶   How does the brand affect customer relationships?

▶   How does the brand influence the Employee Experience?

WHAT DOES THE SERVICE ORGANISATION SHOW AND TELL PEOPLE?

My children used to have a session at school called "show and tell" when they were younger, where they would take in objects that ranged from toys to things found in the garden, and then describe them to their classmates. Well, "show and tell" is an ingredient of the Service Delivery Mix too.

Showing and telling and the Service Experience

The Service Experience is likely to include tangible things other than people, real estate, ICT and other tools & equipment. These could include letters, reports, marketing brochures, menus, business cards, purchase orders, invoices, gifts and promotional material, thank you materials, uniforms, signage etc. These are all part of the Service Experience and may be part of the Service Benefit too.

The logos, pictures, words, language, symbols, colours etc. associated with these materials all have an impact on what existing and potential customers think of the service.

Showing and telling and customer expectations

And what do the words, diagrams, videos, uniforms, etc (attempt to) tell customers about the service organisation? I will discuss in Chapter 11 how perceived failure to meet these expectations is a key source of customer dissatisfaction.

▸ Think of going to a restaurant – you will see the signage, the menu, the bill, the waiters' uniforms and their name badges.

▸ Think of the report you get from your accountant or management consultant.

▸ Think of the letter you get from your Doctor.

▸ At Harvard Business School they give you HBS folders, HBS logoed bags, HBS umbrellas, HBS portfolio cases and HBS certificates, and you can buy lots of HBS gifts, ranging from sweatshirts to ties and cuff links, to pens and paper.

Showing and telling and Employee experience

In the same way that these tangible items, other than people, shape the customer's Service Experience, they also shape what the Employee thinks about the service organisation. For example, are they proud or embarrassed to wear the uniform? Are they proud or embarrassed to give customers the marketing material?

Thus, these other tangible items influence both the customer and employee experience and the organisation's brand.

WHAT DOES THE SERVICE ORGANISATION EXPLICITLY TELL PEOPLE?

Service organisations will almost certainly produce some form of explicit marketing communication material; be that a "flyer" or "brochure", a sign or a website. This will provide both explicit and implicit messages about its SerVAL Proposition.

There are many books and articles on marketing and service marketing that set out "how to do it". So it is not my intention to explore this in any detail, other than to make the obvious but absolutely fundamental point, often forgotten or insufficiently addressed by many organisations, that these messages should:

▶   Clearly set out the Benefits, Experience and Price that the customer can expect, and thus address the VITAL characteristics.

▶   Align with the SerVAL Proposition that will be delivered.

▶   Align with the intended Brand image and meaning.

A service organisation's failure to clearly communicate the SerVAL Proposition being offered is likely to lead to extremely limited sales to customers and/or customer dissatisfaction. I will explore customer satisfaction in Chapter 12.

HAS THE SERVICE BEEN BRANDED?

The other main element of the Service Delivery Mix , the brand, is intangible. Again, branding deserves a book in its own right – and has many. I just want to raise a couple of points about the importance of brands to service businesses.

The most basic point for any service organisation is whether their potential customers have heard of them? This is known as "brand recognition". This isn't just about international organisations, but also applies to local service providers, such as the local gardener. If a customer hasn't heard of him, how is he going to give him any work?

So, a service organisation's brand will influence whether potential customers have heard of it or not.

Once the brand is known, the next question is, what is it known for? At the most basic level, this involves what the organisation does. However, it also includes its reputation for delivering the Service Benefits and Service Experience it promises, for the Direct Price it promises.

Brand reputation, or "brand meaning", represents how a service organisation's SerVAL Proposition is widely perceived – the Service Benefits it delivers, the Service Experience it provides, the direct price it charges, and how consistently it delivers this value proposition.

HOW DOES THE BRAND IMPACT THE SERVICE BENEFIT?

The Service Benefit will contain a core benefit. It may also include an enhancing benefit or two. On top of this, there may be a psychological benefit. This largely relates to the customer's level of assurance concerning the magnitude of the core and enhancing benefits, the probability they will receive these benefits and the promised Service Experience, and how assured they feel about having to pay the expected price. The service organisation's brand is likely to be the key factor in whether or not it provides such a psychological benefit to its customers, and the level of such a benefit.

For example, a service organisation may have a reputation for being very responsive and friendly, very formal or informal, "innovative" or very conservative, and for charging high or low prices. It might also be known for being reliable, having "market experts"or excellent processes for carrying out the work.

"You never get fired for buying IBM."

That is a big psychological benefit to a risk averse purchaser of a high cost IT system. Consider the internet retailers mentioned above. They may be selling the same goods as competitors, but rather than offering these in high street or retail locations, where people can try them out and be attended to by shop assistants, they display their wares on the internet and deliver them. Many of the ingredients are the same (goods, warehouses, logistics, etc) and some are different.

Of course, a service organisation might have a reputation for delivering few benefits, if any, and a poor Service Experience. This is likely to attach a psychological disbenefit to the service.

This will reduce the overall Service Benefit, potentially to a level where the Service Value Equation doesn't balance, and the Total Cost to Customer outweighs the Service Benefit and Service Experience, so that the customer doesn't buy the service or is only prepared to pay a much lower Direct Price.

HOW DOES THE BRAND SHAPE THE VITAL CHARACTERISTICS OF A SERVICE?

Brands can be particularly important for service organisations, as the intangible nature of many services can make them tricky to sell/hard to buy.

Customers want to have some certainty that they are buying something of real value which has some substance to it, and that other people buy it too.

They may only have the service organisation's reputation to go on and what other customers "feel" about the organisation.

They get this from the firm's brand. It tells them, or implies, something about the firm – what it does, how it does it , who it does it for, as well as how good it is at delivering the service, the personality of the people involved etc., and its position in the market vis-à-vis its competitors.

The brand can, thus, significantly shape how tangible the SerVAL Proposition is perceived to be by its customers.

It can also reduce potential customer concerns about service variability, signal the level, nature and "personality" of customer/ service provider interaction, and how long service benefits can be expected to last.

Think how some service organisations use "cuddly characters" as part of their brand image, and how this is able to convey the impression of a friendly, empathetic service.

Think of the use of "classic" and/or "historic" imagery to convey the length of time that an organisation has existed, and by inference, how long its benefits can be expected to last, e.g. "Managing wealth since 1823."

HOW DOES THE BRAND AFFECT CUSTOMER RELATIONSHIPS?

The underlying source of long-term successful customer relationships is the consistent delivery of the expected SerVAL Proposition. However, strong customer relationships also form an important source of customer loyalty and hence, customer value (as I will explore in Chapter 13).

Strong customer relationships allow service organisations to retain and grow customers by offering them more of the same SerVAL Proposition or new and additional SerVAL Propositions. They also enable organisations to recover from those occasions where the delivered SerVAL Proposition didn't quite meet customer expectations.

Fundamentally, these relationships are based on:

▶ The delivery of the expected SerVAL Proposition

▶ Interpersonal relationships between customers and employees of the service organisation

▶ Legal relationships (contracts) between the customer and the service organisation*

▶ Psychological relationship between the customer and the service organisation's brand.

The latter is what is often termed "brand loyalty".

* Legal relationships that aren't based on consistent delivery of the expected SerVAL Proposition will only last, as a maximum, for the length of the contract.

In cases where the level of human interaction between the customer and service provider is low or infrequent, as with many internet-based service organisations, customers are unlikely to build strong relationships with the service provider's employees.

Many services don't involve long-term contracts. Brand loyalty can, thus, be a critical source of long-term customer relationships for many service organisations.

Brand loyalty can be a significant element in the Total Cost to Customer, in terms of the psychological costs of switching.

A service organisation's brand will also strongly influence what current and potential customers expect from the organisation, against which its performance will be measured. I will discuss this more in Chapter 12.

HOW DOES THE BRAND INFLUENCE THE EMPLOYEE EXPERIENCE?

The service organisation's brand is also important for recruitment, as it will attract or repel certain types of people. This is a self-enforcing or self-destructive circle. The brand will attract certain types of people as employees, who will then shape the brand.

The higher the levels of contact between the customer and the service deliverer's employees, the more the people are actually seen as the brand.

This can be a very important consideration if a service organisation is recruiting and retaining large numbers of people who don't match the organisation's culture and brand. It will lead to a change in culture and brand that will reflect the dominant group of people. Retaining cultural and brand integrity can, thus, be a significant challenge in fast growing, people-intensive service businesses.

Brand, therefore, can have a significant impact on the Service/Profit Chain, as discussed in Chapter 5.

SUMMARY

All the tangible elements within the Service Delivery Mix will impact the Service Experience, and also, to varying degrees, the Service Benefit (particularly via their impact on the Brand).

Brand is an important element of the Service Delivery Mix as it can provide significant psychological benefits to customers who buy a service that can be highly intangible. It can also form an important element of the Total Cost to Customer, due to its impact on customer loyalty, and hence switching costs. A service organisation's brand will also influence the type of employees it can attract and retain, and these employees will, in turn, influence the brand.

Furthermore, a strong case can also be made for it becoming an increasingly important component of the Service Delivery Mix, due to the increased levels of ICT and the internet within the mix.

Where the level of human contact is low, such as with internet-based businesses, the brand can be the prime, if not the only way, to convey the "personality" and "character" of a service organisation, as well as all the other messages the organisation wants its customers to hear or perceive. It can form the primary source of "empathy" between the service provider and its customers.

This may explain the use of "cuddly and cute" animals, cartoon characters, etc, or trusted celebrities as brand ambassadors to provide a "human face" (sic) to businesses with whom customers primarily have an impersonal relationship.

The brand may be the only element that personal loyalty can be attached to, and thus generate a psychological cost that can stop customers moving to another service provider. It can help to define the values and expected behaviours of the service provider in the customer's eyes.

The Service Brand is, thus, a key part of the SerVAL Proposition.

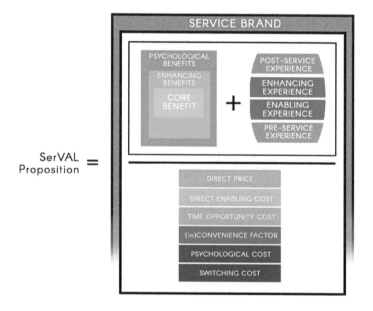

The questions below will help you to consider the current and potential impact of your marketing materials, marketing communications and brand on both your service organisation and your competitors.

CHAPTER EIGHT:
KEY QUESTIONS TO CONSIDER:
MARKETING MATERIALS AND BRAND

▶ In addition to people, process, ICT systems and the internet, real estate, tools & equipment, what other tangible items in your service organisation do your customers see, feel, hear or otherwise directly or indirectly interact with?

▶ How do these impact the Service Benefit?

▶ How do these impact the Service Experience?

▶ How do these impact the Total Cost to Customer?

▶ How might these impact customer loyalty?

▶ How do these impact the Employee experience?

▶ Do these reflect the desired "brand meaning"?

▶ What marketing messages are you explicitly giving?

▶ How well do these explain the Service Benefit?

▶ How clearly do these explain the Service Experience?

▶ How certain can customers be about the price?

▶ How do these messages impact customers' perceptions of their overall Total Cost to Customer?

▶ Do your customers clearly understand your SerVAL Proposition?

▶ Do they understand how it differs from those provided by your competitors?

▶ How might these communications impact customer loyalty?

▶ How do these communications impact the Employee experience?

▶ How well do these communications reflect the desired "brand meaning"?

▶ What do your customers perceive as being the "meaning" of your brand?

▶ Is this the intended "meaning"?

▶ What psychological benefit(s) does your brand provide?

▶ Does this psychological benefit create strong switching costs for your customers?

▶ Can this psychological benefit be made clearer?

▶ Can this psychological benefit be made stronger?

▶ Do your competitors' brands generate high customer loyalty and high switching costs?

▶ How might these switching costs be reduced, relative to the benefits of selecting your service organisation?

CHAPTER #9

DELIVERY MODELS FOR SERVICE SUCCESS

INTRODUCTION

In previous chapters, I described the three core components that comprise the Service Value Equation for any service. I also discussed how the typical VITAL characteristics of a service significantly shape the Service Value Equation. I proposed that each service organisation's specific Service Value Equation be thought of as its Service Value Proposition ("SerVAL Proposition") to its customers. I then went on to consider the basic ingredients that are available to create any service, and how these can be combined into different service "recipes", which I termed the Service Delivery Mix, and their impact on the SerVAL Proposition offered by different service providers.

In this chapter, I will highlight the different types of service models that enable service organisations to combine and deliver their chosen Service Delivery Mix in order to create their chosen SerVAL Proposition. These are often called Service Delivery Models. I will also consider how the Service Delivery Model can influence the VITAL service characteristics. I will touch on how the Service Delivery Model also influences the working experience of the employees in the Service Delivery Mix, which can have a major impact on the Service Experience delivered to customers.

I will then examine the other side of the value creation equation – how the Service Delivery Model influences the service organisation's cost base, profit margins and long-term customer relationships. I cover this in more detail in later Chapters.

KEY QUESTIONS

In order to consider the effect of the Service Delivery Model on the SerVAL Proposition, the questions I address are as follows:

▶ What Service Delivery Models are available?

▶ How does the Model impact the VITAL characteristics of a service?

▶ How does Service Benefit choices impact the Model?

▶ How does the Service Delivery Model impact the Service Experience?

▶ How does the Model impact the Total Cost to Customer?

▶ How does the Model impact the service organisation's Brand?

▶ How does the Model impact the Employee Experience?

▶ How can you apply this to your service organisation?

In order to consider the effect of the Service Delivery Model on how a service organisation creates value for its owners, I then examine the following questions:

▶ How does the Model impact the organisation's cost base?

▶ How does the Model influence the efficiency of service delivery?

▶ What are the implications of changing the Model to reduce costs?

▶ How might the Model impact customer relationships?

WHAT SERVICE DELIVERY MODELS ARE AVAILABLE?

In practice, there is a wide range of Service Delivery Models available to service organisations. Rather than attempt to come up with a definitive list, which would probably not be exhaustive and will soon date, I think it is more helpful to consider the characteristics of different models, as it is these characteristics that shape the SerVAL Proposition. Service textbooks tend to focus on the following characteristics of a service when classifying service delivery models, and I have found them to be quite insightful.

▶ The level of service customisation.

▶ The degree of customer contact i.e. high or low.

▶ The nature of customer contact, e.g. face to face, by telephone, correspondence, the internet etc.

- Where the service is delivered:
  - The customer comes to the service deliverer
  - The service deliverer comes to the customer
  - Arm's length delivery, e.g. the internet.

- Who has the customer contact? Often used to define "front line" and "back office" operations.

- The level of labour intensity involved in creating and delivering the service.

- The level of judgment exercised by, and operational flexibility given to, the service delivered.

- The nature of relationship with customers:
  - Formal relationships (membership, contracts)
  - Informal relationships (public transport, mail, radio)

- The nature of demand for the service compared to supply, in terms of periodic/day to day/irregular fluctuations in demand.

- The period of service delivery:
  - Continuous delivery of service
  - Discrete transactions

You may have noted that this list doesn't include direct service delivery versus outsourcing. These are, of course, different ways of assembling a Service Delivery Model. In essence, however, it reflects who owns and directly controls the different elements of the Service Delivery Mix and Service Delivery Model, rather than its fundamental characteristics.

HOW DOES THE MODEL IMPACT THE VITAL CHARACTERISTICS OF A SERVICE?

In Chapter 3, I set out how services have some VITAL characteristics, namely:

- **V**ariability

- **I**nvolvement

- **T**angibility

- **A**ttainment period for the Service Benefit, Service Experience and Total Cost to Customer

- **L**asting Service Benefit

The Service Delivery Model can shape these characteristics.

For example, the more standardised the targeted Service Benefit and Service Experience, the less variable it should be. The less discretion given to the service provider's employees to make decisions and/or to vary the service delivery process, the less variable the service will be. The less involved the customer is with the process, the less variable it is likely to be. The fewer employees involved with the process, the less variable it is likely to be.

However, the more involved the customer is within the Service Delivery Model, the more tangible the service may appear, and the stronger and longer-lasting the memory of the service is likely to be. The more formal the relationship between the service provider and customer, the more tangible the service may appear. At the very least, there is likely to be a contract document or membership card.

A Service Delivery Model that involves continuous or ongoing provision of service is also likely to align the service delivery, service payment and receipt of Benefits and Experience, and provide a more lasting (continuously current) memory of the service, and also lasting/ongoing benefits.

It can be seen that a degree of trade-off may exist, or be required. Should there be high customer involvement to make the service more tangible, but more variable? Or a short-term service experience that is easier to control and to make less variable, or a longer-term experience, which may be more variable but lead to stronger customer relationships? The Service Delivery Model choice is central to such trade-offs.

HOW DO SERVICE BENEFIT CHOICES IMPACT THE MODEL?

A key strategic decision for any service business is to decide whether it should produce standardised or customised Service Benefits. This process involves the service provider deciding whether or not their customers need, want and can pay for a customised or standardised Service Benefit, and whether or not they can make an acceptable return from providing it. The SerVAL Proposition provided by their competitors also needs to be considered.

The strategic decision that is made concerning standardisation v. customisation of Service Benefits is likely to shape the Service Delivery Model, and the Service Delivery Mix, in the following manner.

It is likely to influence:

▸ **The degree and nature of customer interaction:** customised solutions will typically require higher levels of customer interaction.

▸ **The processes adopted:** customised solutions will require processes that focus on understanding customer needs, designing and delivering solutions, and a relatively high degree of process flexibility, customer interaction and judgment exercised by the service provider's people.

▸ **The type and skills of people involved in the business:** customised solutions require people who can design and deliver a customised solution, and can effectively, efficiently and commercially exercise judgment.

▸ **The ICT systems and internet approach that is adopted by the business:** these will need to reflect the nature of the service being customised, the level of customisation, the processes adopted, as well as the level, form and location of customer interaction.

▸ **The location and nature of its real estate:** this will reflect all of the above and give regard to where these types of customers can be found or are prepared to travel to, as well as and the need to travel, the form and frequency of customer interaction, and where a suitable pool of suitably skilled people can be found.

▸ **The nature of the type of customer relationships required and desired.**

Equally, decisions made about the Service Delivery Model will impact the Service Benefit. For example, will a decision to standardise processes, reduce customer contact levels etc. lead to a reduced ability to deliver customised benefits?

This interdependence can be considered thus:

SERVICE BENEFIT

SERVICE DELIVERY MODEL

HOW DOES THE SERVICE DELIVERY MODEL IMPACT THE SERVICE EXPERIENCE?

The chosen Service Delivery Model will also have a significant impact on the Service Experience and, in service design terms, is the key influence on the Service Experience.

For example, the level, frequency, nature, location and media for contact between customer and service personnel, and the nature of the service personnel will have a significant impact on the Service Experience.

▶   Contrast online retailing with visiting a high street shop.

▶   Contrast visiting a high street shop with visiting a shopping mall.

▶   Contrast visiting a mall with visiting a luxury retailer in a prestige location, such as Bond Street in London.

Decisions on where the service is delivered – at the customers' premises, the service provider's premises or at a third party's premises, such as using hotels and conference centres for meetings – will also have a profound impact on the Service Experience.

Contrast online banking with visiting a bank's offices.

Contrast meeting a traditional banker in a pinstriped suit in his private office in large impressive premises, with meeting a uniformed customer assistant in an open plan branch.

Contrast meeting with your bank manager, who is empowered to make lending decisions, to meeting with a customer assistant, who refers to a computer.

Would you get together with your banker for a meeting in a hotel lobby?

The way that the service organisation chooses to deal with high and/or irregular fluctuations in demand will shape its ability to respond quickly, consistently and reliably to its customers. That will reflect both the timing of when the customer receives the Service Benefit and the customer's perception of the Service Experience.

Imagine phoning your central heating maintenance provider in the middle of a cold spell because you have no heat or hot water, and the maintenance provider tells you that they are too busy fixing everyone else's heating, they haven't got anyone to mend yours for two weeks.

So, service organisations must recognise that their Service Delivery Model is not just a case of putting all the components of the Service Delivery Mix together in a functional and profitable manner. Instead, it has a fundamental impact on the Service Experience.

Changes to the Service Delivery Model can be expected to change the Service Experience, and thus the SerVAL Proposition. This may or may not be something that the customer wants, or is prepared to pay a similar price for.

This interdependency can be considered as follows:

HOW DOES THE MODEL IMPACT TOTAL COST TO CUSTOMER?

Price

The price that a customer is willing and able to pay for the service will fundamentally reflect:

▶   The Service Benefit

▶   The Service Experience

In addition, the relative total cost to them of alternative Service Value Propositions, as well as the customer's available budget. In short, demand and supply.

The Service Model is the means to deliver the Service Benefit and Experience, so the direct impact of the model on price is through the benefits and experience it delivers.

This means that any change to the Service Delivery Model that leads to a significant change in the Service Benefit and/or Service Experience may lead to a change in the price that customers are willing to pay for the Service.

Total Cost to Customer

Equally, if not more, importantly, the Service Delivery Model also strongly influences the other elements of the Total Cost to Customer, namely:

▶   Enabling costs

▶   Opportunity Cost

▶   (In) convenience factor

▶   Psychological costs

▶   Switching costs

The costs that customers incur to enable them to receive the Service Benefit and Service Experience are significantly influenced by the Service Delivery Model.

Think of the travel costs incurred when the service is delivered at the service provider's premises, rather than the service provider coming to the customer. Travel time will also generate a time opportunity cost. Most people can spend their time much more usefully than sitting in a traffic jam, for example. And what about the inconvenience of travelling there, service delays, etc. Inconvenience can also be shaped by the degree of operational flexibility (process rigidity) in the model.

Internet-based Service Delivery Models can have a huge impact on the Total Cost to Customer, significantly reducing travel costs, opportunity costs and inconvenience. It can also reduce the psychological costs connected to concerns about price, as price comparison can be much easier and quicker.

The Service Delivery Model is also likely to have a major influence on the psychological costs associated with using a service or switching service providers. These costs may be high in cases where someone has a high level of personal contact with the same member of staff at the service provider, particularly if that person generates a psychological benefit.

The Service Delivery Model can also shape switching costs. For example, models that involve continuous service delivery, based on ongoing legal contracts, can involve some switching costs. For example, from a utility provider or if you cancel a cleaning contract early. Those involving occasional service provision, where the contractual arrangement is just a point of sale/point of service, may have very limited switching costs, however.

If the Total Cost to Customer, excluding the price, is high, then this may limit the price that customers are willing and able to pay. Equally, if they can be reduced, then a price premium may be achievable.

The price might be reduced by changing the Service Delivery Model.

An example of this is on-line shopping and home delivery services now provided by a number of large super market chains. Paying a delivery charge (which is a higher price) saves the customer the travel costs, travel time and inconvenience of driving to the supermarket. But does this lead to a higher or lower margin for the retailer?

HOW DOES THE MODEL IMPACT THE SERVICE ORGANISATION'S BRAND?

An organisation's brand will ultimately reflect the type, level and nature of Service Benefit and Service Experience it delivers, the Total Cost to Customer, and the marketing communications required to promote this.

If a service organisation's brand "meaning" is to be recognised as symbolising a high volume of standardised outputs, e.g. fast food, then it is going to be difficult to persuade customers that it is also famous for producing more customised food offerings.

The brand's character will be greatly shaped by the Service Delivery Model. For example, if the service provider has a low level of contact between its employees and customers, then building a brand based on "friendly people" is going to be difficult, although not impossible, as discussed in the example below.

An interesting example of how a firm has built an empathetic, personable, friendly brand, despite having an internet-based, low people contact model is comparethemarket.com, a price comparison website in the UK. It has used cartoon meerkats as central characters in its marketing communications materials, particularly TV advertisements. They have thus used the Brand and marketing communications as a way to overcome some of the potential downsides of a low contact, low labour content model.

It is important to remember that, eventually, the substance of service delivery will align any gaps between reality and rhetoric! Putting a "friendly" brand wrapper around an unfriendly Service Experience with a low Service Benefit is unlikely to provide sustained success.

An interesting question arises when firms look to materially change their Service Delivery Model.

If the service organisation is known to deliver a friendly, people-based, service in lots of convenient locations, how will a move to an internet-based, remote service fit with the brand? Or is the brand so strong, perhaps through a reputation for always delivering a high quality service, that it can leverage this into a different model because people trust it? This is a key question as more and more service organisations look to change their cost base by replacing people with technology, and thus changing the contents within the brand wrapper, particularly the Service Experience.

HOW DOES THE MODEL IMPACT THE EMPLOYEE EXPERIENCE?

The primary creators of a Service Benefit are people. That is the case, even if the service is primarily an internet-based service, or a capital equipment intensive service. That is because, ultimately, people design the service, choose and assemble the Service Delivery Mix, and create the elements therein. The skill and motivation of the service provider's people, thus fundamentally underpin the Service Benefit.

Furthermore, one of the main factors influencing the customers' Service Experience is the behaviour of the service organisation's employees, as and when they interact with these customers.

The Service Delivery Model adopted by a service organisation, whether deliberately or inadvertently, through custom and practice and evolution, is going to have a major influence over the day-to-day working experience of all the employees in the service organisation. This might be termed "the Employee Experience". In the section below, I highlight how the Service Delivery Model can influence this Employee Experience, and then explore the huge importance of the Employee Experience on the SerVAL Proposition in the following chapter.

The Service Delivery Model will impact the level of customer interaction that employees have and the format of that customer interaction. For example, are the organisation's employees meeting lots of customers face to face, or do they spend a lot of time on the phone and/or dealing with written communication? Are they travelling a lot to meet customers, or are they meeting customers at the service provider's office?

It will also impact:

▶ The level of creativity and judgment they deploy in their roles. Are they developing customised solutions for customers or providing the same service each time?

▶ The degree of variety in their work.

▶ The quality, quantity and type of tools & equipment and ICT that they use, and thus how easy it is to perform their role.

▶ The quality and location of the real estate they work in.

The level of customer awareness of the employees' service organisation's brand, the brand meaning and brand character is likely to impact the employees' pride in working for that organisation, and thus influence their motivation and behaviour.

Any service organisation that is considering changing its Service Delivery Model should therefore pay close attention to the impact on Employee Experience, as it is very likely to change it, for better or worse.

For example, extrovert employees are unlikely to enjoy working in Service Delivery Models that involve low levels of customer contact, and their performance levels and retention rates are likely to drop, thereby increasing the costs of recruitment to the service organisation.

Introvert employees are similarly unlikely to enjoy the Employee Experience of working in a high customer contact model, and their introvert behavior is unlikely to provide a good Service Experience, leading to poor customer satisfaction and customer retention, which can reduce both the profitability of the service organisation and damage its brand.

Employees who enjoy high levels of autonomy in their roles, for example, professionals, such as lawyers and accountants, may be unlikely to enjoy the Employee Experience of working in a Service Delivery Model, where low levels of autonomy are permitted and little judgment can be exercised.

HOW DOES THE MODEL IMPACT THE ORGANISATION'S COST BASE?

The Service Delivery Model adopted will heavily influence the combination of components in the Service Delivery Mix, namely:

▶ People

▶ Process

▶ IT and Communication systems

▶ Internet

▶ Knowledge

▶ Tools & Equipment

▶ Real Estate & Facilities

▶ Brand

▶ Customer involvement

This will also heavily influence the organisation's cost base, and hence the margins it can achieve from the Price that its customers are willing and able to pay for its SerVAL Proposition.

People costs

One of the most important cost influences of the Service Delivery Model will be the quantity and cost of human resources deployed. The cost of the individual person will reflect the levels of skill required, which is likely to reflect whether or not the service being produced is standardised or customised, and how much judgment is required when delivering the service. All things being equal, using lower skilled people exercising little judgment producing a standard service output and a standard service experience will cost less than using higher skilled people that produce a bespoke output, involving a high element of judgment.

Compare the people cost base of a fast food restaurant with a Michelin starred gourmet restaurant. But compare the Service Benefit and the Service Experience, and the price too. They offer different SerVAL Propositions.

The cost base will also reflect where the labour is located, which in turn will reflect the level, form and frequency of customer/service provider interface. If the latter is low, or via remote communication media, then the scope to locate service providers in lower cost locations is greater.

Labour location will also reflect where the service needs to be delivered. A cleaning service may involve low customer interface, but you can't economically use employees based in South Africa to clean an office in London!

The number of people deployed will also depend on the ability to replace people by equipment and ICT to improve efficiency and effectiveness. However, such an approach may also affect the Service Experience.

Real estate costs

The second major cost for a service business is likely to be the quantity, location and quality of real estate required. The location will be influenced by whether the Service Delivery Model involves customers visiting the service deliverer's premises or vice versa, or no visits to the premises at all.

Remote service delivery with remote communication tends to support the use of cheaper real estate in locations where there is a lower demand.

Think about the different real estate requirements of different types of retailer, from the on-line retailer to the high street retailer, to the supermarket to the luxury retailer. This also gives a different service experience to the customer. What would be the implications of a luxury retailer moving to an out of town retail park? Its real estate costs would go down. Would it sell more or less of the same product, and for the same price?

Providing the service at the customer's premises also means that less real estate may be required.

In the professional services market, management consultants tend to work at clients' premises and at home, and spend less time in the office compared to lawyers, for example, who tend to work from their offices where clients will visit them.

The potential real estate requirements can be quite different, with management consultants being one of the earliest adopters of "hot desking" strategies, for example.

The quantity of real estate will, in part, reflect the nature of the service (for example, cleaning companies need less real estate than lawyers under current business models).

Real Estate costs will also be potentially influenced by the number and skill set of people who are required to deliver the service: large numbers of highly skilled people may only be found in areas where real estate costs are very high.

That is often the case with professional and financial services, which tend to be found in locations such as central London or Manhattan.

ICT costs

The third major cost is likely to be the cost of the ICT and internet that is deployed to deliver the services. In many service businesses, ICT has moved from being a back office tool that supports front line service deliverers (such as word processing) to being a front office tool (such as a help desk), to becoming the actual front office, such as online retailing and online banking, and replacing front line staff, with people becoming the back office to support the front line, as a result.

The use of more ICT and internet in the Service Delivery Mix, through adopting a new Service Delivery Model, may reduce the cost of the business model by replacing people and real estate, or allowing cheaper people and real estate to be used.

It will also impact the SerVAL Proposition by changing the Service Experience.

Being able to shop online and interact with your bank online can save a huge amount of travel time, travel cost and general aggravation. It can also provide a 24/7/365 service and thus increase service accessibility. Think how ATMs have increased the accessibility of cash and mobile phone applications may reduce the need for cash and bank charge cards in future.

Tools & Equipment

The use of tools & equipment in some services can have a major impact on the cost base. This impact arises from a combination of the cost savings, driven by the use of the tools (efficiency and effectiveness) and the costs of the tools.

The use of vacuum cleaners and floor polishing machines has reduced the need for labour in office cleaning businesses, for example, by driving costs down. Vacuum cleaners are relatively cheap to purchase and might be the equivalent of 2 or 3 days wages of a cleaner.

The requirement for expensive rubbish collection trucks, which have relatively low utilisation (a few hours a day, a few days a week) for waste management services can drive the costs up significantly. The cost of these can be the equivalent of 20 years' wages for their operatives!

HOW DOES THE MODEL INFLUENCE THE EFFICIENCY OF SERVICE DELIVERY?

As well as considering the raw cost implications of the Service Delivery Model, it is also important to consider efficiency.

Efficiency is defined by Wikipedia (February 2016) as follows:

"The (often measurable) ability to avoid wasting materials, energy, efforts, money, and time in doing something or in producing a desired result. In a more general sense, it is the ability to do things well, successfully, and without waste."

Efficiency is thus a comparative measure of the unit costs of producing a service, and in simple terms, reflects the level of wasted cost.

I explore how to manage the costs of service delivery and issues of service efficiency, and efficiency/effectiveness trade-offs in Chapter 14. In the section below, I simply highlight how the Service Delivery Model impacts Service Efficiency.

The most efficient service delivery models are those involving:

▶ The production of standardised Service Benefits

▶ The use of standardised processes

▶ Limited numbers of people involved in undertaking standardised tasks with minimal variations

▶ Standardised customer issues/situations to be dealt with

▶ Limited customer/service provider interaction

▶ Predictable, stable volumes of demand.

In short, the service delivery models most aligned to manufacturing/production delivery systems, where high levels of repetition and capacity utilisation are possible. This is the model often described as a "Service Factory". The Service Delivery Models that don't meet the above criteria are going to be relatively inefficient.

But how important is efficiency to your business and its competitive position, compared to the Service Benefit and Service Experience?

Think about mass produced and mass retailed suits compared to bespoke "Saville Row" suits. The production process must be much more efficient for the former than the latter. For the latter, the customer is paying for a higher Service Benefit, such as a better fitting suit and the psychological benefits of wearing it, and the Service Experience of receiving high levels of personal attention from an expert.

However, if the bespoke maker of a suit cannot attract a price premium for this extra benefit and experience, then it is better to be in mass production, where greater volumes can be sought.

The bespoke tailor, however, still needs to be as efficient as possible to eliminate waste from the production process.

WHAT ARE THE IMPLICATIONS OF CHANGING THE MODEL TO REDUCE COSTS?

To reduce costs, in order to protect or increase margins, a service organisation may consider:

▶ Reducing the number and/or cost of people in its Service Delivery Mix.

▶ Reducing the quantity and/or quality and/or changing the location of its real estate.

▶ Replacing people and real estate with (lower cost) ICT and/or other tools & equipment.

▶ Not investing in its ICT and/or its other Tools & Equipment.

▶ Not investing so much in Brand promotion and development.

▶ Removing waste from the Service Delivery Model and Mix.

This could result in:

▶ A more efficient version of the service organisation, delivering the same SerVAL Proposition, but at a lower cost.

▶ Delivering a degraded version of the same SerVAL Proposition that may not prove to be as attractive to customers, but is just good enough to retain most of them.

▶ A different, but similar SerVAL Proposition.

▶ A totally new SerVAL Proposition.

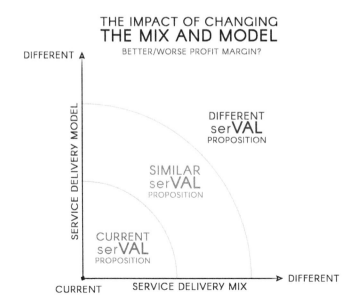

THE IMPACT OF CHANGING
THE MIX AND MODEL

It is important to recognise that if the Service Delivery Model is changed in order to reduce costs and increase margin, then it should not be assumed that prices will remain the same, as the Service Benefits and/or Service Experience may change. A change in Service Delivery Model may not lead to a change in margin.

What happens if you reduce the level of customisation and judgment in a taxi service? You call it a bus service. You then get lower prices and need different vehicles, etc. and thus a different cost base.

What happens if you try and use your routine maintenance personnel to do complicated plumbing work? What will your customer think if you send a highly qualified plumber to change a tap washer and charge a high hourly rate?

What happens if you outsource a large element of your legal service to India, where highly qualified graduates are paid a fraction of those in the UK? Will your clients still be happy to pay several hundred pounds per hour for the service, when they know it is now costing you much less to produce, and their service experience has changed, or will they want to pay a much reduced price?

Changing the Service Delivery Model may have a significant impact on the price the service organisation can charge for its services, as well as the cost of delivering the service, if it changes the Service Value Proposition. Remember the relationship set out below.

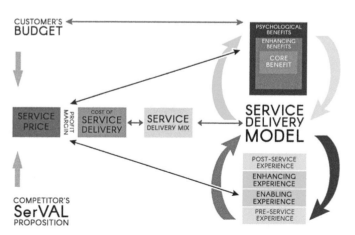

THE SERVICE DELIVERY MODEL'S IMPACT ON CUSTOMER RELATIONSHIPS

In simple terms, the longer the relationship lasts, the better it is for the service provider, assuming they enjoy a profitable relationship with the customer. I explore this in more detail in Chapter 13. In the section below, I consider how the Service Delivery Model may impact the length of such relationships.

It is probably self-evident that the level and frequency of customer/ service provider interface is likely to impact the strength of the relationship between an organisation and its customers.

Therefore, all things being equal, it might be expected that a Service Delivery Model based on continuous or frequent contact between the service provider's employees and its customers is likely to generate stronger customer relationships than a model that involves occasional, ad hoc contact or little human contact.

Without such, there is greater reliance on:

▶ Customers building a strong relationship with the Brand, as discussed above

▶ The SerVAL Proposition being significantly better than those of competitors

▶ High switching costs and/or other barriers to switching

Other barriers to switching can be the structure of the legal relationship between service provider and customer used in the Service Delivery Model. Relationships based on longer-term contracts will guarantee customer retention for a longer period than those based on one-off transactions, subject to the terms of the contract being met.

The Service Delivery Model adopted, thus, has a hugely significant influence on a service organisation's relationships with its customers. Any changes to the Model should bear this in mind.

A number of leading law firms have introduced work processing centres and are also looking at using ICT-based Artificial Intelligence to analyse legal documents. This is expected to reduce costs and increase efficiency.

A potential downside, however, may be that it significantly reduces the degree of human interaction between lawyers and their clients, and this may reduce (traditionally strong) client loyalty, which is usually to people rather than the firm in the legal market, and/or make the firm's brand much more important.

A trade-off may, therefore, be required.

Consider the possible differences in the strengths of customer relationships between the two examples in the diagram below.

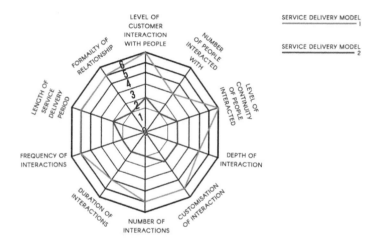

SERVICE DELIVERY MODEL 1

SERVICE DELIVERY MODEL 2

SUMMARY

The Service Delivery Model that a service provider adopts to combine its Service Delivery Mix has a significant impact on the whole Service Value Proposition. It defines the type of Service Benefit provided, directly shapes the Service Experience, and will thus materially influence the Price that customers pay. It can also drive all the other elements of the Total Cost to Customer. It will shape the Brand and can drive brand strategy. It will underpin the nature of customer relationships. It also impacts service performance through its huge influence on the Employee Experience. Finally, it is a major driver of a service organisation's cost base, and hence its ability to create value for the organisation from its customer SerVAL Proposition. Thus, overall, it is a key source of competitive advantage.

Therefore, any changes to the Service Delivery Model, whether evolutionary or revolutionary, planned or unplanned, need to be considered in terms of the holistic impact on the organisation's SerVAL Proposition, Employee Experience and ability to create a sustainable economic position for the service organisation.

CHAPTER NINE:
KEY QUESTIONS TO CONSIDER:
YOUR SERVICE DELIVERY MODEL

	CHARACTERISTIC	DESCRIPTOR	COMMENT
Customer contact and relationship model	Degree of customer contact	Low, Medium, High	
	Frequency of customer contact	Infrequent, Often, Continuous	
	Methods of customer contact	Eg Face to face, by telephone, by correspondence, through the web etc.	
	Who has the customer contact?	Which depts?	
		Which locations?	
		Which individuals?	
	Nature of customer relationships	Structured contracts & membership, or informal use as needed?	
		Personal or organisational?	
Service operations model	Level of service customisation	Bespoke?	
	Location of service delivery	Customer comes to service deliverer, service deliverer goes to customer, arms length (eg web), via third party	
	Nature of service delivery period	Continuous delivery or discrete transactions?	
	Level of labour intensity	Low, Medium, High	
	Level of ICT and internet involved	Low, Medium, High	
	Level of capital equipment involved	Low, Medium, High	
	Level of process flexibility	Low, Medium, High	
	Level of judgement required from labour	Low, Medium, High	

	Level of demand fluctuation	Low, Medium, High	
	Frequency of demand fluctuation	Low, Medium, High	
Demand and supply conditions	Predictability of demand fluctuation	Low, Medium, High	
	Ability to respond to peaks in demand without carrying high capacity	Low, Medium, High	
	Responsiveness of competing supply	Low, Medium, High	

▶ What is the impact on your Service Benefit?

▶ What is the impact on your Service Experience?

▶ What is the impact on the Total Costs to your customers?

▶ What is the impact on and implications for your Brand?

▶ What is the impact on your costs of service delivery?

▶ What is the impact on your customer relationship management strategy?

▶ What is the impact on your employees and the employee experience?

WHAT SERVICE DO YOUR CUSTOMERS ACTUALLY WANT?

INTRODUCTION

The preceding chapters have set out a broad basic framework for understanding services and how to create and deliver a SerVAL Proposition. That is a starting point. However, the success, or otherwise, of any service organisation will depend on providing something that a customer needs, wants and can afford. In short, providing a customer with an attractive SerVAL Proposition.

In this chapter, I am going to consider how a service organisation can gain an understanding of the SerVAL Proposition required by its customers.

KEY QUESTIONS

I will consider how a service organisation can gain such an understanding through addressing the following questions:

▶ Who is the customer?

▶ How many people are involved in procuring, benefiting from, experiencing and paying for the service?

▶ How can we assess what a customer actually wants?

▶ Why and when will a customer buy a Service Benefit?

▶ What price will a customer pay for that service?

▶ What Service Experience does a customer want?

▶ Will the customer tell the service provider what they want?

▶ Does the service provider know enough about the customer to anticipate what they want?

▶ Will the customer develop the Service Experience they want?

▶ How else does the customer impact the Service Experience?

▶ How can you apply this to your service organisation?

WHO IS THE CUSTOMER?

Unfortunately, identifying the potential or actual customer of a service is not always straightforward!

It is necessary to identify whether a single person receives the whole SerVAL Proposition. If not, is it the customer the person who needs the Service Benefit, has the Service Experience or pays for the Service? Or should they all be considered as customers? And what if it is a group of people who each require the Benefit and Experience and share the total costs (for example, a group of friends going to a restaurant)?

HOW MANY PEOPLE ARE INVOLVED IN PROCURING, BENEFITING FROM, EXPERIENCING AND PAYING FOR THE SERVICE?

So what determines the number of people who are involved as customers of a service? Typically, it depends on the service and the market.

In business-to-business service markets there is generally not a single customer or single procurer of a service. It is pretty common that there is a separation between budget holding, procurement and service receipt, and each customer representative will have their own personal objectives and own departmental objectives.

Those who receive the Service Benefit and/or Service Experience may have quite different objectives to those who pay the Service Price.

For an office cleaning contract, this might include a "user" representative, someone from "Facilities", someone from Finance, someone from Procurement etc.

There are parallels in the business-to-consumer market. Most people are all influenced by other people and other factors when making a decision to buy something. This may be their friends, family, peers or aspirational role models. My wife and children certainly express some vociferous opinions on some of my potential (and actual) choice of clothes!

For services to children, typically the parent is the budget holder, whereas the child receives the Service Benefit and the Service

Experience. In some cases, the parent may share the Experience and gain a Service Benefit, albeit one that may be different from the child's, such as having a happy child or time off from child care to do something else.

For public services, there is typically a separation of who pays the direct Price, usually the taxpayer, and who receives the Service Benefit and Service Experience. Those receiving the Service Benefit and Service Experience, however, typically pay the remainder of the Total Cost to Customer, namely the enabling cost, the opportunity cost, the (in) convenience factor and the psychological costs. This can create very complex relationships between customers and customers and the service provider.

In the UK, for care services for children, there can be a situation where the direct Price is firstly paid by the taxpayer to central Government. This may then be paid into the Health Service by the Government and allocated by the Health Service to various bodies.

There can be procurement bodies, such as local doctors, and then service delivery bodies, such as paediatric service providers. So the payer of the direct Price is quite complicated.

In terms of the Service Benefit, there is clearly the child, but also their parents and carers. The child, their parents and carers also experience the Service. What if they want/expect different things? For example, the child may well want a warm and smiling service deliverer, whilst the parent may be more concerned that the person is an expert.

The parents and/or carers are likely to be the ones who have the travel costs to the service provider's premises, the opportunity cost of taking time off work or foregoing other uses of their time, and all the hassle associated with travel, parking, form filling, etc.

Each person involved with the SerVAL Proposition will bring their own personal motivations and objectives to the procurement decision-making and service evaluation process.

What the procurement person wants may be different from the operational person and indeed there may be conflicting requirements, such as one wanting a low price and the other a high level Service Experience.

Some of the people involved with the purchasing decision often do not become involved with the service again until the next procurement process. However, the users of the service enjoy or suffer the consequences for the duration of the contract.

Furthermore, the users want a better service because they are not paying for it; there is a separation between Service Benefit and Experience and Price. This can create major challenges.

This is particularly prevalent in public services.

ARE SERVICE INTERESTS ALIGNED?

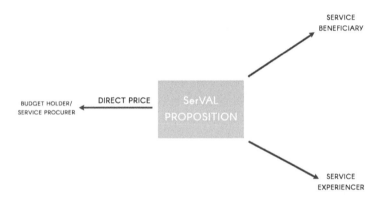

The involvement of multiple customer stakeholders also complicates the process when a service provider is asking its customer whether they are satisfied with the service they are receiving or whether they would like changes.

Who is the prime customer amongst that group of customer stakeholders?

It is, therefore, very important to understand there may be different customers for each element of the SerVAL Proposition, and/or there may be multiple customers for the whole or each element of the SerVAL Proposition, each of whom will bring their own requirements to the procurement decision and to their evaluation of whether or not they were satisfied with the customer.

The service provider, thus, needs to understand what can be termed as a "customer stakeholder map" for their service:

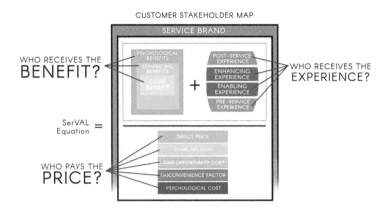

CUSTOMER STAKEHOLDER MAP

Insurance companies will pay the direct price for repair work to a home damaged by flooding, but the householder will suffer the time opportunity costs and hassle factor of dealing with the building contractor. The householder will also receive the Service Benefit, but fellow householders, neighbours and other third parties may also receive the Service Experience, with noise and dust from the works and the presence of contractor's vehicles etc.

With an IT maintenance contract for a business, the direct price is paid by the Finance department, but agreed by the Procurement department, but the time opportunity cost, hassle factor and psychological cost is paid by the IT department. The Service Benefit (functioning IT) is largely received, or not, by the customers and employees of the business, and partly by the IT department. The Service Experience is largely received by the IT department and partly by the employees of the business.

When a group of people are taken to a restaurant to celebrate a birthday, they will all receive the Service Benefit and Service Experience, but are likely to receive different pre-service experiences, unless they all live together. The host will pay the direct Price, but they may all experience different opportunity costs, hassle factors and enabling costs.

With public services, the direct Price is usually paid by the taxpayer, but the transfer to the service provider is normally via an intermediary body, such as central or local government. The person (s) who receives the Service Benefit may bear the enabling costs and opportunity costs. If the service is a health service, then an individual may receive the Benefit, but their relatives and friends are also likely to share the Service Experience.

Having identified who the customers are, their potential SerVAL requirements can then be considered.

HOW TO ASSESS WHAT A CUSTOMER ACTUALLY WANTS?

Failure to understand the customer's needs is a primary and very obvious cause of the failure to deliver what customers expect to receive, as I will show in Chapter 10. Furthermore, it is not that easy to assess what SerVAL Proposition a customer actually wants, as I will demonstrate below! This may be one of the main reasons why it is difficult to point to lots of examples of outstanding service!

However, just because it isn't easy and may not be a precise science, it still needs to be done.

Research methods

Assessing what a customer wants can be done through any, or a combination of, the following methods:

▶   Structured market research

▶   Informal market research, e.g. "there does not appear to be any providers of service X in this market"

▶   Customer requests for a new service from the organisation

▶   Intuition

▶   Trial and error, as is often the case with new services

▶   Trying to find a solution to a need the customer has

The assessment must cover all three elements of the SerVAL Proposition, commencing with the Service Benefit because without a customer need to meet, there is no service requirement, and the customer will not buy the service.

As part of this process, it is worth remembering that sometimes customers will generate needs, and sometimes needs are created for customers, i.e. the customer may define the need or the need may define the customer. For example, people over 2 metres tall and weighing 200kg may have a need for specialist clothing shops and/or specialist tailoring services. New legislation that companies with revenues over $10m must produce an annual report on their carbon emissions will create a group of customers of all companies above that size who may wish to buy consulting/ advisory/report writing services on carbon emissions.

WHY AND WHEN WILL SOMEONE BUY A SERVICE?

A customer will procure a service when they require the Service Benefit and can afford to pay for it. The starting point for any service provider is, therefore, to identify an actual or potential need for a service in a market.

However, identifying a potential need is not sufficient in itself. The level, timing and consistency of demand will also depend on whether the Service Benefit addresses a current need, or a future need, and/or whether that need can be deferred, and how necessary it is to receive the benefit.

In the examples above, there will be demand from people who are already over 2 metres tall and 200kg in weight, as well as future demand from people smaller than this that will grow to this size, such as some children and young adults. And some of the people this large will die. Most current and potential customers will need a specialist shop, but not to have bespoke clothes made for them.

The carbon emission reporting requirement will not become law for another 5 years, when it will become compulsory to have the service, or the directors of the organisation may be sent to prison and the organisation fined.

So what factors influence whether a need is current or future and/ or deferrable, and the importance of the benefit?

Basic needs, distress needs and discretionary needs

Clearly, some customers' needs are basic; ones they will always have. For example, food and shelter. Some service needs are laid down by legislation, for example, the requirement for businesses above a certain size to have an independent financial audit. These needs are current and not optional. Some services are driven by customer distress. For example, heating system failure in the winter drives the demand for boiler maintenance and replacement services. These tend to be current, rather than optional needs, but are more difficult to predict than basic needs. Other needs are discretionary. For example, the need for restaurant services is discretionary because people do not have to eat out, and so is the need for travel agency services because people do not have to go on holiday.

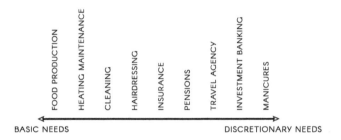

The level of discretion actually exercised will also depend on the cost of the service relative to the individual's budget. For example, whilst a manicure may be less necessary than a holiday, it will constitute a much smaller percentage of someone's budget and may be selected ahead of a more expensive, slightly less discretionary service. The level of discretion exercised may also fluctuate over the economic cycle, as customers' budgets increase or decrease.

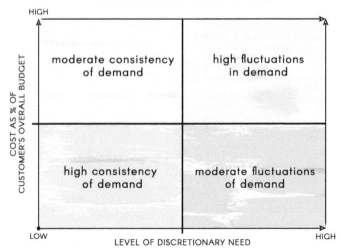

Furthermore, discretion does not necessarily mean that the purchase decision is binary, i.e. buy or not. Demand for many services can also be deferrable.

Many Local Authorities in the UK have decided to only provide refuse collection service on a fortnightly basis, rather than weekly, in order to save money.

The ability to defer a procurement decision will vary from service to service.

Another factor influencing the deferability of a service is the immediacy of the Service Benefit. If a service provides a deferred benefit, such as a pension service for a young person, then procurement of that service is also more readily deferred. In my experience, the strength and form of the relationship between service provider and the customer also influence the level of durability and discretion exercised over the purchase of a service. The more arm's length the service provider, in terms of both customer/provider operational interaction and relationships, and the weaker the brand, the more discretionary the service becomes, as the psychological cost of deferring the purchase is lower. The Service Delivery Model will, therefore, also shape the level of discretion in demand. It is, therefore, very important for service organisations to understand how discretionary and/or deferrable its SerVAL Proposition is in order to understand the level, timing and consistency of any potential demand that may exist.

Furthermore, it should seek to make its services as non-discretionary and non-deferrable as possible.

The ability to pay

The other key factor to consider in terms of demand is the customer's ability to pay for a service. Potential demand only becomes an actual demand when a customer is able to pay for a service. A potential customer may have no budget to pay for a service to meet the need. An existing customer's overall budget may be shrinking, or they may need to, or decide to, spend it on something else.

Where do budgets come from?

A customer can find a budget to purchase a service in the following four ways:

▸   They have an existing budget for the service, as it is part of their historical spending patterns

▸   Their available funds are growing and, thus, creating surpluses to spend on new goods and services, or more of their existing purchases

▸   The need for that service is greater than the customers' needs for something else, and they replace that other requirement in their list of expenditures

▸   The service provider assists the customer to find a budget to purchase the service, such as through cost savings provided by the service, or by providing finance to enable the purchase.

Why and when will someone buy a service?

Therefore, why and when a customer will buy a service is simple: it is because they have a **c**ompelling, **i**mmediate, **n**eed ("CIN") and some money to pay for it, i.e. a **b**udget available to spend that can be delivered by the customer ("CINB").

Note – the ability of the customer to deliver a theoretically available budget should not be overlooked, particularly in business-to-business situations where the potential customer may still need to have their budget signed-off by a third party, such as the Finance, Procurement department or their line manager.

If a customer doesn't have a **C**ompelling **I**mmediate **N**eed and a **B**udget, then they will not buy or cannot buy a service from a provider. At one level, identifying the CINB is clearly a statement of the obvious, but at another, we all tend to forget this from time to time. A lot of pre-sales selling costs are wasted because of a failure to identify a CINB. This applies to both existing services and new ideas. Furthermore, it is extremely important to remember that providers of services (and goods) are not just competing with other organisations that produce similar services, but also for a share of a customer's overall wallet.

An example that really brought the importance of **CINB** home to me, and has served me in good stead ever since, was a business that was trying to sell new heating and cooling systems into schools in the UK in the mid-1990's, funded through energy savings. It had not closed a single sale over a number of years, despite the business model working very well in other countries. A number of prospects had expressed an interest, but were always delaying the decision to proceed.

Was the failure to close a sale down due to an unmotivated or incompetent sales force, or was there something inherently wrong with the concept?

An investigation indicated that the sales force was highly motivated – but losing that motivation fast, due to the failure to close a sale! They were also quite competent, as they could articulate the value that the solution brought and were articulating it to all the right people. So what was the problem?

Firstly, the value being delivered was not high enough. Financial payback took too long and energy consumption and energy costs were not that high compared to the costs of the equipment and associated services. There was also no "green" agenda or legislation driving adoption of more energy efficient/lower carbon solutions.

Secondly, whilst schools were not as warm/or as cool as people would like, this tended only to be for a few days a year, and it had been like that for years, as most schools in the UK at that stage were in old buildings. It was something that needed sorting, but tomorrow would do. Thirdly, there was no budget to work on the legal agreements etc. required to put the scheme in place, either in financial or time terms. And, as ever, the schools were working to tight budgets anyway.

In short, there wasn't a strong enough need or benefit for the solution, and whilst it was a great idea, there was no reason to buy one today, rather than tomorrow. And tomorrow never comes. They also had no budget. The business pulled out of that part of the market.

Opportunistic, immediate purchases, such as a room upgrade in a hotel, an extra drink at a restaurant or a small purchase at the checkout at a supermarket can also be considered in these terms. For a start, someone needs a budget to pay for it, and it may only be a small addition to their budget. Secondly, something triggers a compelling immediate need in their mind for them to think: "I really fancy a bar of chocolate", " a bigger room will give me more benefit, as I can fit my family in with less disruption and get a better night's sleep" or "a more prestigious hire car will make me feel better about the travel experience".

Alternative solutions and substitutes

There is one further consideration that influences whether or not there will be a realisable demand for a service, and that is the availability of alternative means of procuring the Service Benefit.

For many services, the alternative is for the customer to provide the service themselves, as people can do their own gardening, rather than employ a gardener. They can also cook at home and not go to an expensive restaurant, or they can go to a cheaper restaurant. They can bring outsourced services in-house and save the contractor's margin. If it is an in-house service provider, it can be outsourced, providing an outsourcer can demonstrate a better Value Proposition.

New technology, plus globalisation, plus competitive pressures are leading to innovation and the emergence of alternative ways of providing services. Why will people use a travel agency service when they can put their holiday together on the web from the comfort of their own home?

ALTERNATIVE SOLUTIONS FOR PROCURING THE SERVICE BENEFIT

PROCUREMENT OPTIONS	Qualified Doctor	Grow you own food retailer	Do it yourself Painter and decorator Interior Designer	Stay at home Stay with friends/relatives Holiday company Travel agency Self-booking via website
SERVICE	Provision of expert medical care	Provision of food	Interior decorating	Holiday

NO ALTERNATIVE SOLUTIONS

SEVERAL ALTERNATIVE SOLUTIONS

The greater the availability of **a**lternative **d**elivery solutions for the Service Benefit and the lower the switching costs to procure them, the weaker the CINB, all things being equal. The key to demand for a service might thus be considered using the acronym "**CINBBADSS**" (**C**ompelling **I**mmediate **N**eed, **B**udget, **B**etter than available **A**lternative **D**elivery **S**olutions and **S**witching costs). These alternative solutions are the "substitutes" in Michael Porter's famous "Five Forces" model (Porter, M.E. (1980) Competitive Strategy, Free Press, New York, 1980.)

Service organisations, therefore, need to assess:

▸ What their existing and potential customers actually want, when they want it, and what they can afford to pay for it.

▸ Whether they can obtain the Service Benefit through an alternative delivery solution.

▸ What their competitors are charging for the same or similar service.

▸ The SerVAL Proposition of alternative services and goods that consume their customers' budgets.

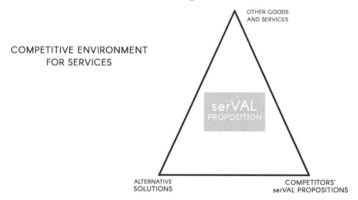

COMPETITIVE ENVIRONMENT
FOR SERVICES

OTHER GOODS
AND SERVICES

serVAL
PROPOSITION

ALTERNATIVE
SOLUTIONS

COMPETITORS'
serVAL PROPOSITIONS

In order to sell more of its services, retain what market share it already has or create a market, a service organisation needs to consider how to position its service so that it:

▸ Becomes less discretionary

▸ Becomes less deferrable

▸ Delivers more value than its direct competitors' SerVAL Propositions

▸ Delivers more value than the SerVAL Proposition of alternative service solutions

▸ Is in a position where a budget is made available by its customers to pay for it.

The power of the SerVAL Proposition and its price element – relative to other SerVAL Propositions and goods – is thus a key determinant of a service organisation's success. A powerful SerVAL Proposition is based on strong CINBBADS.

WHAT PRICE WILL A CUSTOMER PAY FOR THE SERVICE?

The price that a customer is willing to pay for the Service Benefit and Service Experience will depend on five factors.

▸ The level of Benefit and the Experience received.

▸ The price that other service providers will charge for providing the same, or similar Benefit and/or Experience.

▸ The Total Cost to the Customer.

▸ The cost of alternative service solutions, such as doing it themselves.

▸ Their available budget.

In short, demand and supply.

A business will not pay £10,000 for some advice when the expected cost saving is £5000. No customer, given the choice, will pay a high price for a poor Service Experience.No customer, given the choice, will pay more to one service provider than another for exactly the same Service Benefit and Service Experience. However, they may pay a higher direct Price if the other costs are much lower; for example, pay a higher direct Price for the convenience of less hassle and lower opportunity cost of using a local retailer compared to one a number of miles away. That is why the total Service Price needs to be considered.

Customers are much less likely to pay a price for a service that is significantly higher than the cost of them carrying out the service themselves. However, once again, the total Service Price needs to be considered. Customers may pay a high direct price for someone mowing their lawn because the opportunity cost of them doing it themselves is very high, as it means they can spend their weekend going to meet friends, instead of cutting the grass.

In order for a Service organisation to identify the direct Price it can expect for its service, it needs to gain an understanding of the Total Cost to Customer that a customer will pay for a service, the TCC that they would pay if they choose competitors' SerVAL Propositions, and the TCC that they would have to pay for Alternative Delivery solutions, including switching costs between each, and the TCC they will pay for the service provider's SerVAL Proposition.

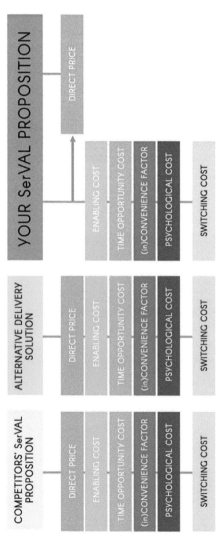

WHAT SERVICE EXPERIENCE DO CUSTOMERS WANT?

It can be very difficult for customers to articulate the Service Experience they want. This difficulty can be due to some of the VITAL characteristics of services, as discussed in Chapter 3, particularly their variability, the involvement of the customer in producing the service, (in) tangibility, and they don't tend to be lasting, other than in the memory.

The variability of services can make it difficult for the customer to describe what they want, or for the service organisation to describe its offering, because each time it is slightly, or significantly, different. This can be a particular issue for services that are variable by design, i.e. bespoke services.

The level of customer/provider operational interaction ("involvement") can make understanding customer needs more complicated too, particularly in cases where high levels of interaction occur.

This might emerge as a statement, such as "I only want John to cut my hair"; whereas what they are actually saying is that they like having John cut their hair because they share the same interests in a particular sport, have friends in common, and/or are much more relaxed with John because he has cut their hair for years. Or, what they may be saying is that they wish is someone who gives them the haircut they want (which assumes an equal level of skill and effective communication of what is wanted) and also shares similar interests and relaxes them. In fact, Jane could do this too.

Intangibility can make it difficult to explain exactly what the benefits of consuming the service are. It is even more difficult to explain a Service Experience because, by definition, these are relatively intangible. Service organisations must, therefore, try and ask their customers' questions and explain their services in a way that makes it as tangible as possible.

This might be through using the different elements of the Service Delivery Mix, and the performance characteristics of the Service (see Chapter 9), such as "how responsive does the Service need to be?"

"I need to have someone come and repair my boiler within 4 hours in the winter because I run an old people's care home and if they get too cold they will become very ill and may die."

"I want a very experienced person dealing with my issue because it is very important to me and it is a complex issue".

"I want a person with good knowledge of the products to serve me in the shop because I understand very little about the differences and find the choice bewildering."

"I want to deal with a friendly person who really understands my needs."

Because services tend not to last, customers will rely on their memory for what they want and what they think of the service they have received before. They may also rely on the memory of other people by asking family, friends or work colleagues what they remember about the service.

The creation of a powerful service memory is, therefore, very important.

So it can be difficult to describe a service. That isn't the end of the challenge, though.

Customers may struggle to articulate what they want because they have no time, interest or experience to help them express their needs, have yet to actually think it through or think their requirements are obvious. It could be because they have yet to procure this type of service, so do not understand what it really can do for them.

A brief to a domestic cleaner can be as simple as, "I want my house clean" or be prescriptive on the inputs (but not the output), such as, "I want it vacuumed twice a week." This may or may not achieve the required level of cleanliness.

They may not specify that they do not want the vacuuming done near the study in the morning, as they are working from home then, and do want certain cleaning materials used because their pet has an allergy to it. Service providers can realise their customers' oversight to their cost.

I want to leave a hairdressers believing I look like George Clooney, smelling great, having had my hair washed by the attractive assistant and drunk a cup of espresso at just the right temperature. I also want to be seen leaving the "right" salon by the "right" people, and being able to discuss how I use the "right" "product" to make me look and smell so good. And the only holiday I want to talk about is mine, in Barbados. Oh, and I want to park my Porsche right outside where everyone can see it, but not touch and scratch it. If someone could wash and polish it at the same time, that would be good too. But the new hairdresser didn't know that when I said, "My usual, please."

Or it may that the customer has simply stated the obvious and assumed the service level and experience that is actually critical to their purchase decision.

Sometimes, the customer does not actually know what they want and needs some help in describing it. This assistance may come from the service provider.

Typically, I will have a rough idea of what I want when looking for some consultancy advice or recruiting someone. I will then want to discuss this with the consultant and develop my thinking with input from them, I will then reject some of my ideas and thoughts some of theirs before arriving at a "final" specification.

It may come from third parties, such as family, friends or acquaintances, from books, consumer advisory organisations and magazines, such as 'Which', and increasingly from websites.

The British Cleaning Council www.britishcleaningcouncil.org. has a standard cleaning specification set out on its website, for example:

The Consortium of Local Authorities in Wales has a modular series of building maintenance specifications on its website (www.claw.gov.uk).

The Australian Bankers' Association sets out common service standards for Australian banks (www.bankers.asn.au).

In a business-to-business context, it is not unusual for consultants to help the customer specify their requirements. Whilst it can, therefore, be difficult to identify what a customer actually wants, it is important to realise that in the vast majority of cases the discussion is not about totally new services that no one has ever bought before, but the evolution of existing services. So, in most cases, the service provider is discussing minor adjustments to its existing service, or a service that someone else already offers.

This makes it easier to discuss because most existing or potential customers will have experienced it before from that provider or a competitor, even though the service may be intangible. This discussion can be articulated in terms of the current levels of Service Benefits received, the Price and the how various elements of the Service Delivery Mix and the Service Delivery Model impact the Service Experience.

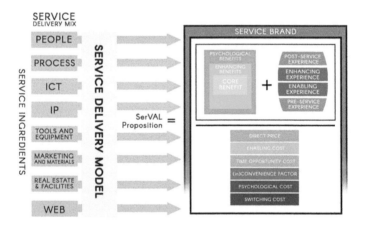

It is also important to contextualise this in terms of what they are willing and able to pay for. Most people would want the best possible Service Experience, as well as the best possible Service Benefit.

However, asking customers what they want ignores the need they have that they don't yet know they have! To paraphrase, Donald Rumsfeld, there are known service needs and unknown service needs!

To quote from Henry Ford, "If I asked my customers what they wanted they would say a faster horse".

WILL A CUSTOMER TELL THE SERVICE PROVIDER WHAT THEY ACTUALLY WANT?

Sometimes, a customer may know what they want, but won't tell the service provider why they want it. It is likely this is because they do not trust the service provider yet.

Consider your own experiences as a customer.

You are more likely to speak freely with someone you have worked with for years and is now a personal friend who has earned your trust, than to someone who you have just met.

This may mean that the customers it has the strongest and deepest relationships with are the best source of feedback on the level of Service Benefits and Service Experience it provides.

Two other good sources of intelligence will be the customers the organisation:

▶   Loses, or who raise complaints, as they will demonstrate where it is failing to deliver an appropriate SerVAL Proposition.

▶   Wins from other organisations, as these will not only highlight factors important to the customer, but also which competitors are failing to deliver.

If a customer will not tell the service provider the SerVAL Proposition they want to receive, the Service provider will have to try and anticipate their wants.

In order to do so, it needs to understand them as best it can.

DOES THE SERVICE PROVIDER KNOW ENOUGH ABOUT THE CUSTOMER TO ANTICIPATE WHAT THEY WANT?

Does the service provider understand the customer's environment?

It is important to understand the environmental factors impacting individual consumers. For example, what is happening to wages and salaries (the customer's ability to pay), socio-demographic changes (e.g. increasing/decreasing birth rates, increasing/decreasing longevity), and the changing availability and use of technology?

A social housing organisation I have been associated with identified that whilst a significant percentage of its customers did not have immediate access to computers and the internet at that time, the vast majority had basic mobile phones. Their phones could, therefore, be an important means of communication and service delivery via calls and text, whereas email or the web was less useful. This situation would change again, as more and more obtained smartphones.

In a business to business context, it can be difficult to gain an effective understanding of the needs of a customer, and the benefits that the provision of a certain service can bring that customer, if the service organisation does not understand the customer's industry and/or their organisation very well.

Many years ago, one of my ex-colleagues had to write a maintenance specification for petrol filling stations. Having worked with them for some time, he understood that one of the key sources of revenue and profit were the fridges they sold food from. The most common and most expensive equipment failure was the fuse for the fridges. In fact, a blown fuse, which only costs a few pounds, could lead to lots of lost revenue and wasted food. One piece of strategic analysis I undertook for a client illustrated that a key driver of demand for their services was less due to general economic circumstances, as he had assumed, and more down to particularly competitive challenges and market circumstances in particular industries, along with cultural factors in particular countries.

Well-known tools for strategic analysis, such as "PESTEL" (Political, Economic, Social, Technological, Environmental, Legislative factors), can be very powerful ways that you can use to gain an understanding of underlying drivers of customer needs.

Does the service provider know enough about the customer as an individual?

It is necessary to understand the customer as an individual to a certain degree in order to anticipate what they need, whether in a business-to-business or business-to-consumer context, and to help them articulate these needs.

This understanding comes over time, as a relationship and trust is built between customer and service provider. It also comes from asking and receiving answers to insightful questions, as well as intuition, experience and empathy.

My experience is that it is possible to anticipate what customers want to some degree, even if they do not explicitly say it. For example, in a business-to-business context, there is typically a business equivalent of Maslow's "Hierarchy of Needs". This looks something like this:

Will a risk-averse individual, just two years away from retirement, really want to procure a radical new service solution and maybe lose their job and destroy their legacy if it goes wrong? Will a rapidly rising star employee want to maintain the status quo? Will someone whose job is on the line if they don't reduce their departmental budget by 15% really support an increase in service levels and higher expenditure, even if there are longer-term benefits? Will a user representative, whose constituents are complaining that their area of the building is too hot, really support a reduction in energy consumption through lowering the use of air-conditioning? In the end, whose decision is it?

The Service provider may also have information about similar services it offers to similar customers that may give an insight into what its customers need or want.

Market research can be very advanced in the business-to-consumer sector. For example, large retailers generally have a very good idea of what their customers are buying and the demographics of their markets.

Business-to-business service organisations that best understand the markets of their customer, the organisational needs of that customer and the needs of the individual within the customer organisation, are the most likely to deliver the SerVAL Proposition their customers need, want and can afford.

This means that service organisations in the consumer services market need to really understand the socio-economic environment their customers live and work in, as well as their needs, budgets and personal circumstances.

This means that customer research, customer analysis and understanding customers are core skills of successful service organisations.

WILL THE CUSTOMER DEVELOP THE SERVICE EXPERIENCE THEY WANT?

The involvement of the customer in the service means that they can, deliberately or inadvertently, start to shape the service experience.

A key customer of one service business that I have led insisted all documents should be sent and received in an electronic format from a particular date. This led to a change in the way that we interacted with that customer, and developed our capabilities to deal with other customers in the same way. And, whilst it was a customer-driven innovation, the solution was a co-innovation between the customer, our firm and our competitors, who also served them.

SUMMARY

The identification of the customer of a service is not necessarily straightforward, as a number of different people may receive the Service Experience, bear different elements of the Total Cost to Customer, and possibly receive the Service Benefit. This applies as much to the consumer services market as it does to the business-to-business service market. However, failure to identify all the customer stakeholders in the SerVAL Proposition is likely to lead to some failure to meet their needs.

The customer's requirements and expectations will cover all three elements of the SerVAL Proposition. However, the starting point must be the Service Benefit, as the demand for a service derives from a customer need. Sometimes, customers will generate the needs and sometimes needs are created for customers, i.e. the customer may define the need, or the need may define the customer.

It is important to recognise that some needs are fundamental and others are discretionary. The demand for some needs can also be deferred for a period. The more discretionary and deferrable a need, the harder it will be to persuade a customer to buy a service. Furthermore, a customer may have a need for a service but no budget to pay for it. Without a budget, the demand is not realisable. Service organisations don't just fight with competitors for that budget, but also with all the other goods and services the customer spends their budget on. They also compete against alternative ways of obtaining the Service Benefit.

Like with goods, customers will buy services when they have a compelling, immediate need, they have a budget to do so and don't have a better alternative delivery solution to meet the need, and/or where switching cost is low ("CINBBADSS"). Without the necessary CINBBADSS, a service organisation will not make a sale.

Having identified the customer (s) for the service and the need that is driving it, it can still be difficult to gain an understanding of the Service Benefit and Service Experience required by a customer for a number of reasons. Firstly, the VITAL characteristics of services (intangibility, perishability etc.) make it difficult for a customer to describe what they want. Secondly, they may not know exactly what they want. Thirdly, they may assume the service provider knows what they want. Fourthly, they may not yet be prepared to tell the service provider exactly what they want as their relationship may not be strong enough.

The Service Experience they require will partly depend on what is required to deliver the Service Benefit – the enabling experience – and what is offered by competitors and alternative solutions. It can, however, be hard to describe and may be best assessed through reference to the Service Delivery Mix, Service Delivery Model and service performance measures, such as responsiveness (which will be discussed in Chapter 12).

The Direct Price that customers can be expected to pay will depend on their budgets, the level of benefit received, the Total Cost to Customer and also the TCC of alternative delivery solutions and switching costs – that is demand and supply. The Direct Price they will pay will also reflect the other price elements in the service provider's SerVAL Proposition.

Identification of needs and budgets can be obtained from having a robust understanding of the customer's personal and/ or business (for business-to-business services) environment, using well-known strategic tools, such as PESTEL analysis, as well as customer research, customer feedback, intuition, and/or trial and error. Obtaining a detailed understanding of customers is a core skill that is required of successful service organisations.

Although this can be difficult, don't forget that it is not about creating new services in many cases, but enhancing or developing variations of existing ones. This can be done by improving the Service Benefit, making it more obvious, improving the Service Experience, or adjusting the Price to offer greater value to the customer, without destroying value to the service organisation.

But do not forget that one of the main reasons why service organisations fail to deliver what a customer wants is because they don't understand what that is. I explore this gap further in the next chapter.

Ask yourself the following questions about your service organisation and the services offered by your competitors:

CHAPTER TEN:
KEY QUESTIONS TO CONSIDER:
WHAT SERVICE DOES YOUR CUSTOMER WANT?

CINBBADSS

▶ What need does your service benefit meet?

▶ Who has that need?

▶ Why do they have that need?

▶ When do they have that need?

▶ Who is involved in the customer stakeholder group?

▶ What is the involvement of each person in the group?

▶ How does the service benefit each of them?

▶ How do they influence the buying decision and process?

▶ How compelling is that need?

▶ How immediate/deferrable is that need?

▶ Do they have a budget available to meet that need?

▶ Can they create a budget to meet the need?

▶ Can you help them create a budget to meet the need?

▶ What service experience are they looking for?

▶ Why?

▶ Which members of the customer stakeholder group will receive which parts of the service experience?

▶ What direct price are they willing and able to pay?

▶ Why?

▶ When?

▸ What are their other Total Costs when purchasing the service

▸ How does the Total Cost to Customer compare to the value to them of the Service Benefit?

▸ How does the Total Cost to Customer compare to the value to them of the Service Experience?

▸ How well do you think you know what they want, and if they are willing and able to pay for it?

▸ How and why do you think this?

▸ How can you find out more about their needs?

▸ How many customers require such a SerVAL Proposition (how big is the market?)

▸ What alternative delivery solutions are available to these customers?

▸ How do these compare in terms of the level of value provided?

▸ What switching costs are there to move to your service/away from your service?

WHAT CAUSES A FAILURE TO DELIVER WHAT CUSTOMERS WANT?

INTRODUCTION

In the previous chapter, I considered how to identify the SerVAL Proposition that customers will want to buy. However, as customers, we all know that having bought a service, many service organisations then fail to deliver the one we were expecting.

This might be because they failed to deliver the expected Service Benefits, or we just did not know what Service Benefits to expect. It may be that the Service Experience wasn't as good as we expected and/or we didn't know what Service Experience to expect. It could be because the Direct Price or the Total Cost to Customer was higher than we anticipated. Or it could be due to a combination of all of these reasons.

In this chapter, I am going to consider why this can happen, other than as a result of a deliberate intention to mislead by the service provider, by examining the following questions.

KEY QUESTIONS

▸ What SerVAL Proposition are the customers expecting?

▸ What are the five gaps that mean the customers may not get what they expected?

▸ How can there be a gap between what the customer wants and what the service organisation thinks they want?

▸ How can there be a gap between what the customer wants and the service organisation sets out to deliver?

▸ What causes service delivery failure?

▸ How can there be a gap between what the customer receives and what the customer thinks they have received?

▸ How can there be a gap between what the customer perceives they have received and what the customer expects to receive?

▸ What can be done to prevent this happening?

▸ How can you apply this to your service organisation?

WHAT SerVAL PROPOSITION ARE CUSTOMERS EXPECTING?

In the previous chapter, we established that a customer will buy a service when they have a CINBBADS – a **C**ompelling **I**mmediate **N**eed, a **B**udget, and **A**lternative **D**elivery solutions – to obtain the benefit that is less attractive to the customer than the service organisation's SerVAL Proposition, or the **S**witching costs are too high. But how do they know what to expect from the service organisation's SerVAL Proposition when they decide to buy it?

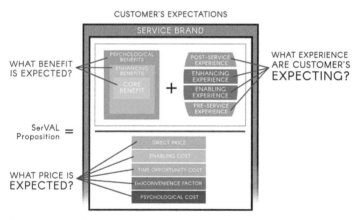

The customer's expectation will be based on the SerVAL Proposition that the service organisation explicitly tells them it will deliver. It will tell them this through general or customer specific marketing communications and/or sales proposals, and contract specifications, etc. If they are an existing customer, then their expectation will also be based on the SerVAL Proposition they have received previously from the service organisation – their "Service Memory".

These points require little explanation. However, three other factors will also influence customers' expectations. Sometimes, these will be the only factors that shape customers' expectations if the service organisation has not explicitly told them what SerVAL Proposition it will deliver.

These three factors are the SerVAL Proposition that:

▶ **Other people tell them** that the service organisation will deliver

▶ **Competitors have delivered to them**

▶ The service organisation **implicitly tells them** that it will deliver to them.

When you visit a restaurant for the first time, your expectations will be set by the location, the building's appearance, the menu, the staff, the appearance of other clientele there, and what you have read and heard about it, and your experience of other restaurants. There is no explicit communication to you about the SerVAL Proposition from the service provider.

"Other people" will include friends, relatives, colleagues, acquaintances, general word-of-mouth, as well as unknown third parties via social media, the internet and traditional media. These third parties may include consumer watchdogs and specialist commentators, such as restaurant critics.

The customer's experience of the service organisation's competitors' SerVAL Proposition will also shape their expectations.

A customer's expectations of a hairdresser's services are shaped by visits to other hairdressers. A customer's expectations of a hotel's services are shaped by visits to other hotels.

Customer expectations will also be shaped by the tangible elements of the service organisation's Service Delivery Mix, such as property, people, tools & equipment and websites.

A customer's expectations of the SerVAL Proposition of a hospital are likely to be shaped by the appearance and condition of the hospital buildings, and the appearance and behaviour of staff. Their expectations of the SerVAL Proposition of a law firm are likely to be shaped by the behaviour and appearance of the law firm's employees at the initial meeting. A customer's expectations of the SerVAL Proposition of a builder are likely to be shaped by the appearance and condition of the builder's truck.

Last, but not least, customer expectations will be influenced by the communications associated with the service organisation's brand.

Thus, there is a wide range of factors influencing customers' expectations and all of these will come into play each time a customer procures a SerVAL Proposition. So, how do service organisations fail to meet these expectations? Of course, as discussed in the previous chapter, there can be multiple customer stakeholders involved with the SerVAL Proposition.

SERVICE ORGANISATIONS FAIL TO DELIVER WHAT THE CUSTOMER EXPECTS BECAUSE OF FIVE GAPS

The best explanation I have seen of why service organisations fail to deliver what their customers expect to receive is set out in the SERVQUAL "5 Gaps" model, developed by Zeithaml, Parasuraman and Berry ("Delivering Service Quality ", Free Press, 1990).

This is represented diagrammatically below.

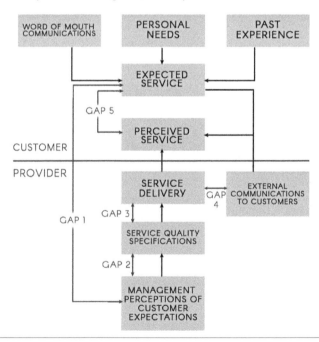

From DELIVERING QUALITY SERVICE by Valarie Zeithaml. Copyright (c) 1990 by The Free Press. Reprinted with the permission of Free Press, a Division of Simon & Schuster, Inc. All rights reserved

The first gap arises because the service organisation doesn't know what the customer wants and expects from the service.

The second gap arises because, whether or not the service organisation knows what the customer wants and expects, the service organisation fails to specify this clearly to the part of the organisation that delivers the service.

The third gap arises when the organisation fails to deliver to that specification. This can occur even if the customer's expectation is fully understood and specified.

The fourth gap can arise even if the service organisation delivers to the required specification. This gap is where the service organisation has either directly or indirectly given the customer an expectation that the SerVAL Proposition will be different from the one that is actually delivered. This is a classic "over promise" and "under deliver" scenario. It should also be noted that the often advised "under promise" and "over deliver" scenario will also create issues, because the next time the service is purchased, customer expectations will be higher but the service specification may not reflect this.

The fifth gap is where the customer perceives that they haven't actually received what was specified and promised. This is a situation that can arise because of some of the inherent characteristics of the services, namely that they are intangible and perishable, so a customer doesn't know quite what they have received and/or can't remember exactly what they have received.

I went to visit a customer who wanted some advice, but he wasn't quite sure exactly what he needed. He thought he wanted to merge his business with another and some advice on how to do it. I listened to what he had to say, and framed it in my own mind. I thought I knew what he wanted. I then returned to the office and explained to the consulting team what I thought the client wanted. They interpreted what I told them, and delivered some advice based on what they understood I had said. You can see already the potential emerging gaps; the customer not really sure what they want and/or unable to articulate it clearly, which can be a frequent challenge due to the intangible nature of services, and I misunderstand what they wanted and/or superimposed my own belief of what they actually needed. I then give an imprecise briefing to my team, who thought they understood what I had told them and/or superimposed their own beliefs of what they thought needed to be done. So they delivered a service based on their "specification". The next potential gap can be caused by the firm's marketing communications activities. If we say we only use consultants with 20 years industry experience, and then engage some newly qualified MBAs on the project – who are more than adequately experienced and skilled to do the element of work assigned to them – and the customer is aware of their involvement, they may believe they are not getting the "promised" service.

The final gap comes when the customer perceives he has received a service different from the one he expected. Note this is perception and not necessarily reality.

All bar one of these are fundamentally communication gaps. The exception is the gap between delivering what is specified and what is actually delivered, which can be due to operational causes, i.e. failure to deliver.

A slight variation between what the customer wants and expects, and what is passed on at each stage, is a business form of the children's game of 'Pass the message'; each time the customer's requirement is "passed on" in the organisation, it can change slightly, so the end result can be quite different! The SERVQUAL model illustrates that it is important for service organisations to recognise that customer dissatisfaction can be caused by communication failure, as much as by operational failure.

GAP ONE: HOW CAN THERE BE A GAP BETWEEN WHAT THE CLIENT WANTS AND WHAT THE SERVICE ORGANISATION THINKS THE CUSTOMER WANTS?

We have seen in the previous chapters that the intangible and perishable nature of services can make it difficult for customers to have a clear understanding of the Service Benefit or Service Experience that they require, or if they do have such an understanding, it can be difficult to articulate. Sometimes, the only tangible element of the SerVAL Proposition is the direct price element. The variable nature of services doesn't help either because each procurement of the service, whether from the same or a different service provider, may have been slightly or significantly different.

This gap may also be due to a failure of the service organisation to understand their customer's personal and/or organisational environment. As discussed in Chapter 10, such an understanding provides the context for the customers' needs and expectations. There is a double danger here, however – knowing too much or too little about the customer.

Knowing too little can clearly lead to a gap, as the service provider fails to understand their real needs.

I recently had my haircut in a small provincial town, by a fashionable young lady. I gave her a briefing of what I basically wanted. Now, I should point out that I had been hill walking and was relatively scruffy, and my hair was windblown at the time.

I ended up with a haircut that she obviously thought that a casual fashionable young (well that bit I am making up!) man would want, and probably was wearing locally. It was described by my wife and kids as a "sort of Mohican", but a bit longer on the sides.

I spent the next half an hour trying to flatten it and reshape it, and then got it recut to look something like a haircut that a "respectable" middle-aged executive might normally have.

Now, this was as much my fault as hers but I will not go back there, as she had superimposed her views of what she thought I wanted.

Knowing too much can be a problem too. This issue arises because a customer wants what they think they need and then expects to be given it. However, it is not uncommon, particularly for 'expert' services, such as medicine, law, architects and other 'Professional Services', for the 'experts' to have a more detailed knowledge of what is required than the customer, particularly if the customer is not a regular purchaser of such services.

If the service provider then fails to explain to the customer what they need, or explains the need, but fails to persuade the customer about what is required, then a gap can emerge. This is a version of the Rolling Stones' lyric, "You can't always get what you want, but sometimes you get what you need."

A further challenge for some services, particularly Professional Services, such as law, accountancy, medicine, etc. is that such practitioners can be sued if they are professionally negligent, so there is a big onus on the professional to persuade the customer what it is they actually need.

A core skill for any successful service organisation is, therefore, the ability to clearly understand what the customer needs, wants and expects, and to articulate this back to the customer and onwards into the service delivery part of the service organisation.

GAP TWO: HOW CAN THERE BE A GAP BETWEEN WHAT THE CUSTOMER WANTS AND WHAT THE SERVICE ORGANISATION SETS OUT TO DELIVER?

The specification challenge

Let us assume that the service organisation's management team, or sales and marketing team, accurately understands the requirements of the customer, which can be difficult, as we have established. This then needs to be turned into a 'specification' to be given to the people who will actually deliver the service. So why might this be difficult?

Well, with services being intangible, even after gaining an understanding of what the customer needs, articulating it in meaningful terms can still be difficult. This might be what is termed the "service specification challenge".

It is also important to remember that there are three elements of the SerVAL Proposition that need to be specified.

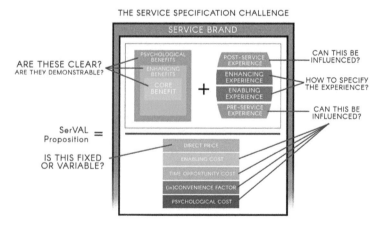

THE SERVICE SPECIFICATION CHALLENGE

There can be a danger that, instead of specifying a Benefit, the service provider will just specify an output because this is easier to specify, and can be more tangible measurable. But, as discussed in Chapter 1, the output may have little value to the customer.

For some services, a fixed price will be specified. It is clear to the customer what they will pay for the Service Benefit and Service Experience (even though these may be unclear!). However, for other services, a variable price that is based on a range of factors (e.g. time spent by the service provider) may be specified.

A window cleaner is likely to provide a fixed price to clean all the windows in a house.

A lawyer tends not to provide a fixed price for some services, and traditionally didn't for any services.

Where a variable, and hence uncertain, the price is combined with an unclear benefit, then the opportunity for customer dissatisfaction is much higher than for a service with a clear benefit and a clear fixed price.

With the former, the customer doesn't know quite what benefit they have received and isn't sure how much they are going to pay for it.

There is also the challenge of specifying what the Service Experience will be like. As we have discussed previously, describing an experience is not easy. However, the Service Experience can be explicitly specified to a degree. For example, the level, frequency and nature of customer interface, and whom that will be with, and where it will occur, can be specified, as can certain elements of the behaviour of the ingredients in the Service Delivery Mix, for example, the responsiveness of people and processes.

It is not unusual in Facility Management contracts for it to be specified how often the customer will meet with the management team of the service provider, who will attend such meetings, what will be discussed there, where it will occur, etc. They often set out service levels, including response times and the behaviour of staff. ("The receptionist will be friendly and courteous, greet everyone with a smile, be available at all times between 8am and 6pm, and provide all visitors with a cup of coffee or other drink if required.")

Typically, when a customer makes an appointment at a hairdressers they will be told who will cut their hair, when and where. This will shape the Service Experience. "No, actually, I would prefer John to cut my hair, and at your salon, at location X, not location Y."

The Service Experience may be implied by the tangible ingredients of the Service Delivery Mix, the Service Delivery Model and the Brand.

An internet-based service delivery model implies that the Service Experience is unlikely to involve much interaction with people.

Property with a very high specification in a fashionable location implies that customers who visit it will enjoy a luxurious Service Experience.

The Sales/Operations divide and Operations/Operations divide

There is a further complication beyond the service specification challenge. In how many organisations do "operations know better than sales"?

Sometimes rightly, sometimes not!

There is the danger that even if the sales and marketing function clearly understands what the customer wants, and specifies this clearly to the service delivery team, the operations team either do not trust the sales team, and think "the customer can't really want that, he must want this..." or "the customer shouldn't want that, she really needs this..." In the latter case, they may be right, but the customer did not ask for that!

This typically occurs where significant elements of the service are not delivered by the individuals who interacted with the customer to identify their needs and expectations and then drafted the specification.

That can be a typical operating model in many business-to-business services.

It may also arise because the service delivery team has not been provided with the service specification and/or this hasn't been clearly explained to them.

My experience in the business-to-business service market certainly suggests the latter can be an issue. It is not unusual in business-to-consumer services either, for different service personnel to deal with the customer at various stages of the service delivery process and/or each time they purchase the service.

This might be considered an "operations/operations" divide.

How often in a restaurant have you had the wrong meal delivered, your steak cooked to the wrong specification or the wrong drink delivered because the order hasn't been clearly passed to the kitchen or bar?

How often have you had to repeat your issue to a telephone-based call centre or been put through to several different departments and had different people in each department take the same details down each time you call them.

It is vital, therefore, that service organisations ensure the people actually delivering the service understand what the customer wants and expects, and this is clearly recorded and shared with all the relevant personnel.

GAP THREE: WHAT CAUSES SERVICE DELIVERY FAILURE?

The customer may not always get what they expect because the Service Delivery System fails to deliver the expected service. This failure could be because the resources in the Service Delivery Mix fail to perform as expected.

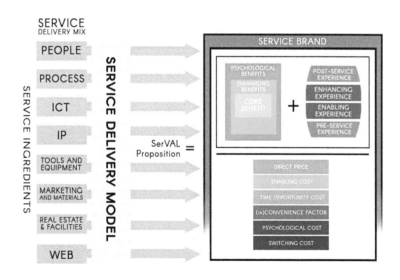

Let's start with the people in the Service Delivery Mix. The (modified) Service Profit/Chain model, discussed in Chapter 5, illustrates how the performance and behaviour of people in the Service Delivery Mix are key, and how creating the right working environment, with the right role descriptions, recruitment, rewards, recognition and retainment of the right people, influences this. But people also create variability.

It could be due to process failure or process variability (see the comment above about people and variability). It could be due to real estate failure. This might be as simple as the parking spaces being full or toilets being unclean, etc, through the Service Delivery Mix.

It could be because the Service Delivery System, which translates the Service Delivery Mix into performance, has failed to work effectively.

The various Service Delivery System models, covered in Chapter 9, were based around:

▶ The degree of customer contact i.e. high or low.

▶ Who has customer contact? (This is often used to define "front line" and "back office" operations).

▶ The nature of customer contact, e.g. face to face, by telephone, correspondence, through the Web etc.

▶ The period of service delivery:
  ▶ Continuous delivery of service
  ▶ Discrete transactions

▶ Where the service is delivered:
  ▶ The customer comes to the service deliverer
  ▶ The service deliverer comes to the customer
  ▶ Arm's length delivery (e.g. through the web)

▶ The level of service customisation.

▶ The level of labour intensity.

▶ The level of judgment exercised by, and operational flexibility given to, the service deliverer.

▶ The nature of demand for the service compared to supply, in terms of the periodic/day to day/or irregular fluctuations in demand.

▶ The nature of the relationship with customers:
  ▶ Formal relationship (membership, contracts)

Service Delivery System failure might be due to the level and/or duration and/or nature of customer interface being less or more than expected.

It is not uncommon for professional service businesses, such as law firms, to explicitly or implicitly promise customers high levels of contact with senior lawyers, only then for minimal contact to occur, or with junior staff, and then send out a bill that includes work undertaken by lots of lawyers who the client has never met and wasn't aware would be working on the project. Or the reverse can occur, where customers choose to use an internet-based service, and then find that they still need to meet with the service provider's employees or telephone them to resolve important issues. That has certainly happened to me with banking services, for example.

It may be due to a failure of the service provider to travel to the customer at an appropriate time or frequency, or vice versa. It may be because a high degree of customisation was expected, but the customer was given a standard service.

Think of the bespoke dress designer whose customer arrives at a party to find someone else wearing a very similar dress. Or the consulting firm that promises its client a highly specialised senior team, who are experts in the client's industry and will spend a lot of time getting to understand the client's business, and then sends in a team of generalist young MBAs who work to prescriptive methodologies.

It may be due to the level or quality of judgment exercised by an employee, probably because they don't have the right experience and expertise. Or that the employee isn't able to exercise any level of flexibility when requested by the customer.

Another challenge is that services are inherently variable (as discussed in Chapter 3), particularly the service experience, when they involve a high level of human input and/or a high level of customer/service provider interface. So the Service Benefit, and particularly the Service Experience, may well have been delivered in a different way than before.

It may be because there is insufficient capacity in the system to deliver the Benefit and Experience as expected.

This can be an issue for service organisations that experience significant peaks and troughs in demand, where at times they don't have enough people, tools and equipment, network capacity or real estate available to service the customer's needs.

It can also be an issue for fast growing service organisations that may be exacerbated by high immediate demands for labour or the recruitment of people who don't meet the required performance and behaviour requirements, which leads to the Service Profit Chain breaking down.

The Service Delivery System must, therefore, be developed and stress tested, with regard to these issues.

In the same way that the availability of capital may limit the speed of growth, service organisations may wish to limit their speed of growth, having regard to their ability to obtain the appropriate ingredients in their Service Delivery Mix at a sufficient speed.

GAP FOUR: HOW CAN THERE BE A GAP BETWEEN WHAT THE CUSTOMER RECEIVES AND WHAT THE CUSTOMER THINKS THEY HAVE RECEIVED?

Some of the major causes of a potential gap between what the customer receives and what they think they have received are once again rooted in the VITAL characteristics of services – intangibility, perishability and simultaneity.

For example, if the benefit is not particularly tangible, the customer may feel that they have not received much of a benefit.

Equally, if the benefit is deferred, then again the customer may not feel they have received a benefit (which is true at that point) and wonder whether the benefit is actually worth it.

What is the benefit of saving for a pension if I see the value of the pension pot fall due to a fall in the stock market, and the value of the potential annuity fall due to falling gilt yields, and my life expectancy reduce and/or I will have to work for much longer, and I know the Government will give me a pension too, and furthermore, my current disposal income is shrinking and I could do with some short-term benefits from other services?

Another key cause can be the level of customer/service delivery interaction, and in particular the visibility of the service delivery process.

Where the process is not very visible to the customer, they may not be aware of the level of resources committed to it by the service organisation, or the volume of activity that has been undertaken to generate it.

A good friend of mine engaged a major international law firm on a very large property transaction involving the acquisition of a property company and some of its assets. He met around 5 of the team, including two Partners. He was shocked to receive a bill for the work for 28 people over a weekend to get the deal done.

He hadn't been made aware that this many people were working on the transaction, had seen none of them personally, nor the work they had done.

This part of the Service Experience was totally invisible to him. The most visible part of it was the invoice.

Services can also be perishable, so what is delivered may just disappear. Was it even delivered?

"This floor was clean 30 minutes ago.".

"No it wasn't. You haven't cleaned it."

This provides a service organisation with three objectives: firstly, it must understand the SerVAL Proposition that the customer thinks they have received.

Secondly, it must demonstrate, as far as it is able to, that this is the service that was agreed with the customer and, thirdly, show that they have actually received it.

GAP FIVE: HOW CAN THERE BE A GAP BETWEEN WHAT THE CUSTOMER EXPECTS TO RECEIVE AND WHAT THEY PERCEIVE THEY HAVE RECEIVED?

There can also be a gap if the customer expects to receive a certain service benefit or a specific service experience, for a given price, and then does not feel that they have received it. This can be due to the intangible and perishable nature of services, as mentioned in the cleaning example above, or it can be another communication challenge, as outlined below.

Customer perception of what to expect is based on a combination of factors, including their past and current experience of the services of the service organisation and also that of its competitors. This is where the **service memory** is so important.

It also comes from the reputation of the service organisation. This will be based on word-of-mouth from their own network and what independent third parties tell them, which is why social media is becoming so important.

It will also be based on their perception of the brand, which will in part reflect word-of-mouth and also how the organisation presents itself.

It will also be based on what the organisation tells them to expect; whether that be that the relationship leader, the sales force, the marketing communications material, the operational people delivering the service, the sales proposal, the service specification and/or the written contract.

If a Professional Service firm claims in its marketing communications that its services are "Partner led" and "Partner intensive", then the customer may expect that the majority of her interface with the service organisation will be with a Partner.

Even though she gets a good service output and a great service experience for the price expected, if she perceives she has less Partner contact than expected, she may perceive that she did not receive the expected service...

What the Professional Service firm meant was a greater level of Partner involvement than delivered by its competitors, but still a relatively low Partner input, and not exclusively Partner input.

And, as mentioned in an earlier paragraph, it will be also based on the ingredients in the Service Delivery Mix, and what the Service Delivery Model implies to the customer.

Service organisations must ensure there is no gap between the Service Benefit and Service Experience that their marketing communications & Brand promises to a customer, and what it actually delivers.

WHAT CAN BE DONE TO PREVENT THIS HAPPENING?

In simple terms, it is key that service organisations do not create any of the five gaps identified or allow such gaps to emerge.

This means that excellent customer service is founded on:

▶ A robust understanding of customers' needs.

▶ Development of a clear SerVAL Proposition that meets those needs.

▶ Clearly specifying the SerVAL Proposition and communicating that both to the customer and the service delivery teams.

▶ Developing and maintaining a Service Delivery Mix and Service Delivery Model that can and does deliver the expected SerVAL Proposition.

▶ Demonstrating to the customer that the specified, expected, SerVAL Proposition has been delivered.

▶ Ensuring that explicit and implicit, direct and indirect, marketing communications do not both "over promise" and "under deliver", nor "under promise" or "over deliver".

SUMMARY

The SERVQUAL model provides a simple and clear understanding of how communications breakdown, as well as operational delivery failure, can lead to customers perceiving that the service organisation is failing to deliver what they expected to receive. Even a relatively small gap at each level can open up a significant variance overall.

The inherent VITAL characteristics of services – namely intangibility, perishability and simultaneity, variability and the customer/ service provider interface – increase the likelihood that the five communication gaps identified in the SERVQUAL model will open up, and service organisations will fail to deliver what their customers expected to receive. Together, these form one of the reasons why "excellent" customer service can be perceived as rare – it is very difficult to achieve.

To ensure that your customers perceive you have delivered what they expected, you need to ensure the five communications gaps remain closed, and, of course, you actually deliver what you say you were going to in the expected manner. The more tangible and clearly specified you can make your service output and service experience, then the easier this will be to achieve.

If the Service Delivery Mix and Service Delivery Model of an organisation cannot deliver what it promises, or if it allows even a single communication gap to open, then it will not deliver what its customers expected to receive. This will damage the organisation as it could lose customers and money rectifying issues that should not have arisen, as well as damage its brand, reduce the potential to win new customers or retain existing ones, and threaten the price it can charge them.

In short, service organisations must deliver, and be perceived to deliver, the expected SerVAL Proposition.

CHAPTER ELEVEN:
KEY QUESTIONS TO CONSIDER:
MIGHT YOU BE FAILING TO DELIVER WHAT YOUR
CUSTOMER WANTS AND EXPECTS?

▶ Who is your customer/customer stakeholder group?

▶ Does your customer know what they actually want?

▶ Do you clearly know what they want?

▶ Can you articulate this clearly to your service delivery team?

▶ Have you articulated it clearly to your service delivery team?

▶ Do your service delivery team understand it?

▶ Do your service delivery team believe it?

▶ Do they accept it?

▶ Are you delivering what is required?

▶ Do you have the right Service Delivery Mix to deliver it?

▶ Do you have the right Service Delivery System to deliver it?

▶ Are your employees performing as required?

▶ Do they have the right systems, processes, tools & equipment etc. to perform as required?

▶ Are these all working as required?

▶ Are your employees behaving as required?

▶ Do your customers perceive they are receiving the service expected?

▶ How do they know they have received what they expect?

▶ Is there a gap between the rhetoric in your marketing communications and the reality of what you can and do deliver?

▶ Is this leading to customer dissatisfaction?

▶ How can you close this gap?

HOW WILL CUSTOMERS ASSESS THE SERVICE THAT THEY RECEIVE?

INTRODUCTION

In the previous two chapters we considered how to identify the SerVAL Proposition required by a customer, and how service organisations can fail to deliver it.

In this chapter, I am going to examine how customers will assess the SerVAL Proposition they receive.

KEY QUESTIONS

To achieve this, I am going to consider the following key questions:

▸ How do customers of service organisations evaluate performance?

▸ How do customers assess the Service Benefit?

▸ How do customers assess the Service Experience?

▸ How do the components and characteristics of a service impact these measures?

▸ How does the Service Delivery Model impact these measures?

▸ Are these absolute or relative performance measures?

▸ Are these performance measures of equal importance for different services?

▸ Are these performance measures of equal importance for different customers?

▸ Do customers make a trade-off between Benefits and Experience?

▸ How do customers assess the Price that they paid?

▸ What are the consequences of failing to deliver what customers expected?

▸ How can you apply this to your service organisation?

HOW DO CUSTOMERS OF SERVICE ORGANISATIONS EVALUATE SERVICE PERFORMANCE?

One of the leading models for assessing customer satisfaction for service organisations, the SERVQUAL model of Ziethaml, Parasuraman and Berry, highlights quality as the only relevant customer assessment of the service that is received.

"Customers do not evaluate service quality solely on the outcome of a service (e.g. how a customer's hair looks after a haircut) they also consider the process of service delivery (e.g. how involved, friendly, and responsive the Hairdresser was)."

"The only criteria that count in evaluating service quality are defined by customers. Only customers judge quality; all other judgements are essentially irrelevant." Delivering Service Quality, Zeithaml, Parasuraman, Berry, Free Press, 1990.

Whilst I would take issue with their comments about service outcome, believing that it should be Service Benefit – the biggest flaw in this statement, I believe – this model appears to ignore the impact of price on the customer's assessment of service quality (although perhaps it is implicit in the assessment of service quality). If the haircut was extremely expensive, compared to what the customer expected to pay, then they would not be very pleased! I believe that it is vital that all three elements of the SerVAL Proposition must be considered when assessing service quality, because the Total Cost to Customer provides a context to the level of Benefit and Experience received.

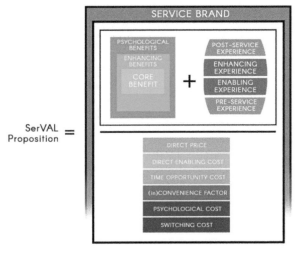

If you go to a well-known fast food outlet, and get the food and service experience you expect, but at a price commensurate with a Michelin starred restaurant, you will not be satisfied.

Conversely, if you go to a Michelin starred restaurant and pay a price commensurate with a fast food outlet, you are likely to be extremely satisfied. However, this is probably not economically sustainable for the restaurant! I will discuss the cost of service provision in a later chapter.

HOW DO CUSTOMERS ASSESS THE SERVICE BENEFIT?

As explained in the preceding chapter, this process starts with there being a clear understanding between the service provider and customer of both the customer's need and what the service provider will do to meet that need, i.e. the Benefit the customer will receive and the Benefit the service organisation provides.

The customer will start by assessing the Benefit they perceive they have received against that which has been specified. As set out in the previous chapter, the intangible nature of services means that, unfortunately, the Benefits are often not clearly specified!

In the absence of a clear specification, customers will make their assessment on the basis of what they expected to receive, based on their previous occasions of receiving such a service, word of mouth from other customers, and what the service provider has implied through its marketing communications and Brand. In short, the customer will create their own expected specification to assess the Benefit received.

However, in order to compare the Benefit received against a clear specification, or their own, often less clear, expectations, the customer needs to know they have actually received a Benefit. So, how do they know they have?

Intangibility may mean it is difficult to see that the expected Benefits have been received. The perishable nature of services can also mean that it may be difficult to prove that the Benefit has been delivered.

How do you know what Benefit you have received from a counselling or advisory type service? How do you know whether or not your condition has improved anyway? What if other events occur which override the Benefits you may have received? One way of addressing this is simply for the counsellor to ask, "do you feel better?" or "give me some examples of your improvement?", as this will highlight to the patient the Benefits they have (or haven't!) received, as well as enabling changes to treatment etc.

Compare that to the potentially more obvious Benefits that are received from a physiotherapy service, such as enhanced mobility.

How do you know that you received the Benefits of a cleaning service? The area may have become dirty again. That is why it is important to get the client to acknowledge that they have received the output – the clean area.

In such circumstances, it may be that the service provider can make the service outputs very tangible, and the ensuing Benefits are relatively obvious. Or they may need to make the Benefits obvious too. They may even guarantee the outputs as part of the process of making the Service Benefit more tangible, as in the "Bugs Berger" case described below.

A further challenge is that the Benefits are often not a direct result of the service, but are either consequential or implied.

Consider pest control. There is a famous Harvard Business School case study called "Bugs Berger" where a pest control guarantees the absence of pests for its customers. The absence of pests is an output. The Benefits of a lack of pests include hygienic conditions, which will be important for restaurants etc, employee satisfaction (who wants to see a cockroach in their office?), lack of tenant complaints in rented domestic properties etc.

The firm's restaurant customers will know what the Benefits are, as will its landlord customers, etc, so is there any benefit (sic) in spelling out the Benefits that flow from the outputs?

Another challenge is that some services may provide preventative Benefits, so the Benefit is an event that hasn't occurred. So how does the customer know that the event hasn't occurred; because of the service provided to them?

A security guarding service is to prevent your house, office, factory etc. from being broken into or damaged. What if it never is? Is that because of the guarding service, or was it never likely to happen?

For other services, the Benefit is an "insurance policy" that only becomes available if an event does occur. How does the service provider show that the "insured event" was probable, and therefore worth insuring against if it didn't happen? This is where the psychological Benefit may become very important. The Benefit is that customers can "rest assured/sleep easy" and not worry about what would happen if an event does occur.

A medical insurance firm might claim "another year has gone by during which you didn't need to worry about the consequences of falling ill". An auto breakdown recovery organisation might tell its customers something similar, that "another year has gone by when we have been on standby to rescue you should your vehicle have broken down". Retailers advertising "24/7" opening hours for their convenience stores are providing the psychological benefit of the availability of food and other consumables should their customers need it. For some customers, such as those that work unusual hours, there may be an actual Benefit of being able to buy food at 2am on a Sunday.

The challenges described above arise where Service Benefits are immediate.

But, as discussed in earlier chapters, some services may be providing deferred Benefits. How does the customer know that they are going to get that Benefit, or indeed will even need it then?

It can be seen that it is not a straightforward process for customers to know they have received the expected Service Benefit.

These challenges are major barriers that need to be overcome in order to be seen to deliver excellent service.

To build, and sustain a reputation for providing excellent service, it is, therefore, key that a service provider needs to both clearly understand what Benefit a customer expects, and also demonstrate, as best they can, that they have delivered it.

In the UK, train companies publish their achievement of scheduled departure times for trains.

This is an attempt to demonstrate that their service delivers the part of the expected Benefit for the vast majority/all of time, i.e. that it leaves and arrives on time/as expected, so people can accurately plan their travel arrangements.

"Our customers completed their journeys on time for 99% of our services throughout the year." Another Benefit may be that the journey was without incident.

An ex-colleague of mine in a law firm produces annual reports to his clients showing the number of cases he has fought for them (he is a litigator), the success rate of those cases, the damages he has won/costs he has saved for them, risks he has managed for them, the feedback he has got from those involved with the case, and the fees charged for performing the work.

Schools typically publish the academic results achieved by their pupils and the Benefits of achieving such results, such as successful applications to prestigious Universities and Colleges.

Of course, this doesn't show what type of person the school is producing. How do those schools that seek to produce "well-rounded individuals", rather than academic high performers, show that?

A hospital might show that 95% of its patients made a complete recovery within a given time from a particular procedure dealing with particular issues.

HOW DO CUSTOMERS ASSESS THE SERVICE EXPERIENCE?

A good starting point towards understanding how customers assess the Service Experience is to consider the way that we assess a Service Experience ourselves. After all, we all have the advantage of being customers for a whole range of services on a daily basis, so that we can readily put ourselves in the position of a customer!

Think of some of the services you have experienced recently. Your last trip to the shops or a restaurant, your last haircut or your last interaction with your bank. Your last conversation with the facility manager at your office, or the last management consulting assignment you awarded.

Furthermore, most of us work for organisations or departments within an organisation that provide services, so obtain some of the feedback from your organisation's customers or some of the reports produced about your industry. Write down the kind of things that were important to you as a customer, and/or customers in your industry.

When I have done this exercise in workshops, or for services I have experienced, the type of words used to describe the service experience include:

▶ "Always turn up on time" / "always late".

▶ "Always do what they say they will do" / "nothing was too much trouble" / "only did the least they could".

▶ "Took ages to answer the phone" /"didn't respond to my letter for weeks" / "we queued for hours" / "they answered the phone instantly".

▶ "Didn't seem to know what they were talking about or doing" / "really seemed like an expert".

▶ "Didn't trust a word he said" / " felt I could totally rely on what I was told".

▶ "Was really rude and didn't want to talk to me" / "really charming and asked me about XXX, which she remembered from last time".

▶ "Didn't seem to understand or care that my mum's heating not working for a few days in the middle of winter was not acceptable and told her to wear an extra sweater" / "she really cared and came round in the evening to make sure the heating was working and my mum was ok" / "they didn't have a clue about my business needs" / "they really understand the pressures in my industry and my personal goals in the firm".

▶ "Their offices were really large and plush, no wonder their fees are so high" / "their offices were really large and plush, they must be really successful" / "his van was old and dented and rusty and really dirty, don't want him making a mess in my house" / "the waitress had food stains all down her skirt, hope the kitchens aren't that dirty" / "the cover fell off the report they sent me, and the appendices were a different type face to the main body, and there were lots of typos"/ "the receptionist was really smart and friendly with a big smile."

Are there any themes?

A major study of how customers assess service performance, covering a broad range of business-to-consumer and business-to-business services, was carried out in the USA in the late 1980s by Zeithaml et al., along with the "Five Gap" model discussed in Chapter 11.

It was also published in their book, "Delivering Service Quality, Balancing Customer Perceptions and Expectations" (Free Press, 1990).

They found the same performance measures applied across most service businesses, which they summarised as follows:

▶ Responsiveness

▶ Reliability

▶ Assurance

▶ Empathy

▶ Tangibles

This can be more readily remembered if slightly changed in order to become RATER. (How does a customer RATE your service? The customer is the RATER of your service.)

This is well worth a read. Like most models, it has been criticised since I became aware of it in the mid-1990's.

I have found it an excellent mental model and practical way of considering (primarily) the Service Experience. It reflects my own experiences as a consumer of both business-to-consumer and business-to-business services.

It also reflects what the customers in the businesses that I have run or advised have said too, even if the words used to describe performance may vary from industry to industry.

So what do these **RATER** performance measures actually mean?

"Responsiveness" is pretty self-explanatory.

By **"reliability"** they mean that the promised service is performed both dependably and accurately. The other three measures need a bit more elaboration.

By **"assurance"** they mean that the service provider is **competent, credible, risk and doubt free, courteous** and their performance and behaviour is seen as **trustworthy.**

"Empathy" refers to the service provider **understanding the customer, being accessible and being communicative.** Personally, I would put courteous in this category.

"Tangible" relates to the appearance of the physical components in the Service Delivery Mix, such as property and facilities, equipment, personnel and communication materials.

A more recent publication by the customer relationship specialists, Don Pepper and Martha Rogers (Managing Customer Relationships, A Strategic Framework, Wiley, 2011), indicates that their research and experiences suggest that customer trust is based on the following formula:

$$\text{CLIENT TRUST} = \frac{C + R + I}{O}$$

Where:

C= Credibility

R= Reliability

I= Intimacy

O= Orientation/Motive

Their use of credibility corresponds closely to assurance and intimacy corresponds to empathy in Parasuraman et al's SERVQUAL model. Orientation/motive is a useful addition/clarification to the RATER list, in which trustworthiness forms part of "assurance".

What Pepper and Rogers mean by this is that customers will trust their supplier of goods or services if they trust their motives, i.e. that their supplier is not trying to take advantage of them (such as "mis-selling" or delivering less than what is promised to enhance profits), but rather has the best interests of the customer at heart, as well as the supplier's commercial interest. Again, this chimes with my own experiences.

There have been a huge number of issues relating to orientation/ motives (collectively termed "mis-selling") that took place in the Financial Services industry from 2010-13, where it has been claimed that the service provider was selling services that its customers did not need in order to make a profit.

It can be seen that a number of these RATER performance measures relate more to the Service Experience than to the Service Benefit, albeit "Assurance" is an important psychological Benefit and reliability applies to both. In summary, therefore, customers will typically assess the Service Experience with regards to how *responsive, reliable, assuring* and *empathetic*, they perceived the service provider to be, with regard to the appearance of the *tangible* elements of the Service Deliver Mix, compared to their expectations. They will also consider whether or not they trust the motives of the service provider.

HOW DO THE COMPONENTS AND CHARACTERISTICS OF A SERVICE IMPACT THESE MEASURES OF SERVICE EXPERIENCE?

I have considered in previous chapters the different components and characteristics of services. Having regard to the SERVQUAL model above, it should be apparent that these can, and will, have a major impact on the way customers assess the Service Experience. I will now examine this in more detail. I will also illustrate how they are closely interrelated.

Reliability

Reliability is a key performance measure for many services. Achieving reliability can be a major challenge for service providers, because as we have already identified, one of the typical characteristics of services is variability! In the SERVQUAL model, reliability refers to dependability and accuracy. I would argue that these two measures relate more to the Service Benefit than the Service Experience. For example, a train service is reliable because for 95% of the time the trains arrive and depart within 5 minutes of the scheduled time.

However, I think that another key measure of reliability is the consistency of the Service Experience, in terms of each Service Experience being identical/very similar each time, i.e. the degree of Service Experience variability.

An internet-based service provider, such as an online bank, which is subject to the performance of its website (see below) can be expected to provide a dependable, accurate and consistent service each time for its customers.

A collection of untrained, poorly paid, poorly motivated, poorly managed cleaners may be expected to deliver an unreliable service, both in terms of the output, the Service Benefit and the Service Experience.

In terms of the Service Delivery Mix, systems and processes would obviously be expected to have a major influence on reliability. The more consistent and stringent the systems, the more reliable the service might be, all things being equal.

However, as discussed in earlier chapters, there are some potential consequences of service organisations becoming too systemised, such as the impact on the Employee Experience and, flowing from that, via the Service-Profit chain, how the Employee Experience influences employee behaviour and performance.

Understanding this is important because reliability isn't just a result of systems and processes. It is also about people committing to always doing what they have promised to do, when they have promised to do it. It is also about them being trained to perform the service in a given way and adopt specific behaviours when delivering the service. Reliability, or lack of it, can thus be a major reflection of an individual employees' motivation within service organisations and the organisation's culture. This also links back to the Service-Profit Chain model. There may, therefore, be a process/systems and people trade off to be made to ensure reliability.

Furthermore, the level of reliability of a service will not just be down to systems, processes and people, but will also reflect the tools and equipment, and ICT used by the service provider.

A garden maintenance service, which utilises old, poorly maintained lawn mowing equipment, transported in an old, poorly maintained truck, may fail to deliver a cut lawn on many occasions if they fail to arrive due to a breakdown, or their equipment doesn't work when they get there.

For example, in the train company used earlier, one of the key factors influencing reliability will be the performance of the train and the tracks.

The reliability of the internet, local network connections and the customer's computer, as well as the bank's own systems, will have a major impact on the reliability of an internet-based bank service.

The Service Delivery Mix thus has a major impact on reliability, and the selected foundations of service reliability, people and/or process, requires considerable thought, as the latter can have wider implications for the Employee Experience and, through this, the Service Experience.

Assurance

How do service organisations provide "assurance"? That is, how do they demonstrate competence and credibility, and "acceptable risk" to a customer? This is the "Trust me"/ "Don't get fired for buying IBM" aspect of its service. This is particularly important the more intangible, perishable and potentially variable the service is. In such cases, the customer isn't quite sure what Service Benefit and/or what Service Experience they will receive, and/or what price they will pay.

The tangible elements of the Service Delivery Mix can be very important for contributors to provide the customer with some "assurance". Marketing communications and brand will be an essential element of this. For example, providing examples of previous successes, the qualifications of employees if relevant, the identity of other customers (the customer thinks "they act for XYZ, so they must be good"), the organisation's experience, the quality of its systems and processes etc.

Doctors, dentists, opticians, etc tend to have their certificates of qualification on the walls of their surgeries. Look at many firm's websites and they will provide examples of who their customers are. They will typically also highlight quality accreditations, such as ISO.

The appearance of these tangible elements can also provide assurance. For example, a prestigious building in a high profile location may send a signal, rightly or wrongly, to a firm's customer that it is a very successful and sustainable organisation because it can afford to rent or own such a property. The appearance of the service provider's people can also provide or reduce assurance, as can the tools and equipment they use.

As mentioned in the bank example in Chapter 7, an organisation's premises can convey an image of conservatism or of being dynamic, innovative etc. Many people like their lawyers to look like lawyers, with dark suits, smart, conservative haircuts etc. These days, people like their car mechanics to have a comprehensive, smart, clean, tool kit and a laptop for diagnostics. Not just an oily rag, a spanner, a screwdriver and a hammer.

Another important source of assurance will be the recommendations or comments from the customer's friends, family and acquaintances, or references from other customers, or from other advisors or third parties in the market. Social media can be an important source of this. That is why firms want people to "like" them on Facebook, for example. These are all key elements of building a Brand, and Brands can be a very important provider of assurance.

As well as the assurance that can come from the tangible elements of the Service Delivery Mix, and the sense of confidence that can come from the less tangible Brand, service organisations might also provide some assurance by guaranteeing the Service Benefit. If this is not possible, then they may guarantee the output, such as in the Bugs Berger example above. This is typically done by making some or all of the Price elements of the SerVAL Proposition contingent on achieving the Benefit; the service provider puts some 'skin in the game' by incurring a monetary risk through investing in achieving the stated Benefit. This approach is typically associated with transaction-based services, such as Real Estate brokerage, sales of businesses, sales of Equities and Securities etc. No Benefit (i.e. no sale), then no fee. Service organisations must think very carefully how their Service Delivery Mix and the particular characteristics of their service impact the level of assurance provided to their customers.

Tangibles

The core components of the Service Delivery Mix will largely influence the tangible element of the Service Experience, particularly the service organisation's people, premises, tools & equipment, IT system, and brand.

▸ Are your facilities appropriately large, fitted out to the right standard, clean, warm etc to meet your customers' expectations?

▸ How does the design of your facilities impact the customer/ service provider operational interface?

▸ Is the lighting and ambient music in your restaurant in keeping with the rest of the image and type of food served, time of day and target clientele?

▸ Does your staff dress in a way that conveys the right impression to the target customer group?

▸ Is your website easy to use?

▸ Are your vans clean and smart?

▸ Do your communication materials, both hard and electronic copy, give the intended impression?

It is important to remember that the customer's assessment of the tangible element of the Service Experience is unlikely , to be made in isolation, except possibly for first-time buyers, but will be compared to the tangible elements of the service provider's competitors' Service Experience, and also against best in class for that element.

Think of some of the "value" supermarkets, such as Aldi and Lidl, and compare their stores to a "premium" supermarket, such as Waitrose.

The different Service Experience of finding that tins are still in boxes, which are left on pallets, reinforces the idea that this is a "value" offering, as well as reducing costs to enable "value" to be delivered profitably.

If you go into the showroom of a car dealer that sells brand new, prestige cars, then into the showroom/yard of a dealer selling second-hand vehicles, you will consciously or sub-consciously, make a comparison of the showroom as part of the Service Experience.

One of my clients provided me with the example of a heavily built, heavily tattooed, highly qualified male nurse that used to carry out home visits for their care organisation.

Despite his high levels of skill and empathetic nature, a number of patients did not like to be treated by him because of his appearance, which they felt to be intimidating.

Empathy

Empathy is:

"The power of entering into another's personality and imaginatively experiencing his or her experiences; the power of entering into the feeling or spirit of something and so appreciating it fully." (The Chambers Dictionary (1999), Chambers Harrap Publishers Ltd, Edinburgh).

More generally empathy is taken to also include basic human politeness, manners, courtesy, friendliness and interest in other people, and being sympathetic too.

The importance of empathy, and the level of empathy expected by a customer, will depend on the service in question, and also the customer in question.

▶ I don't expect or require much more empathy from a fast food service provider's employee, other than politeness and friendliness.

I don't expect or require much more than this from my hairdresser. Other people, so I am told, require much higher levels of empathy from their hairdresser.

I do expect a high level of empathy from my doctor.

In order to move beyond politeness and friendliness, should that be required, a service organisation is required to gain a deep understanding of their customer and their needs.

My experience suggests that there are three aspects of customer knowledge, as follows. Having a good understanding:

▶   Of a particular customer issue or situation.

▶   Of the customer's industry and organisation (in the case of business-to-business situations) or of their socioeconomic, domestic and personal circumstances (in the case of business-to-consumer services).

▶   Of the customer as an individual, to such an extent that a two-way relationship is established.

This experience also suggests to me that it is possible to achieve the first point and the second point, certainly at an intellectual and practical level, without achieving the third point.

Consider your own experiences. If someone is impolite or unfriendly and has no real interest in you, and does not understand your issue, and in a business context does not understand your industry or organisation, or in a personal context doesn't understand your situation, then you are not likely to perceive them as being very empathetic.

▶ It can often be the case in very technical services that the deliverer of the service can have a great understanding of his customer's industry, firm and even the customer, but have little interest or ability in building empathetic relationships with the customer. I have seen this with some highly qualified heating engineers, whose perceived attitude can be "get out of my way, customer, and let me fix your heating system".

In the UK, lawyers are known, in general, for having extremely high IQs but much lower EQs (Emotional Quotients) and, thus, are not seen as being particularly empathetic.

It also possible to be superficially friendly and not achieve any of the above. The level of empathy demonstrated by a service organisation will be highly dependent on the people and process element of the Service Delivery Mix; firstly, the performance and behaviour of those of its employees who interact with its customers and, secondly, the organisation's systems and processes, and recruitment and training regime, which enable these employees to gain this understanding.

The Service Delivery Model will also have a huge impact on the level of empathy experienced by customers, as the model will shape the level and nature of customer interaction. Those models that involve minimal levels of interaction between people are likely, all things being equal, to generate a service experience with lower levels of empathy than those models involving high levels of interaction.

A really interesting challenge for 21st Century service businesses, as technology becomes an increasingly important part of the Service Delivery Mix and Service Delivery System, is the implication it has on relationships with customers. How much empathy do you get from a website?

Empathy is also based on a two-way relationship between service provider and customer. If there is an in-depth and strong relationship, then a customer will also empathise and sympathise with their service provider when the provider has a problem. Empathy can, thus, be extremely important in terms of dealing with customer issues and complaints about service.

The following two studies of medical malpractice law suits in the USA, indicated that those doctors who provided a (marginally) longer initial consultation, and those that could build a two-way communication with their patients were much less likely to be sued for malpractice than those who did not.

▶   Brennan, T, Relation between negligent adverse events and the outcomes of medical-malpractice litigation. New Eng. J Med. 335(26):1963-67, December 26, 1996.

▶   Levinson, W. Physician-patient communication: the relationship with malpractice claims among primary care physicians and surgeons. JAMA. 277(7):553-59, February 19, 1997.

This was confirmed in another study in Italy in 2011, using the Jefferson Scale of Empathy (JSE), developed in 2001 as an instrument to measure empathy in the context of medical education and patient care. This validated instrument relies on the definition of empathy in the context of patient care as a predominately cognitive attribute that involves an understanding of patient's concerns, pain and suffering, and an intention to help. The scale includes 20 items answered on a seven-point Likert-type scale (strongly agree = 7, strongly disagree = 1).

These are examples of a (lack of) empathy creating service dissatisfaction, particularly when the Service Benefit of improved health was not delivered.

Responsiveness

The responsiveness of a service organisation is the easiest aspect of performance to measure.

However, whilst it is clear, for example, whether the measure of answering a telephone in less than, say, 3 rings is met, the measure becomes less meaningful if the operator then hangs up the phone without saying anything! So, determining what aspect of responsiveness to measure, and how best to measure it, in a meaningful way, is the real challenge.

One of the challenges in a maintenance business, whether it is maintaining equipment for another organisation or a private individual, can be selecting a meaningful measure of responsiveness. Some of the most sophisticated measures of this can be found in Private Finance Initiative & Public/Private Partnership arrangements in the UK.

In such contracts, it would be typical to measure how long it took the "help desk" to answer a phone call or email requesting responsive maintenance, or cleaning, then how long it took the maintenance or cleaning operative to attend the location to investigate the issue. That in itself is no help if they then fail to resolve the issue when they get there.

So, it is also necessary to measure when the repair or the clean is done, and this may involve both a temporary repair and a permanent repair, e.g. to shut off a leaking tap, and then to replace the leaking tap.

As well as understanding what is the correct measure of responsiveness, another factor that service organisations need to consider, regarding the intangible and perishable nature of services, is how visible the response is. Does the customer know the service organisation has responded?

A good example of perceived service failure that relates to the "invisibility" of service delivery, is an office building managed by a Facility Management company I led. It was an old building and had problems with temperature levels – it was too hot in summer and too cold in winter. A member of staff of the firm occupying the building would call the Facility Management Help Desk and request the temperature to be increased or decreased. The Help Desk would contact the heating engineer who would then go to the basement boiler room, adjust the temperature and return to his previous activities. As temperatures do not change quickly in large buildings, and no one had seen the engineer go to the basement, the Help Desk would get another call from the same person half an hour later, saying that the temperature had not changed and nothing had been done about it. This was unsurprising, since they had not seen the heating engineer go to the basement boiler room!

We addressed this issue by requiring the heating engineer to go and speak to the person who had placed the request to the Help Desk and tell them what he had done, and if they were not there to leave a "calling card". In short, we just made the service more visible. The number of repeat calls plummeted and satisfaction with the service experience increased. The customer could see that they were not being ignored and the response was quite fast.

The Service Delivery Mix has a key influence on the level of responsiveness of service organisations.

For example, the location of the service organisation's premises will have a major impact on responsiveness.

An ambulance station located in a town centre might be close to potential patients, but may get stuck in traffic.

The type and amount and capabilities of equipment utilised by the service organisation (vehicles, etc) will also, impact responsiveness, as will the capacity of IT and Telecom systems etc.

An ambulance station with only one ambulance and one crew available may not be very responsive in out of hours times, or if the ambulance has already been called out. How often do you get stuck in queues when phoning service organisations? "Your call is important to us, you are number 5 in the queue, and we will be with you in 20 minutes."

The number of people that are employed, where they are employed, and their attitude to customer service, will also impact responsiveness. If the organisation has insufficient capacity at times of peak demand, then its ability to respond will be reduced. Its location will also impact responsiveness, as discussed above.

In my experience, responsiveness can also reflect the organisation's culture and the behaviour and performance of its employees. We have all been in shops, restaurants, banks, garages, offices, etc, where the receptionist/assistant/teller has not been busy (or not appeared to be, which can be an important issue when considering facility design and the customer/service deliverer interface), but has not paid us any attention for some time, or allowed the phone to ring and ring in the background. That representative of that service organisation is capable of responding in a timely manner, but has chosen not to.

HOW DOES THE SERVICE DELIVERY MODEL IMPACT THESE PERFORMANCE MEASURES?

We identified in Chapter 9 that the main categories of Service Delivery Model reflect the:

▶ Degree of customer contact.
▶ Nature of the relationship with customers:
  ▶ Continuous delivery of service
  ▶ Discrete transactions
  ▶ Formal relationship (membership, contracts)
  ▶ Informal relationships (public transport, mail, radio)
▶ Where the service is delivered:
  ▶ The customer comes to the service deliverer
  ▶ The service deliverer comes to the customer
  ▶ Arm's length delivery (e.g. through the web)

- ▶ Nature of demand, compared to supply.
- ▶ Level of customisation.
- ▶ Level of labour intensity
- ▶ The level of judgment exercised by, and operational flexibility given to, the service deliverer.

These all will have a significant impact on the **RATER** measures.

The level of Reliability will depend on the level of customer contact, where the service is delivered (and thus whether the environment is controlled by the service provider or not), whether or not this is a people or a system based (with people generating variability), the levels of operational flexibility permitted to service delivery employees and the levels of customisation.

The way that a service organisation manages its capacity to deal with peaks and troughs will impact reliability. If a service provider has too few people to deliver its service, they will become overstretched and become less reliable and less responsive.

This can be a significant issue, in my experience, in fast growing organisations, or organisations that experience pronounced peaks and troughs in their workloads. It also has a huge impact on organisational profitability.

The way that Assurance is provided should also reflect the Service Delivery Model. For example, where there are low levels of customer contact, on an infrequent basis, then Brand recognition and reputation will be very important, as will the quality of the service delivery process. Formal relationships, such as explicit contracts containing performance measures and guarantees, can also provide assurance.

If the service is delivered at the service provider's premises then the appearance of the property will impact assurance. Where the service is labour intensive, then the experience and qualifications of the service provider's workforce will provide assurance, especially where high levels of judgment are required.

The exposure of customers to the Tangible elements of the Service Delivery Mix will depend in where the service is delivered, and the level and nature of customer interaction.

Accordingly, the importance of the appearance and functionality of ICT systems, including the internet, and of tools and equipment, including vehicles, and the service provider's employees will also vary.

I provided the earlier example of a male nurse doing home visits. For that service organisation, its customers didn't visit the service provider's premises, and the service provider didn't provide company vehicles, nor a uniform, nor have a website. The only tangibles were the nurse, what he chose to wear and drive, and any paperwork or materials left with the customer. And an identity badge.

If the Service Delivery Model involves very low levels of customer contact and/or very superficial levels of customer contact, then the level of Empathy experienced by customers might be expected to be lower than for those SerVAL Propositions, where the level of customer contact are higher.

But this also depends on whether the service is based on high levels of labour or not; that is whether or not the customer/service provider interface involves large amounts of interpersonal contact, or say, high levels of interaction with a website.

It is not just the quantity of customer/service provider interface that is important, however. It is also the quality of that interface. The level of perceived empathy is likely to reflect the degree of discretion and flexibility exhibited by the service provider.

This can be reduced in a heavily system/process based businesses, or where decisions are being made in the background by people that the customer cannot see or access.

How much empathy do you feel with a call centre operative when they "check with their supervisor" for any decision, usually only to give a "no" based answer?

To really understand this point, in a humorous manner, check out the British TV show "Little Britain" and their "the computer says no" sketches.

However, empathy can come at a cost; of reliability (variability), responsiveness and efficiency.

The more people are involved, the higher degree of customer interaction with these people, the more variable, and hence less reliable (consistent) the service can be. So a degree of trade-off between these two performance measures may be required.

Furthermore, if the Service Delivery Model involves high levels of judgment being exercised by the service deliverer's employees, and high levels of operational flexibility being permitted, then the customer will require high levels of empathy from these people, or else they are likely to exercise their judgment or be perceived to exercise their judgment, very poorly.

Without high levels of training and robust process to support this judgment, then the less reliable and more inconsistent the service may be. A similar scenario exists where high levels of customisation of the service are expected.

These factors can prove to be a major challenge where high levels of service delivery efficiency are being sought.

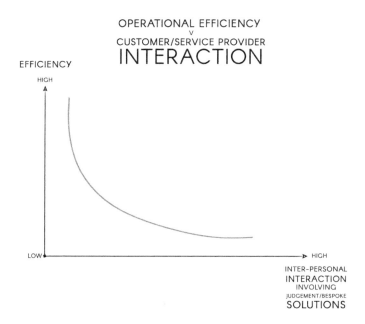

OPERATIONAL EFFICIENCY
v
CUSTOMER/SERVICE PROVIDER
INTERACTION

EFFICIENCY

HIGH

LOW — HIGH

INTER-PERSONAL
INTERACTION
INVOLVING
JUDGEMENT/BESPOKE
SOLUTIONS

Where the service is delivered continuously and/or over a long period of time, again customers may expect higher degrees of empathy from the service provider.

And where high levels of empathy are required, it may be difficult to maintain responsiveness (or empathy), particularly in periods of high demand, if responding to a new customer requirement requires an existing customer interaction to be cut short.

Many of us will have been in a situation where we are being served by someone and their phone rings and they answer it to speak to another customer. The manner in which this is done, how often, the length of interruption and the explanation for it, will impact the level of empathy, and importance, that we feel as a customer.

Responsiveness will be influenced by how the service provider manages the capacity in its organisation, and particularly the peaks and troughs of demand.

This can range from the number of people, vehicles and tools available, through to the capacity of phone lines and ICT systems. It can also reflect the availability of materials, or products. For those service organisations that are distributors of goods,- such as retailers,- the responsiveness of their supply chain will also be key influences of their own responsiveness.

One example of daily peaks and troughs of demand occurs with Facilities Help Desks. Typically, in office buildings, the peak of calls are from about 8am to 10am, and then from 2pm to 3.30pm. Why is this? This reflects the times when people arriving at work and returning from lunch, and finding that their office is too hot/ too cold, or their wastebin has not been emptied, or a light bulb has failed etc. A key operational decision is, thus, how to resource the Help Desk in a way to meet these peaks of demand, without having excess capacity, and thus wasted cost, during the rest of the day.

Those organisations which seek to manage peaks and troughs of demand through a queuing/appointment system may be seen as being less responsive. The importance of responsiveness to the customer, therefore, needs to be considered when designing the Service Delivery Model. No one wants to queue for an ambulance, but will do so for a taxi.

ARE THESE ABSOLUTE OR RELATIVE PERFORMANCE MEASURES?

These performance measures are also relative; relative to people in similar jobs, relative to those provided by competitors, relative to context, and relative to what people expect from someone undertaking that service.

The greater use of technology in the Service Delivery Mix may make services more Reliable (consistent) over time. Better technology may also make that element of the service more reliable with, for example, greater "uptime" or processing speed. So customers' expectations of reliability may increase over time.

The level of Assurance required may vary depending on the context, even for the same customer and the same service.

In legal services, for example, for some business transactions, many customers have been quoted in surveys as saying that they are more than happy with the level of assurance provided by a "mid-tier" commercial firm. For "bet the business" advice, however, they are likely to use one of the five "top-tier" firms, as they know these are the best, and if the transaction goes wrong they cannot be accused of using a legal advisor who was not quite good enough.

The expected appearance of Tangible elements of the Service Delivery Mix will depend on what competitors offer.

In the UK, many new hospitals were built during the 1990s and 2000s. This made the experience of going to the ones which had been built in the early and mid-20th century, and had previously been the "norm", much less satisfactory than before, as there was now a "new and shiny" alternative to compare the experience to.

People will generally require and expect a different level of Empathy between, say, a cleaner and a Doctor (and often be pleasantly surprised and disappointed respectively, when they get the opposite!).

A good level of Responsiveness for answering telephones might be five rings, if your competitors and all the other organisations answer in seven rings, and so on.

Over time, depending on competitive pressures, these will change. Telephone responsiveness may decrease to three rings as a norm, and two rings as excellent.

So these measures are very relative, with levels of customer expectation generally rising over time due to both competitive pressures and technological improvements.

ARE THESE PERFORMANCE MEASURES OF EQUAL IMPORTANCE FOR DIFFERENT SERVICES?

Zeithaml et al, do not claim that these measures have equal weighting of importance in each service type. This seems a reasonable assumption, borne out by plenty of examples.

Reliability is likely to be more important for an ICT service than for a lawn mowing service.

Assurance is clearly more important for brain surgery than for cleaning services.

Tangibles, which as clean tables, plates, cutlery, floor, are likely to be more important for a restaurant than a warehouse.

Empathy is likely to be more important for psychology services compared to brain surgery.

Responsiveness is clearly more important for an ambulance service or emergency plumbing service than it is for a hairdressing service.

ARE THESE PERFORMANCE MEASURES OF EQUAL IMPORTANCE FOR DIFFERENT CUSTOMERS?

I would go further and suggest that the measures also vary in importance between customer groups, and can be one way to segment customers.

One of my ex-colleagues was very clear about her requirements from a hairdresser – she doesn't want the chatty, empathetic type; she wants the silent type.

I was on a train with a longstanding friend and colleague. In my experience, one of the characteristics of the service experience on the trains run by that particular operator, ,is that the staff are "characters" who have some fun interface and banter with the customers on the train.

I think this is great and I much prefer that aspect of their service experience to that provided by other train operators.

My friend commented, however, when we left the train, how much the banter of the staff annoyed him, saying: "I wish they would just sell me a cup of coffee and move on".

So, we had two totally contrasting views on the same customer experience.

There is one very important difference between the two examples above, however. In the hairdressing example, my ex-colleague had the choice of using a different hairdresser, and matching the Service Experience with her needs.

In the train example, my colleague and I had no choice, as there was only one train operator for that journey.

If my colleague and I are equally representative of their customer group, then only 50% will enjoy that part of the Service Experience.

So it is important for service organisations to establish the relative importance of each of these measures to target customer groups, and then establish how these are evaluated by the customers, recognising that some elements can more easily and objectively be measured, responsiveness for example.

Whereas others are not so easy to measure and can be much more subjective, such as "empathy".

I have also illustrated how some of these performance measures may need to be traded off against others – empathy v. reliability, for example.

DO CUSTOMERS MAKE A TRADE-OFF BETWEEN BENEFIT AND EXPERIENCE?

Earlier in the book, I made the point, using a quote from Michael Hammer of MIT about limousine drivers and cars, that no matter how good the service experience, the basic requirement is to deliver the service output/Benefit.

Sasser, Heskett and Schlessinger (The Service Profit Chain, The Free Press, New York, 1997) make a similar point, using a similar analogy.

"The quality of the processes for delivering the results, including the attitudes of those in direct contact with customers, is important. But no amount of congeniality or empathy on behalf of an auto-dealer's service manager will substitute for the failure of the car."

I can personally testify to this, having had exactly had such an experience with a dealer for a world leading car manufacturer. And, to the immense credit of the dealer, when I pointed this out, they purchased the car back from me, as they didn't have a suitable replacement.

But, whilst this is a core truth, for many services the Service Benefit is not binary, by which I mean the customer doesn't either receive or not receive it. Cleaning is a great example of this.

Two different people clean a floor and one may make it slightly cleaner than the other, but in both cases it is clean. The question is whether it is clean enough in both cases to meet the needs of a particular customer. And then there is the Service Experience. The person who cleaned the floor not quite as well (but well enough) was really friendly and smart, and sought out the customer for a chat.

They always turn up exactly on time, whereas the second one is a bit sullen, keeps himself to himself, is occasionally late, and is slightly dishevelled in appearance. How does the customer compare the two?

These kinds of situations occur all the time, not the least because services are intangible perishable, and variable, with different levels of customer/provider operational interface. In practice, therefore, as long as acceptable levels of Service Benefit and Service Experience are being achieved, there is some form of conscious or sub-conscious, trade-off being made by customers.

▶ Bad haircut plus good hairdressing experience = don't go back again/refuse to pay

▶ OK haircut plus ok hairdressing experience = may go back again

▶ OK haircut plus good hairdressing experience = probably go back again

▶ Good haircut plus ok hairdressing experience = probably go back again

▶ Good haircut plus good hairdressing experience = go back again

All the above, of course, are subject to the price paid and availability of alternatives.

This suggests that the relationship between Service Benefit and Service Experience may look like this:

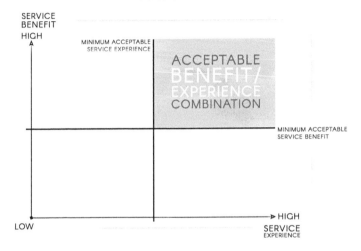

SERVICE BENEFIT v SERVICE EXPERIENCE
TRADE OFF

I have personally experienced two good back to back examples of this.

I went into a branch of my bank to pay in a cheque but didn't like the Service Experience particularly. The layout was cramped, it didn't give much privacy, the staff were friendly, but very young and scruffy, with "high fashion" haircuts (sounds vaguely similar to an earlier experience?). I thought, do I really trust these people with my money, do they really know what they are doing? In my perception, the tangibles were poor, the assurance was low, the empathy was superficial and the bank's IT system had very publicly crashed a few weeks before, so I was not sure how reliable they now were. They were responsive, however, and I didn't have to queue for long. They also helpfully pointed out how I could use automated paying in machines for cheques in future. The Service Output met my needs. The cheque was paid in and credited to my account. So, on balance, it was an OK Service Experience and I received the desired Service Output.

I then drove to my local car dealer as there had been a product recall. As a middle-aged car buff, I perceived the Service

Experience as great. The premises are well located and fitted out to a high, designer specification. The reception staff are very friendly. While you wait you are served cappuccino and biscuits, and have TV to watch, newspapers or car magazines to read, or you can work using their WIFI.

I had to wait twice as long as I was told, which was irritating, but overall the experience was good, in fact, much better than the bank. The output however was less good. The car had no problems relating to the recall. However, they told me that a light bulb had failed and asked if I would like to book in to have it replaced. How long would it have taken them to tell me they had found it and fixed it? Did they think I had so much free time that I could bring the car back again – involving a 45-minute journey – and wait for another hour just to replace a light bulb? I thought this was poor, but not so poor I wouldn't go back again, unless I had a much easier alternative. But poor enough to tell you in a book.

In both cases, I thought the service was OK overall. But, in both cases, there was a trade-off between the experience and the output. If the garage had given me a bad service experience, I almost certainly wouldn't have gone back, given a choice.

The level of what is acceptable will be determined by customer need, price and competition. In a monopoly situation, then any standard will be accepted, if there is no alternative to the service, and any price will be acceptable, subject to affordability and the level of need for the service – the alternative being to go without.

Service Providers need to position themselves somewhere in that acceptable Benefit/Experience zone or the organisation will not survive or will need to change.

The minimum level of Benefit required is likely to vary from customer group to customer group, which may support customer segmentation. For example, an acceptable haircut is likely to be very different between a US Marine Corps training camp and a West End of London hairdressing salon, as is the quality of experience expected!

Service providers, thus need to understand the Service Benefit v. Experience tradeoffs that their customers are prepared to make.

This can also be another opportunity to differentiate from competitors, by offering a different trade-off combination in the SerVAL Proposition. Anywhere in the acceptable combination zone, as shown in the diagram above, will be acceptable to specific customers.

The third element of the equation involved in the trade-off is the price.

HOW DO CUSTOMERS ASSESS THE PRICE THEY PAID?

Customers will first assess the price before purchasing the service. So how do they do it? Firstly, never forget that you are a customer too, so what do you do?

If a vendor proposes a price, then you compare it to other prices for the same or similar services. If you are making an offer, you consider other prices in the market to identify the "going rate".

You also compare it to what you have paid before to the same vendor and/or to its competitors. This is where the "service memory" can be really important. Can a customer remember exactly what he received for his money; potentially the only tangible reminder of the service is the invoice!

What we tend to do is to compare the price against several others, if available, so that we have a range of prices against which to compare this price. Now, one of the difficulties in comparing prices for services, compared to, say, prices for cars, is the intangible nature of the service. For a car, it is easy. You have a particular make and model and specification of car in mind, and you visit or phone a few dealers, or search the internet and find a range of prices for exactly the same product. Price information is readily available. If you want to compare models of car, that is relatively easy too. For a bigger engine, which will give you a specified difference in performance, it is clear what the extra price is.

It is up to the individual car purchaser whether it is rationally, or irrationally, worth paying say £3k more for leather seats, or extra 10mph top speed or one second quicker to 60mph, or an extra 5mpg.

If you are comparing different makes of car, then it is slightly harder because, as well as evaluating the hard facts, comparing performance – whether you get air-conditioning, electric mirrors, etc – you are also deciding whether you prefer the looks of the vehicle and also the brand. Do you want a BMW or a Mercedes, a Ford or a Toyota?

There is one more element to pricing that needs consideration. It derives from what customer psychologists* term "transaction utility theory".

*Richard Thaler (1983),"Transaction Utility Theory", in NA - Advances in Consumer Research Volume 10, Eds. Richard P. Bagozzi and Alice M. Tybout, Ann Arbor, MI: Association for Consumer Research, Pages: 229-232.

In layman's terms, it reflects whether the customer feels they received the 'enjoyment'/'Benefit' from the actual transaction that they expected.

This is not the same as whether they thought they received value for money overall, that is when the Service Value Equation is in balance. This is best demonstrated by an example.

I have a lot of experience of buying cars. Recently, I had identified a car I wanted to acquire, and having considered the range of prices I could afford and the marginal Price/marginal Benefit differences within that range, had selected a particular vehicle.

The dealer was asking £10,500. I was determined to pay just under £10,000. We got to a stalemate of me offering £9,800 and him wanting £10,000.

I bought the car, but I didn't enjoy the negotiation, as I felt he was being intransigent. I got good value for money, but didn't quite feel great about the transaction.

Now, my expectations were inflated, second-hand car sales are a low margin business and every pound makes a difference to the dealer, but not too much difference to me.

However, I am a competitive person and I wanted to achieve something in the deal too. If he had settled at £9,999 I would have felt so much better about the whole deal.

This does not only apply in those situations where you can negotiate. Think about all those retailers who offer 'BOGOF' (Buy One Get One Free) deals, discounts, special sales periods etc. People like a "bargain". They feel they have got something extra from the transaction.

Another way of considering this, but to the same effect, is that "satisfaction with the deal" forms part of the customer's evaluation of the "Post-Service" experience.

Not only do customers assess the price prior to the transaction, but also during and following receipt of the Service Benefit and Service Experience.

Once they have received the service, they will then be able to compare:

▸ The Total Cost to Customer which they expected to play against the TCC, they actually paid (if there was no fixed price, nor any variations); and/or

▸ The Benefit and Experience they actually received to the TCC they paid, compared to the Benefit and Experience they expected to the TCC they actually paid.

If the Benefit and/or Experience they received was worse than expected, then the Price also looks expensive, and the SerVAL Proposition is worse than expected. If the Benefit and/or Experience they received was better than expected, then the Price looks better than when they agreed to purchase the service, and the SerVAL Proposition is better than expected.

Customers may also feel that other elements of the Total Cost to Customer, which may well be outside of the service provider's control, have also been higher than expected. Travel may have cost more, taken longer and been more difficult than expected. A better alternative use of time may have emerged, increasing the opportunity cost, etc.

The SerVAL Proposition, therefore, may be considered, in terms of the Total Cost to Customer, as follows:

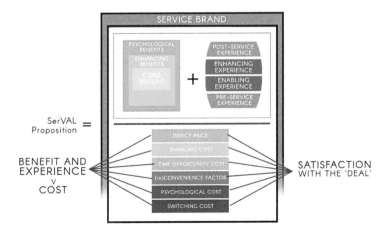

Evaluating all three elements can provide a significant challenge when the Direct Price is nil, as it typically is in the case of Public Services. If you are not paying for something, then how can you consider whether the Service Benefit and/or Service Experience represents good value?

WHAT ARE THE CONSEQUENCES OF FAILING TO DELIVER WHAT CUSTOMERS EXPECTED?

There are a number of potential consequences for a service organisation that do not deliver the SerVAL Proposition the customer expected to receive.

Short-term direct financial impact

One consequence can be short-term financial issues. Firstly, it can be expected to cost the service organisation additional money to resolve any issues raised by the customer. This reduces profitability and/or the budgets that are available to do other things.

It is also likely to involve the short-term diversion of resources (management, frontline customer service and support) to resolve the issue. This will have an opportunity cost, as well as the direct cost mentioned above. Secondly, in more extreme cases, it can create cash flow issues if a customer refuses to pay their bill.

Long-term direct financial impact

It may also lead to the loss of the customer and the loss of the expected future income from that customer. It will also generate the cost and effort of having to replace that customer.

Negative impact on the Service Benefit and Service Experience

Another consequence of customer dissatisfaction is that the morale of the service organisation employees is likely to be negatively affected, as no one likes receiving complaints. This can be expected to impact their performance, and/or their behaviour, which according to the Service-Profit Chain, is likely to have an impact on the SerVAL Proposition delivered to for other customers.

The Service Benefit may not be as good and the Service Experience is likely to be less good, which, in turn, needs to be rectified, and so on.

Long-term consequential financial impact – damage to Brand reputation

Failure to deliver the expected SerVAL Proposition may also lead to:

▶ The dissatisfied customer telling others about their dissatisfaction, leading to negative "word of mouth"

▶ Other existing customers leaving because they have heard negative things about the organisation, and they were not committed to the organisation anyway

▶ Potential new customers choosing not select the organisation ahead of its competitors.

In an ever more competitive world, lost customers will be ever harder to replace economically. The loss of current and potential customers, and the damage to the organisation's brand is thus much more significant for the organisation than just the short-term costs of rectifying service dissatisfaction. Moreover, the risk of customer dissatisfaction has increased significantly in the age of social media and the internet. It is very easy for dissatisfied customers to broadcast their dissatisfaction very widely, very quickly, to millions of people. Negative word of mouth (NWOM) has thus become exponentially more powerful, as has positive WOM (PWOM) in the age of social media.

Depending on the nature of the failure to deliver what the customer expected, it could also lead to lawsuits that will increase one-off costs and/or increased regulation, which may be expected to increase future ongoing operating costs. The Financial Services industry is experiencing these consequences at the time of writing (2012-2016). It could also lead to an increase in future insurance premiums, or even an inability to insure. This latter point is a challenge particularly felt by professional service organisations.

THE KEY MEASURE OF SUCCESS

This leads neatly into some key research by Frederick Reichheld, summarised in The Harvard Business Review article, 'The One Number You Need to Grow', in December 2003, which indicates that, ultimately, there is only one key measure of customer satisfaction, namely:

How likely is a customer to recommend the service (or goods) provider to a friend or colleague?

Reichheld recommends that customers are asked to measure their response on a scale of 1 to 10. A score of 9 or 10 would be received from a positive promoter. A score of 6 or less would be received from a detractor. The aggregate of these can be totalled to identify whether or not the organisation has a positive or negative Net Promoter score, which is a key determinant, according to Reichheld, of growth. All other measures are diagnostic and explain the above.

It might be argued that customer behaviour, whether or not it is loyal, may be a better measure. However, this ignores the fact that customers may remain loyal because they have no choice, or the alternatives are not seen as very good, and/or switching costs are too high to justify a change. Customer loyalty in such situations is a result of the customers being, in effect, "hostages". Unless a monopoly position has been created through significant outperformance in service excellence, then it is unlikely their loyalty is a sign of service excellence.

SUMMARY

The most important measure of customer satisfaction, which underpins customer loyalty, is the Net Promoter Score. Basically, this means that your customers are so satisfied that they will recommend you to other customers.

Customers will perceive whether they have received all the elements of the SerVAL Proposition in the expected combination when assessing the performance of a service provider.

Fundamentally, they will be concerned whether they have received the expected Service Benefit, or not, and the Total Cost to Customer paid for that The more clearly specified, tangible and obvious the receipt of, the Service Benefit, and the clearer and, preferably, less variable the Total Cost to Customer, the easier it is for them to make such an assessment.

Assuming they perceive the Service Benefit has been received at the expected level, they will also be concerned about the Service Experience. In addition, unless receipt of the Service Benefit is binary, the customer is likely to require a minimum acceptable level of Service Benefit and a minimum acceptable level of Service Experience, with some degree of trade-off between them.

These minimum acceptable trade-offs will be largely dictated by competition and alternatives to buying the service, as well as by the Total Cost to Customer that is being paid for the service. The trade-offs and minimum levels of performance may vary between markets and selected customer groups, and these variations can allow market segmentation and differentiation.

Customers will assess the Service by having regard to the Responsiveness, Assurance, Tangibles, Empathy and Reliability that they experience relative to their needs and expectations, and whether or not they trust the motives of the service provider.

The key determinants of the ability of the service provider to meet its customers' expectations in terms of this Service Experience are the Service Delivery Mix and the performance and behaviour of the components therein, and the Service Delivery Model adopted to deliver the service.

The level, nature and location of the customer/service provider interface, coupled with the strength and basis of the relationship the service provider has with its customers, are particularly important elements of the Service Delivery Model in terms of shaping this Service Experience.

When considering the Service Price, not only will customers compare it to service provider competitors and alternative services, they will also compare it to the Service Benefit and Service Experience that they expect to receive, and consider whether the SerVAL Proposition represents a balanced Service Value Equation. And they will consider the whole Total Cost to Customer, not just the direct price element.

Furthermore, not only will customers evaluate the Total Cost to Customer compared to the expected Service Benefits and expected Service Experience in advance of buying a service, they will also evaluate it post-transaction in terms of the TCC paid v. TCC expected, and the actual Benefits and Experience received. Their assessment of direct price will also include how well they think they did on the "pricing deal".

CHAPTER TWELVE:
KEY QUESTIONS TO CONSIDER

- ▶ Who is your customer?

- ▶ Who else is in the customer stakeholder group?

- ▶ How will they each measure their satisfaction with your SerVAL Proposition?

- ▶ How might this be weighted in an overall view of satisfaction?

- ▶ How satisfied are they at present?

- ▶ What is your current Net Promoter Score?

- ▶ Do you deliver the expected SerVAL Proposition?

- ▶ What, if any, trade-off is your customers making between being satisfied with the Service Benefit, Service Experience and the Total Cost to Customer?

- ▶ Do your customers Trust your organisation's motives?

- ▶ Is your organisation suitably Responsive?

- ▶ Does your organisation provide your customers with the required level of Assurance?

- ▶ What do your customers think about the Tangible elements of your Service Benefit and Service Experience?

- ▶ Is your organisation suitably Empathetic?

- ▶ Is your organisation suitably Reliable?

- ▶ What is your current customer retention rate?

- ▶ What is the length of relationships with your customers?

- ▶ Why do you lose customers?

- ▶ Why do you win customers?

- ▶ Why do you retain customers?

- ▶ What service satisfaction measures do you currently obtain?

- ▶ Do you trust the robustness of these?
- ▶ Do these allow you to diagnose the reasons behind customer satisfaction levels?
- ▶ Do you have different customer satisfaction and loyalty levels in different parts of your customer group/market segments?
- ▶ Why?
- ▶ How satisfied are your competitors' customers?
- ▶ How loyal are they?
- ▶ Should you be targeting them?

WHAT IS A CUSTOMER WORTH?

INTRODUCTION

In the previous section of the book, we discussed how to create value for a customer. As well as how to give them what they want for a price that they can afford and are prepared to pay.

But this is only one side of the equation. What value does the service provider receive in return? This is equally important because, without receiving some form of value in return, the service organisation will ultimately cease to exist or choose not to exist.

In the chapters in this section, I am going to consider how service providers can create value from an individual customer.

And, remember, ultimately the value of any organisation is the sum of the value of its current and potential future customers.

KEY QUESTIONS

I am going to explore what is the value of a customer by addressing the following key questions:

▶ What direct financial value does a customer bring to a service organisation?

▶ What is Customer Lifetime value?

▶ How can we assess Customer Lifetime Value?

▶ What use is a CLV calculation?

▶ How important is individual customer profitability for service businesses?

▶ What indirect financial value can a customer bring to a service organisation?

▶ How can you apply this to your service organisation?

WHAT DIRECT FINANCIAL VALUE DOES A CUSTOMER BRING TO A SERVICE ORGANISATION?

This isn't a trick question, but it is a tricky question! The direct financial value that a customer brings to a service organisation is the profit margin, turned into cash, generated from serving the customer. The tricky part can be calculating this margin, but I don't want to get into detailed management accounting arguments in this book. The hardest part is normally what costs need to be allocated to a customer and how much of these costs should be allocated. I will, however, highlight some of the challenges.

Firstly, can the organisation assess the direct costs that the customer has consumed? This tends to be relatively easy to assess in some service businesses. For a hairdresser it will be the time taken to cut someone's hair, , and the cost of that time, plus any hair product used. For a lawyer, it will again largely be a function of time spent and the cost of that time. For a logistics service business, it will be the time taken by the truck driver and the cost of the fuel and depreciation of the truck. In other businesses, such as a retailer, it can be harder. How does a retailer efficiently calculate the time a checkout person has spent on a customer, or the shop assistant help someone to select some shoes? In cases such as these, should the costs of service just be treated as an overhead?

And how do organisation's allocate overheads to customers, should all overheads be allocated to them, or should it be done at all? Also, what about the overheads that represent the capacity to take on new customers or Research and Development? And what about the overheads required for governance purposes and/or regulatory compliance?

Even after allocating overheads, the answer generated may give rise to some tricky questions. What if a percentage of the organisation's customers make a negative contribution to net margin? Should it just get rid of those customers? Such an approach would lose those customers' contribution to overheads, unless the service business can offset them by shrinking their overheads, which would reduce the profitability of the other customers.

Customer profitability can also be expected to vary over time, for several reasons. Firstly, customers may spend different amounts of money with an organisation over time. Secondly, they may need different levels of support, such as the level of time invested in a relationship over time, due to changing needs or personnel. Thirdly, they may buy a range of services with differing profitability for each service, and this may also be on a cycle. Fourthly, the service organisation may have just invested in additional overhead to support growth or business change, and if allocated at that period, will reduce customer profitability.

Most overheads are relatively "lumpy", so tend not to be scaled in a linear way. What if a big customer is lost, then all of the overheads that were being allocated to it now need to be covered by the organisation in some way. If allocated across all the remaining customers, then they will appear less profitable than before, even though the cost to serve the customer has not changed at all.

And when the organisation takes on more customers, without requiring additional overhead, the overheads will be spread over more customers, so, each may appear to be more profitable, even though nothing directly related to the customer has changed.

So what?

So customer profitability analysis can be tricky. That doesn't mean it shouldn't be done. It just means it needs to be carefully thought through, and the reasons for the variations understood clearly, prior to any conclusions being drawn and action taken. But without undertaking some form of customer profitability analysis, it can be much more difficult to efficiently and effectively build value in a service organisation.

WHAT IS CUSTOMER LIFETIME VALUE?

We have considered the value of a customer in a particular period, or at a point in time. However, the value of a customer isn't just the benefit the service provider receives in one time period.

A customer may purchase the service more than once or over an extended period of time, and thus generate profits in several time periods. Customer Lifetime Value (CLV) is a really simple concept that recognises profit can be earned from customers over a number of periods.

CLV is the financial value of a customer to an organisation over the length of the relationship with the customer (the customer lifetime). In simple terms, if the annual financial value of the customer is £100 and the relationship is for five years, then the customer lifetime value is £500.

Customer	Margin in year					
	Year 1	Year 2	Year 3	Year 4	Year 5	Total
One	£100	£50	£20	£10		£180
Beta	£50	£100	£200	£100	£50	£500
Gamma	£150	0	0	0	0	£150
Epsilon	£70	£70	£70	£70	£70	£350

The table above illustrates different Customer Lifetime Values. It also illustrates that different levels of profit in a particular year are not necessarily a good reflection of the value of the customer to the organisation.

It can be seen that Year 1 Beta is the least profitable customer and Gamma the most profitable. Which customer is the most valuable to the organisation?

HOW TO CALCULATE CUSTOMER LIFETIME VALUE?

A lot of articles have been written about Customer Lifetime Value and there has been a lot of debate by academics about it. A lot of this debate has focused around whether the direct financial value of the customer should be calculated based on gross margins, operating margins, net margins or some new form of margin calculation that is based on actual overhead absorption, stripping out overheads that are not directly needed for that customer etc.

This is a great intellectual debate for management accountants – and quite a useful, practical debate too – as service providers do need to understand what customers are actually contributing.

Having calculated margins in both historic and current periods, it is then necessary to forecast what these direct financial values will be in future periods.

How can a service organisation do this if it doesn't know its customers very well and there is an uncertain economic environment? Also how long will this cash flow last, how long will a customer be retained and how loyal are they? I review customer loyalty in Chapter 15 below. Like all forecasts, it is necessary to make an informed (or ill-informed) guess.

Once a potential future cash flow from a customer has been identified, the next debate is whether this cash flow should be discounted or not? Yes, would be the view of many accountants, using a risk adjusted Weighted Average Cost of Capital, or some other appropriate discount rate.

BUT WHAT USE IS A CLV CALCULATION?

CLV calculations can be of considerable use.

Firstly, they can help with an organisation's budgeting, as they are a very granular consideration of future revenues.

Secondly, on an organisation wide basis, they can also indicate where resources might be allocated to increase value or to limit damage to a firm's reputation. In the example above, why is Gamma not going to spend more money with the firm? Why invest lots more time to retain Gamma than Epsilon? Why does Beta, who is a very similar customer to Epsilon, spend significantly more with the service organisation?

On an individual customer basis, they can form the basis of investment appraisals: how much time needs to be invested in retaining and developing a customer.

The calculation can also demonstrate whether it is worth investing in trying to win a new customer, and how much it is worth investing. This can also make the choice between new and existing customers more informed.

We have all been told the "accepted wisdom" that it costs "5 times" more to win a new customer compared to retaining an existing customer. Whether or not this is true, does it matter?

Customer	Existing	New
Cost to retain/win	£20	£100
Year 1	£50	£10
Year 2	0	£50
Year 3	0	£100
Year 4	0	£100
Year 5	0	£100
CLV	£30	£260
ROI	250%	360%

CLV analysis can show that even if winning a new customer costs 5 times more than retaining the existing customer, it is worth focusing on if it generates an acceptable investment return and payback period.

CLV also shows how returns on resources can be increased, i.e. how to manage the yield from the Service Delivery Mix.

There is always the danger that a percentage of a service organisation's resources are "busy fools".

HOW IMPORTANT IS INDIVIDUAL CUSTOMER PROFITABILITY FOR SERVICE ORGANISATIONS?

Clearly, customer profitability is important for all organisations. But is it more important for service organisations than manufacturers, or for certain types of service businesses compared to others?

Well, let's consider the impact of the VITAL characteristics of the services discussed in Chapter 3. In particular, that services can be varied and involve close interaction with a customer.

What this means in practical terms is that the amount of resources committed to delivering a service each time is delivered can vary and is often driven by the customer.

So whilst the price that a manufacturer might get for a washing machine may vary, the cost of producing each identical washing machine will be the same.

For a service provider, however, each time they deliver a service they may or may not get the same price, and they are also likely to incur a different cost for producing the "same" service.

Significant margin variance can thus occur. So it is key to work for customers who pay the highest price relative to the resources consumed, i.e. the most profitable customers.

This is particularly the case when the cost input is most variable, which tends to be when one of the key resources in the Service Delivery Mix are people and the level of customer interaction is high.

This can be represented as follows.

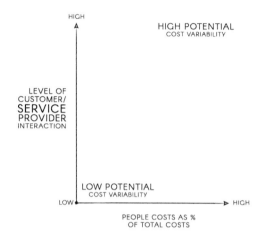

CORE DRIVERS OF CUSTOMER
COST TO SERVE VARIANCE

HIGH

HIGH POTENTIAL
COST VARIABILITY

LEVEL OF
CUSTOMER/
SERVICE
PROVIDER
INTERACTION

LOW POTENTIAL
COST VARIABILITY

LOW   HIGH

PEOPLE COSTS AS %
OF TOTAL COSTS

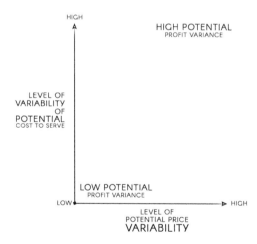

CORE DRIVERS OF CUSTOMER
PROFIT MARGIN VARIANCE

HIGH

HIGH POTENTIAL
PROFIT VARIANCE

LEVEL OF
VARIABILITY
OF
POTENTIAL
COST TO SERVE

LOW POTENTIAL
PROFIT VARIANCE

LOW   HIGH

LEVEL OF
POTENTIAL PRICE
VARIABILITY

These relationships will vary from Service Delivery Model to Service Delivery Model. For example, the models that involve low levels of customisation can be expected to experience lower cost variance and lower price variance. As one of the main drivers of variability are people, then the models with lower labour intensity would also expect, all things being equal, to have lower cost variances. The other main driver of cost variability is the level of customer/service provider interface, so you would expect that reducing this would also lead to lower cost variability.

Organisations, therefore, often seek to reduce cost and price variability by moving to more standardised service "products" by replacing labour content with tools and equipment, ITC and the internet, and so reduce the level of customer interaction. This is the "service factory" model.

However, such an approach can materially change the SerVAL Proposition to the Customer. The Benefit may or may not change, but the Service Experience will almost certainly. But will customers in receipt of a significantly different Service Experience reduce the price they are prepared to pay for it? If so, the quest for less margin variance can lead to more consistent but lower margins, unless of course, the cost of producing the service also falls significantly in order to maintain margins.

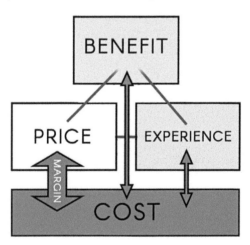

The inherent nature of services can make individual customer profitability and hence, customer selection and customer management, relatively more important for service organisations than for other types of organisation, and this is particularly the case for service organisations that adopt a Service Delivery System which is labour intensive, has high degrees of customer interaction, and allows or necessitates a wide degree of operational freedom to its service operatives, such as professional service organisations, like lawyers.

WHAT INDIRECT FINANCIAL VALUE CAN A CUSTOMER BRING?

So the direct financial value that a customer can bring to a service provider can be summarised in a CLV calculation. However, not only do customers provide **direct financial value** to the organisation, without which it wouldn't exist, but they are also the source of **indirect financial value**. By this I mean they contribute value that leads, ultimately, to additional direct financial value, normally through other customers.

Firstly, customers can be the source of **positive word of mouth (PWOM)** about a service organisation amongst their direct human network. This may lead directly to new customer being attracted to the organisation or members of that network may tell other people (creating a "ripple effect") that leads to the people told becoming customers. The further the ripple gets from the organisation, the more it is about building a reputation and brand, rather than direct referral. That is equally important and not mutually exclusive.

Secondly, customers use social media to communicate positive things about the service organisation to a much bigger group of people. This is increasingly the case and the positive opinions of (sic) opinion setters in a market can be very powerful.

Thirdly, a service provider can obtain and use PWOM from its customers. It can obtain positive references in writing or by video/podcast, etc. that can be used in its marketing communications. Where the customer is a well-known name (say a celebrity that uses a hairdressing salon or a FTSE 100 company using a service) then just referencing the customer's brand can be important, and can either directly attract new customers or strengthen the service provider's brand, which will in turn indirectly attract new customers and aid customer retention.

A fourth, but very important, source of value is that an organisation's most demanding and/or important customers can be a key factor that drives innovation. If a service provider has one customer that contributes say 40% of its profits and they demand a price reduction or an improvement or variation in services, then the service provider is likely to try very hard to find a way to do it, with "necessity being the mother of invention".

Also, if a service provider works for some of the most demanding customers in the market, then the best practices it develops to support them will put it in a good position to work for less demanding customers. In my experience, both of these factors can be key drivers of excellence in the business-to-business service markets. This is the reverse of what many people think, i.e. that they want inexperienced or not very demanding customers.

A fifth reason is that having the best known, most demanding, most attractive customers in the market can be an important attraction for attracting and retaining the best employees in some service businesses, particularly professional service businesses. This then becomes part of a virtuous cycle of success.

SUMMARY

The value a customer brings to any organisation is a combination of direct and indirect financial contribution that is received over a period of time. This is termed Customer Lifetime Value. The longer the period of time the customer is retained, and/or the higher the contribution in a period, then the higher the lifetime value of that customer.

Whilst direct Financial contribution can be tricky to measure, as it involves judgment calls about overhead consumption and allocation, it should be measured as it provides an extremely valuable (sic) insight into value creation and return on resources in service businesses. Assessing the potential length of a customer relationship is also an exercise in judgment, but this judgment can be informed through obtaining a detailed understanding of a customer, their personal economic or business environment, and through assessing and understanding historic expenditure patterns.

Assessing CLV is an extremely valuable exercise to support organisational and individual client budgets and resource allocation, and enables better investment decisions to be made concerning customer retention and customer acquisition.

The indirect financial value that a customer can bring is even harder to measure, but that doesn't mean it doesn't exist! This too will vary from customer to customer, and will also depend on the service organisation's own requirements.

It is important to recognise that all customers don't have the same value to an organisation, and that any organisation will have a portfolio of "customer assets" of varying historic, current and potential future value. This value can be assessed and managed, both in aggregate and individually. The basis of the value of any organisation is the aggregate value of all its existing customers and future customers. In the following chapter, I discuss how to increase the value of an individual customer.

CHAPTER THIRTEEN:
KEY QUESTIONS TO CONSIDER:

WHAT ARE YOUR CUSTOMERS WORTH?

▶ How much "cash gross margin" (cash contribution to overheads and profit) does each of your customers contribute?

▶ How does this fluctuate over time?

▶ Why does this fluctuate over time?

▶ Can you influence or control these fluctuations?

▶ Can you accurately forecast these fluctuations?

▶ How can you increase this contribution?

▶ How long can you expect to retain each of these customers at present?

▶ How might you increase customer retention?

▶ What is the current Customer Lifetime Value of your customers?

▶ What could it be?

▶ How?

▶ Can you serve these customers with a lower overhead?

▶ Can you reduce the overhead cost per customer through growing customer numbers?

▶ Can you replace low gross contribution customers with higher contributing ones to increase the yield from your overheads?

WHAT FACTORS DRIVE THE COST OF SERVING A CUSTOMER?

INTRODUCTION

In the book so far, we have assessed how the ingredients in the Service Delivery Mix and the nature of the Service Delivery Model impact the Service Benefit, the Service Experience and the Total Cost to Customer. We have also considered how they affect the way that customers assess the SerVAL Proposition they perceive they have received.

This analysis provides the basis for understanding how service organisations can produce a SerVAL Proposition that its customers will want in preference to those offered by its competitors or alternative delivery solutions available to obtain the same Service Benefit.

The other side of the equation, which I will now review, is how to produce this SerVAL Proposition at a reasonable cost, so that the service organisation remains economically viable.

In simple terms, anyone should be able to produce a great SerVAL Proposition if they are able to throw resources at it, with no regard for cost or cash flow. However, such an approach isn't sustainable. Therefore, it is critical in the long run for the service provider that the Direct Price it receives from delivering the SerVAL Proposition is at least as great as the cost of producing it. That Direct Price may be received directly from customers in the market, from funds provided by central or local government for public services, or a budget allocated to an internal department.

In this chapter, I am therefore going to explore the factors that influence the cost of production of a service. It will not include a detailed analysis of costing, financial or managerial accounting, or the costs required to win or retain customers, which are beyond the scope of this book.

This overview is designed, like the rest of the book, to provoke thought, and to make it clear that costs should be considered holistically. All proposed changes to a service organisation's cost base should be assessed in terms of the impact on the SerVAL Proposition, and Customer Lifetime Value, not just the immediate bottom line.

KEY QUESTIONS

To gain a better understanding of the factors influencing the costs to produce a service, I will consider the following key questions:

▶   Which factors drive the cost to serve a customer?

▶   How do People costs impact the cost to serve a customer?

▶   How do Processes impact the cost to serve a customer?

▶   How do Tool & Equipment costs impact the cost to serve a customer?

▶   How do ICT & Internet costs impact the cost to serve a customer?

▶   How do Real Estate costs impact the cost to serve a customer?

▶   How do Customers impact the cost to serve a customer?

▶   How does the Service Delivery Model impact the cost to serve a customer?

▶   What is the **Efficiency trap**?

▶   What costs the most to produce – the Service Benefit or the Service Experience?

▶   What is the impact of Fixed and Variable costs/Costs of Sale & Overheads based analysis on cost management in service organisations?

▶   What can be the impact of cost savings on the SerVAL Proposition?

▶   What can be the impact of cost savings on margin?

▶   What can be the impact of cost savings on customer retention?

WHICH FACTORS DRIVE THE COST TO SERVE A CUSTOMER?

The cost to serve a customer is primarily a function of the activities that are undertaken to serve the customer. An Activity Based Costing approach is thus a good approach to gain an understanding of the cost to serve a customer. Fundamentally, the two factors that drive the cost of an activity are how long the activity takes and the cost of the resources deployed to undertake the activity.

Cost to serve a customer = f (time taken to serve, cost of resources deployed)

The time it takes to service the customer reflects how effective an organisation is in using these resources to perform the activity. It also reflects how the level of customer interaction, and the customer's behaviour during that interaction, impact efficiency. A high customer contact model is inherently less efficient than low customer contact models because of the "uncontrolled" greater involvement of the customer. The cost per unit of time reflects how efficient the organisation is combining and utilising the ingredients in the Service Delivery Mix, i.e. the amount of waste in the service delivery process.

A simple example with just people in the Service Delivery Mix.

Customer	Time taken to serve	Current cost to serve per minute*	Actual Cost to serve	Efficiency factor	Potential cost to serve***
Alpha	5 mins	£1	£5	90%**	£4.50

*This is total employment costs divided by the number of minutes worked.

** This reflects the amount of wasted time due to, say, inefficient processes, low labour productivity or time wasted due to customer behaviour.

*** This assumes 100% efficiency.

The efficiency factor is that which is specific to the organisation and not inherent to the Service Delivery Model. The resource costs are the costs of the ingredients in the Service Delivery Mix, namely People, Real Estate, Tools & Equipment, ICT Systems & Internet, Process and Brand. These resources are either directly consumed in the service delivery process; for example, the amount of time someone spends serving a particular customer, or are allocated to a customer on some basis. For example, allocating property

costs by employee headcount and then turning this into an hourly
cost based on the hours worked serving customers.

	Total annual costs (000's)	No of employees	Cost per employee	No of hours spent serving customers per employee	Cost per hour
Property	£1,000		£10,000		£10
ICT	£200	100	£2,000	1000	£2
Tools & Equipment	£150		£1,500		£1.50
Brand	£100		£1,000		£1
TOTAL	£1,450		£14,500		£14.50

Assuming that these employees each cost £100,000 to employ,
then the hourly cost of serving the customer would be £114.50.

In the example above, it would, of course, be possible to go
directly to the total number of hours spent serving customers.
However, by doing so, the analysis might miss out some insight
on how employee numbers drive costs. For example, if you could
increase productivity by 10%, then that could enable a reduction
in the number of employees by 9, which could then enable a
reduction in Property, ICT and Tools & Equipment costs by 9%. It
is unlikely to have any impact on the costs of Brand building and
maintenance.

	Total annual costs (000's)	No of employees	Cost per employee	No of hours spent serving customers per employee	Cost per hour
Property	£910		£10,000		£9.09
ICT	£182	91	£2,000	1100	£1.81
Tools & Equipment	£136		£1,500		£1.36
Brand	£100		£1,098		£1
TOTAL	£1,328		£14,598		£13.26

The hourly cost of serving the customer would then be £91 + £13.26= £104.26. The balance of these resources and the amount of time they are allocated to a customer are shaped, in part, by the Service Delivery Model. For example, a high customer contact and highly labour intensive Service Delivery Model will consume more people resource than a low customer contact, IT-based Service Delivery Model, and the time taken to serve a customer may be longer than in a low customer contact model.

It is also important to recognise the difference between organisational wide costs to serve a customer, i.e. those inherent in the strategic choices that the organisation has made in terms of its Service Delivery Mix and Service Delivery Model, and general organisational efficiency, and those specific to serving a particular customer, which are influenced by the way that that particular service assignment is delivered, and the way that specific customer behaves.

*Cost to serve a generic customer = f (cost of a Service Delivery Mix, Service Delivery Model) * organisational efficiency and effectiveness*

*Cost to serve a specific customer = f (cost to serve a generic customer) * assignment efficiency*individual customer behaviour.*

The Service Delivery Model adopted will have a major impact on the degree of variance between the cost to serve the generic and specific customer; a low variance would be expected for "standardised" services involving low customer contact, and a higher variance for "bespoke" services with high customer contact. In statistical terms, assuming a normal distribution of costs, the difference might be as follows:

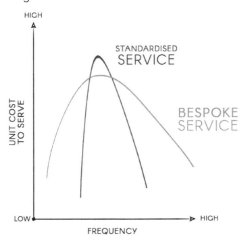

HOW DO PEOPLE COSTS IMPACT THE COST TO SERVE A CUSTOMER?

People can be the major cost of many service businesses. A major cost driver will, therefore, be the number of people employed and how much they are paid, including employment taxes.

A primary cost management strategy for many service businesses is, therefore, to employ fewer people and/or pay them less and/or employ less costly people.

This was a major driver during the first decade of the 21st century for the "offshoring" of services, or elements of services, such as call-centres, from North American and European economies to locations where employment costs were lower, such as Asia and South Africa.

Although, at first glance, utilising cheaper people might seem to present the means to lower the cost of producing the service, it is important to consider whether such an approach, in practice, necessarily achieves that objective.

If it takes a lawyer an hour to write a letter and to employ that person costs £100,000 per annum. If they work 1500 hours per annum, then the cost per hour is £66 per hour. The basic cost of the task, before overhead allocation, is £66.

So you replace your £100,000 pa lawyer with one costing £50,000 pa, and your cost per hour is £33. However, this lawyer is not experienced and needs to spend more time checking his facts and legal reference books, as well as redrafting his letter, which takes two hours to write. Therefore, the cost of producing the letter is still £66.

If you pay a cleaner £7 per hour, then (including employment costs of approximately 15%) it costs you £8 an hour. If it takes an hour to clean a floor, then the cost of cleaning the floor is £8 (excluding cleaning materials etc.).

If you buy your cleaner a floor washing machine that means he cleans the floor in 15 minutes, the labour cost of cleaning the floor is £2. As the allocated cost of the machine is £2, the cost of cleaning the floor is now £4.

For any service activity that is primarily undertaken by a person, the cost of a task will reflect two elements — how long it takes the person(s) to undertake the task and the cost of the person (s) undertaking the task. The latter is largely a reflection of the employment market. The former is a reflection of the individual and the organisation.

The factors which drive the time it takes a person to undertake a task to a given standard, namely their productivity, will vary from service to service.

However, there are a number of generic factors influencing that time, including:

▶ The skills of the person undertaking the task

▶ The efficiency of the Process used to undertake the task

▶ The Tools and Equipment used to undertake the task

▶ The ICT systems used to undertake the task

▶ The Suitability of the Real Estate where they are undertaking the task

▶ The Experience of the person undertaking the task

▶ The Motivation of the person to undertake the task.

Clearly, having the appropriate skill to undertake a task will be an important influence on both the SerVAL Proposition delivered to the customer and the cost of delivering it.

The influence that experience has on productivity was suggested in the lawyer example above. It is further illustrated by the experience curve example below.

The experience curve is a simple, but powerful, model of the common sense concept that we all have experienced (sic), that people become more efficient at performing a task, up to a point, the more times they repeat it.

The potential power of experience in reducing service delivery costs is illustrated by the following example.

Assuming a 10% reduction in labour time is required to undertake a task for each doubling of experience, then after a task has been repeated 10 times, the hours taken to complete it has reduced to approximately 70% of the initial amount, and after 100 repetitions it can be completed in about half the time it took in the first instance.

The resulting experience curve is shown here.

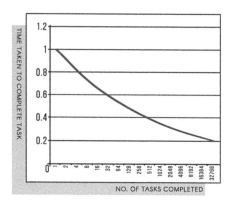

The experience curve suggests, therefore, that replacing more expensive experienced people with cheaper inexperienced people may not reduce the unit cost of producing the service. Service organisations must, therefore, seek an understanding of the experience curve for their service, or elements of their service, which will vary, before making any changes to the mix of people they engage to deliver their service.

The experience curve for a brain surgeon is likely to be far more significant than for a hospital cleaner, but they both form part of an overall health care service.

It is also important to recognise that productivity can be expected to vary from person to person, as everyone is different. The key to consistent productivity is to minimise this range, by employing people with a similar level of experience and skill to undertake the same roles and tasks. However, experience and skill are not the only the people related driver of unit costs. Two people who are equally experienced and skilled, that cost the same, working to the same processes and with the same tools, may not take the same time to complete a task, nor do it equally well. Their motivation to perform productively is also of huge importance. I considered the motivation of employees to perform in some detail in Chapter 5 in terms of how, through the Service/Profit Chain, motivation can impact the Service Experience and the Service Benefit delivered to the customer. The impact of an individual's motivation is not just on the customer side of the equation, however; an individual's motivation to perform a task efficiently and quickly will also impact the cost of providing the service. For the purposes of clarity, I have separated Employee Productivity from Employee Performance (delivering the Service Benefit and Experience) in the diagram below.

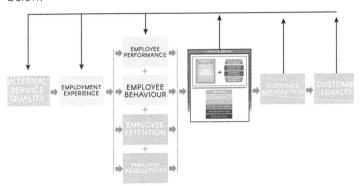

In my experience, motivation related labour productivity is not just a reflection of an individual's motivation, or a team's motivation, but it can also a reflect the local and general employment markets. In part, this reflects the desire and need for people to work, and how hard they do so.

The other key people element that drives the costs of producing a service, as flagged up by the Service Profit Chain, is Employee Retention. Poor Employee Retention can impact customer service, as well as the morale and, hence, the behaviour of other employees. From a cost perspective, a low level of Employee Retention will both increase recruitment costs, and is also likely to reduce average productivity. New employees will go through the experience curve mentioned earlier, and then, as they become demotivated and preparing to leave, their productivity is likely to fall. This can be considered as follows:

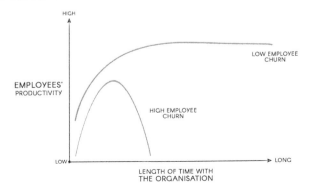

The processes adopted by the people, tools and equipment used by them, etc. will also clearly have an impact on the cost to deliver the service, and I cover these below.

Service organisations should, therefore, not only focus on the raw employment costs of their people when assessing the cost of service delivery, but also gain a good understanding of the drivers of the time it takes to deliver a service to a customer, particularly the motivation, skill and experience of their employees, as their productivity is a key driver of the unit cost of service production.

*Cost to serve = f (raw cost of resource * productivity)*

There are significant implications for recruitment, training and development, job design and recognition and reward, as set out in the (modified) Service Profit Chain model.

Labour Productivity = f (Service/Profit Chain, Employment market)

In the sections below, we will explore the other factors shaping productivity, such as the processes and tools and equipment.

HOW DOES THE EFFICIENCY OF PROCESSES IMPACT THE COST TO SERVE A CUSTOMER?

It is self-evident that inefficient processes will increase the cost of serving a customer. It is also a truism. The Oxford English Dictionary (online version 2014) defines efficiency as follows:

"Achieving maximum productivity with minimum wasted effort or expense."

So, all things being equal, those service organisations with less efficient processes will have a higher cost to serve their customers than those with efficient processes.

In manufacturing, process efficiency is typically driven by the mass production of standard products with very high levels of plant and machinery up-time. This is based on predictable demand, minimal spare capacity, just in time delivery of materials and components and using standardised, highly consistent, production processes in a controlled environment.

The VITAL characteristics of a service mean that such an approach is a challenge for services. However, that is not the case! Firstly, the Service Delivery Mix and Service Delivery Model can increase variability. That is akin to bespoke or batch production of goods. Secondly, the customer's interaction with the Service Delivery process will impact efficiency. i.e. It is not a controlled production environment like a factory.

The intangible nature of services means they cannot be produced and stored in advance of demand, thus making it very difficult to create a production process that can run at full capacity, i.e. without waste. Where the service in question is demanded at short notice with a fast response time, and so it is difficult to predict when the customer wants to attain the SerVAL Proposition, the capacity management and full capacity utilisation is also difficult.

We all know (but sometimes forget!) that people aren't machines, need frequent breaks (often stipulated through employment legislation) and their productivity can vary throughout the working day.

The service process efficiency challenge is increased further for services where people are a key element of the Service Delivery Mix. In my experience, people don't like working to inflexible standardised processes by and large. The adoption of this can be demotivating and lead to high levels of employee churn, as has been the case in many call centres, for example.

Seeking absolute process efficiency in services in the same way, as it is achieved in manufacturing, can, therefore, be both very difficult and potentially counterproductive, as it can lead to a reduction in the performance and change the behaviour of service delivery employees.

Service efficiency is not, therefore, necessarily founded in process efficiency, unless it is based on replacing people within the Service Delivery Mix with ICT and tools and equipment. In short, the fewer people involved in the Service Delivery Mix, then the more service efficiency can be driven by process.

That is not to say that services cannot be efficient or "lean", it is to say that efficiency – as defined at this beginning of the chapter – may arise through highly motivated peoples' productivity, using the right tools for the job, rather than through rigid process efficiency.

That isn't to say that standardising processes cannot add significant value to service organisations without demotivating its employees, but it needs to be done carefully.

HOW DO TOOL & EQUIPMENT COSTS IMPACT THE COST TO SERVE A CUSTOMER?

The cost of the relevant equipment will be dependent on the market for these tools. For hairdressers, the cost of scissors is dependent on the market for scissors, and for refuse collectors, the cost of trucks depends on the market for such trucks, etc.

When considering the use of equipment, however, the analysis should include a comparison with the alternative; by which I mean, do the productivity benefits generated by the equipment outweigh the costs of an alternative method? It also involves identifying whether there is any additional value added to the customer from the benefits of using the equipment, particularly if they will pay for it.

A floor scrubbing machine enables a cleaner to clean a floor in one hour, rather than two. The cost per hour of the cleaner is £7.50, the cost per hour of the floor scrubbing equipment is £5. So, a cleaner can clean the floor using the equipment for a cost of £12.50, rather than £15. It is clearly cheaper to use the equipment. What if the equipment cost £10 per hour, though? Should the service organisation use one?

What if there is only 1 hour available to do the work? Should they use two cleaners? What if they can only get one?

What if the floor scrubbing machine cleans the floor that much better? There will be a higher level of cleanliness, the results more consistent and the use of "hi-tech" equipment will impress the customer about the overall quality of your service operation. If the level of cleanliness is really important to the customer because they have lots of their customers in the area, will they pay a premium for having a cleaner floor?

Without the ability to clean the floor in an hour, there is no sale. If the customer does have two hours available, but is only willing and able to pay £16 to have the floor cleaned, then the service organisation will make a £1 margin without the machine, and a £2.50 margin with the machine – a 150% increase in margin. If the customer is willing to pay more for a cleaner floor, say £17, then the margin is £3.50, which is 250% higher than just employing two cleaners, or one cleaner for two hours.

In the example above, the equipment is both facilitating the productivity of another element of the Service Delivery Mix, i.e. the cleaner using the machine, and also substituting another element of the Mix, i.e. the extra cleaner not being required.

It can be seen that adding another element to the Service Delivery Mix – in this case, some equipment – can change the cost to serve the customer and/or the ability to serve the customer in the time the customer will make available to serve him. It may also change the Service Experience if, in the above example, the machine is noisy or reduces the contact between the service provider's people and the customer.

Service organisations need to consider how tools and equipment, and all other elements of the Service Delivery Mix, can facilitate the productivity of other elements of the Mix, and also substitute for other elements of the Mix, in order to create a higher and/or more sustainable margin.

Have your employees got the best tools for the job? Has your ditch digger got a spade and shovel or a mechanical digger? Has your cleaner got a mop and bucket or a floor scrubbing machine? Has your Real Estate appraiser got some valuation software, a calculator or pen and paper?

HOW DO REAL ESTATE COSTS IMPACT THE COST TO SERVE A CUSTOMER?

Real estate costs are typically – after people costs – the second or third highest cost of many service organisations. The drivers of real estate costs are straightforward the world over, namely:

▶ Location

▶ Quality of space occupied

▶ Quantity of space occupied

▶ Running costs

▶ Local property taxes

▶ Utilisation levels.

Location, through the mechanism of demand and supply, drives rental and capital values per unit of space occupied. The quality of the space occupied, in terms of how highly specified it is (e.g. air conditioned or not) and what condition the property is in, will influence the relative rental or capital price per unit of space for specific real estate units in that location. The quantity of space occupied will then drive aggregate rental or capital costs.

The next factor driving real estate costs are the non-rental/capital costs involved with running a building, such as heating, lighting, ventilating, maintenance, cleaning costs etc. These will reflect its specification, condition, location and size. Local property taxes may also vary from location to location, building type to building type, specification to specification, and according to the amount of space occupied.

And the final factor is how well the real estate is utilised, be that the number of occupants, and/or the number of customers that visit it. Utilisation levels can reflect building design and specification, as well as the occupation policy of the organisation.

The shape of buildings, the location of stairs, lifts, toilet and washroom facilities, the number of columns and pillars, the number of internal structural walls, the capacity of its cooling and ventilation systems, and local building and fire regulations etc, will all influence how many people can be accommodated in the building. The cost per customer, however, is also influenced by how productive the people in the building are, and/or the number of customers that are able to visit the building.

The rental costs of an office in central London might be £50 per square foot, with local property taxes at £20 per square foot, and running costs at £15 per square foot. Thus, there is a total occupation cost of £85 per square foot and a building of 10,000 sq feet would cost £850,000 per annum to occupy. If it is occupied by 100 people, then the cost per person is £8500 per annum. If it is only occupied by 50 people, then the cost per person is £17,000 per person.

If each person in that building provides a service to 100 customers per annum, then the average cost per customer in the first example is £85. In the second example, it is £170.

However, if the building in the second example is designed to enable people to be more efficient because they are given more space, so they can concentrate better, and more of the building is given over to space that will allow more customers to visit the building and be served by any individual, then the number of customers each person can serve in a year might be 200. So, the average cost to serve a customer would be £85 per annum.

The productivity of the individuals in a building will be influenced by a range of factors, including:

▶   The location of the building

▶   The design and layout of the building

▶   The specification of the building

▶   The ambience of the building

▶   Other services within the building

▶   The location of people within the building.

The location of the building will influence productivity in a number of ways. If the building is located in an area where the "best", "most motivated" people in an industry don't want to work, and/or the labour pool in that location is small and/or unskilled, then the people that can be attracted to work in that location may be less productive than others in that industry who are based in other locations.

The location can also influence employee "downtime", be that I mean time lost due to traffic or other transport problems while getting to the building, or travel time to get from the building to visit customers.

One of the key factors for labour productivity for mobile maintenance service businesses, such as gas appliance maintenance services, is the number of visits that a vehicle based technician can make in a day. This is influenced, amongst other things, by the location of the depot relative to the customers.

Location can also have an impact on the number of customers that can or will be served by a service organisation. Retailing and restaurant services are good examples of this.

Rents for retail units are lower in less prime locations. However, a retailer located in a tertiary pitch will, all things being equal, sell fewer goods and/or lower value goods than one in the prime pitch.

If the rent and other property costs for a prime retail unit are £100, 000 per annum and it serves 10,000 customers per annum, then the cost per customer is £10.

If the rent and other property costs of a tertiary retail unit are £20,000 per annum and it serves 1000 customers per annum, then the cost per customer is £20.

Of course, there are other costs to factor in, such as labour costs etc, as well as the gross margin on the goods sold.

A fast food outlet in the middle of nowhere will sell very few meals. This is because there will be fewer customers.

The design and layout of a building can influence how productively people can work within it. For example, small cellular offices can reduce team work. Large open plan space can hinder concentration for "brain work". Tall buildings with small floors can require a lot of travel between floors by lifts, which is non-productive time.

The specification of a building can directly impact peoples' productivity, and also indirectly impact productivity via its effect on their morale and motivation. Consider the impact of a poorly maintained building that is in need of decoration, or is painted in dark colours, or is too hot or too cold, or has too much or too sunlight? And what about if there are lots of cellular offices with shut doors, so that people rarely see their colleagues, or where the organisation's competitors occupy better places to work?

The design and layout of the property will also influence the number of customers that can be served. "Drive through" fast food outlets are examples of service organisations that seek, amongst other things, to increase the number of customers they can serve and their speed of service. But also think about the design and layout of retail outlets, banks, supermarkets, hairdressers, doctors' surgeries, hospitals, airport check-ins etc. Indeed, any service type which involves customers visiting the building.

The number of meeting rooms, checkouts, washbasins, the size of the waiting room, layout of queuing systems and number of car parking spaces, will all have an impact on the efficiency with which the organisation can deal with its customers. This will also have a major impact on the Service Experience, which I will return to further below.

A service organisation's real estate can be considered to be far more than just its offices, retail outlets, distribution centres, depots and yards, data centres, hospitals, surgeries, etc. It can also involve the use of third parties' properties, such as where they hold meetings, including hotels, coffee shops or restaurants. It can also involve using employees' properties; for example, for home working.

It can include the real estate used by its suppliers. If a service organisation outsources call centre services for its customers to a third party, then it will be charged for the costs of that real estate and also benefit/disbenefit from all the factors described above concerning the productivity of their outsourcer's employees.

It can also include "virtual" real estate, such as online meeting rooms, chat rooms, and the use of video conferences and teleconferences to create virtual meetings. This leads me neatly to my next point.

Along with people, real estate is one of the historic core elements of the Service Delivery Mix that is being replaced by ICT and the internet, in particular. Examples include online retailing, online travel agents, online banking, online insurance firms, online public services and public administration, such as completing tax submissions.

Real estate is generally one of the highest costs in the Service Delivery Mix, if you consider it just in terms of its total cost, and how that total can be reduced can be a mistake, as I have hopefully illustrated.

It has a knock-on effect on the rest of the Service Delivery Mix, and the costs and performance of such. We have also identified in Chapter 7, how it influences the Service Benefit and the Service Experience.

HOW DO ICT AND INTERNET COSTS IMPACT THE COST TO SERVE A CUSTOMER?

Like tools and equipment and people, these costs are driven by a combination of the market for "off the shelf" systems or research & development costs for self-developed systems, operational and support costs, relative capability and capacity of the systems, and how much the system is utilised by an individual customer.

In practice, such costs tend to be allocated to a customer through a management accounting exercise rather than be specifically consumed by the customer except if specific elements of hardware are dedicated to a customer, or additional licences etc. are required for a specific customer. It is important to ensure that such allocation is, as far as possible, reflective of "actual consumption", and also that it is costed on a similar unit basis to other elements of the Service Delivery Mix, or else it is difficult to identify the possible benefits of substituting one element of the Mix for another.

Let's say that the people cost element of a bank teller serving a customer is £1 a minute (based on the total employment cost of the teller for a year, divided by the number of minutes he works in a year) and that customer A interacts on average with a bank teller for 5 minutes each visit to the bank. The cost to serve that customer, per visit, is £5.

If the cost of the customer doing online banking is £0.5 per minute, based on the bank's total internet system costs divided by the number of transaction minutes, the system can support in a year, then the cost to serve that customer in that way for 5 minutes would be £2.50.

However, when the customer banks online he is much quicker as there is no conversation, and it only takes 3 minutes, so the cost to serve per visit is £1.50.

However, the customer only visits a branch bank once a month, so the annual cost to serve is £60. But if he becomes an online bank customer, due to the ease of use of the system and his ability to use it on his mobile device, he goes online once a week, so the annual cost to serve is £75.

That is unless an increased usage by all customers lead the bank to invest more in IT capacity and it gains more economies of scale, so the cost per minute per customer falls...

Note: these are not supposed to be real costs, just illustrative calculations! For the sake of simplicity, I have also ignored the costs of real estate etc. that would vary between the models.

I have also not considered how ICT systems can be used as a tool by the bank teller to facilitate service delivery, as the principle is the same as the floor cleaning machine.

Without such systems, it might take 15 minutes to serve each customer.

With ICT systems, as for other tools and equipment, it is important to consider how these can facilitate the productivity of other elements of the Service Delivery Mix, particularly people.

HOW DOES THE COST OF THE BRAND IMPACT SERVICE DELIVERY COSTS?

David A. Aaker, in his well-known book Building Strong Brands, (Pocket Books, 2010) identifies five major brand asset categories, namely:

▶   Brand name awareness

▶   Brand loyalty

▶   Perceived quality

▶   Brand associations

▶   Other proprietary brand assets.

The first three categories are relatively self-explanatory. The fourth quality is literally the images and feelings etc, that customers associate with the brand. The fifth category covers assets, such as the distribution channel relationships and Intellectual Property associated with the Brand.

All of these must be linked to the name/symbol/logo etc of the organisation to be a brand asset.

The cost of the brand is thus all the costs associated with the creation of these assets. For service organisations, these will be the costs of service delivery that impact service quality and, hence, customer satisfaction and/or loyalty, and also distribution channels etc.

It also includes the cost of creating brand awareness and brand associations, and perceptions of service quality, such as marketing communication costs, including marketing and other communication material costs, and the costs of other communication media, such as ICT, the internet, Social Media and "traditional" print and TV media etc.

HOW DO CUSTOMERS IMPACT THE COST TO SERVE A CUSTOMER?

Customers can have a major impact on service efficiency objectives. The level of this impact will reflect the degree of "inseparability" of the service from third parties.

That is the level of the customer's (and other people's) interaction with those producing the service.

I undertook a study in a law firm, across a range of services, that demonstrated a huge variation in the time taken to undertake the work from assignment to assignment for the same service. The main causes of these variations, across all the services examined, included:

▶ The experience of the client

▶ The quality and timeliness of information provided by the client

▶ The number of people involved in the client organisation

▶ The number of other third parties involved, e.g. other advisors for the client, witnesses, providers of finance and their advisors etc

▶ The experience and expertise of these third parties

▶ The availability of these third parties

▶ The motivation of these third parties

▶ The quality and timeliness of information provided by these third parties

▶ The efficiency and effectiveness of the third parties processes

Without too much trouble, we can all identify similar examples. Think of your personal experiences of queuing in a Post Office, supermarket or on the phone. The time taken to serve the customers in front can be very dependent on how that customer behaves.

You go into a bank and join the queue to see the teller. The customer at the front is trying to pay some money in and make a large cash withdrawal but can't find his proof of identity, has brought the wrong paying-in book and enters his PIN number incorrectly into the card reader. He argues with the bank teller, whilst she tries to identify his account and verify he is who he says he is. When she eventually identifies his other account, he finds his proof of identity, which was in an inside pocket of his jacket, and she pays him his cash in £20 notes.

He then changes his mind and wants some in £50 notes, some in £10 notes, and also some coins for the parking meter, so she has to go to another till to find them. Well, firstly, sorry – that was probably me! Secondly, consider how I have impacted on the efficiency of the bank teller, particularly compared to the well-organised lady (my mother) behind me, who had filled in the paying in slip, knew her PIN number off by heart and decided what notes she wanted.

A number of service organisations try to manage this interaction by introducing a greater level of "self- service" and, thus, limit the contact between their employees and customers.

This can range from customers selecting their own goods in supermarkets, rather than having everything behind the counter as used to be the case in small retail outlets, through to using technology for services, such as self checking-in at airports and self- service checkouts at supermarkets.

A lot of this "self-service" is now driven by technology.

The queue in the bank has been automated and the service made available 24/7 through the introduction of the ATM.

The lower the level of customer/employee contact and/or the lower the frequency or the number of external people involved with the service, then the more service efficiency can be driven by process – using technology, rather than by other means.

HOW DOES THE SERVICE DELIVERY MODEL INFLUENCE SERVICE DELIVERY MIX COSTS?

I have suggested above how the different elements of the Service Delivery Mix, namely People, Process, Real Estate, Tools & Equipment, ITC & Internet and Brand, drive the costs to serve a customer.

I have also illustrated how the involvement of customers in the Service Delivery Model can also influence costs. The Service Delivery Model also influences the requirements for different resources in the Mix, as set out in the table below.

Service Delivery	Model factor	People	Real Estate	Tools & Equipment	ITC & Internet	Brand	Process
Degree of customer / employee interaction	High	Type of people- cost depends on labour market	Higher cost	Higher cost	Medium cost	Medium cost	Depends on level of judgement and customisation
	Low		Lower cost	Lower cost	Higher cost	Higher cost	
Level of labour intensity	High	High % of costs	Higher cost	Lower cost	Medium cost	Depends on level of customer / employee interaction	Medium
	Low	Low % of costs	Lower cost	Higher cost	Higher cost		High
Where service is delivered	Close to customer	Higher cost locations	Higher cost	Depends on cost of transporting equipment	Medium cost	Medium cost	Medium
	Remotely	Lowest cost locations possible	Lowest cost locations possible		Higher cost	Higher cost	High
Levels of customisation	High	Higher cost people	Higher cost	Depends on whether high cost equipment used to standardise or for bespoke	Higher cost	Depends on cost of brand building in that market	Low
	Low	Lower cost people	Lower cost		Medium cost		High
Levels of judgement exercised by employee	High	Higher cost people	Higher cost	N/A	Medium cost	Depends on cost of brand building in that market	Low
	Low	Lower cost people	Lower cost		Higher cost		High
Nature of relationship with customer	Frequent	Type of people- cost depends on labour market	Higher cost		Medium cost	Medium cost	
	Infrequent		Lower cost			Higher cost	

WHAT IS THE EFFICIENCY TRAP?

Hopefully, it is apparent from the commentary set out above that service organisations can face an "Efficiency Trap".

Through seeking to drive down unit costs, usually in response to high levels of competitive price pressure in their markets, they change their Service Delivery Mix and/or Service Delivery Models. Typically this involves:

▶   The replacement of high cost people with lower cost people and/or

▶   Introducing standardised processes and rigid workflow systems.

The first point may also involve relocation to lower cost geographic areas and sometimes "offshoring".

However, the first strategy potentially ignores the experience curve factor and may not lead to lower unit costs, particularly if greater levels of supervision are then required, thus building costs back in. It may also reduce the level of Service Benefit produced.

The second, and often associated, strategy may lead to reduced motivation and productivity from employees, and potentially higher employee churn. Hence, this means higher unit costs. It can also potentially lead to changes in employee behaviours, a key element of the Service Experience.

If such changes are associated with a Service Delivery Model with a high level of customer interface, it is likely to impact:

▶   **Responsiveness** – lower levels of experience may increase the time taken to do work, and the reduced flexibility that results from rigid processes can reduce responsiveness (although this can equally increase responsiveness).

▶   **Assurance** – the people who provide the service are less experienced.

▶   **Empathy** – the people who provide the service may have a lower understanding of the customer's needs due to being less experienced and so have lower operational flexibility.

▶   **Reliability** – standardised processes, etc, can increase reliability but may, at the same time, reduce the amount of bespoke services to meet the individual customer's needs.

They are also typically associated with reducing the level of customer interface and increasing the standardisation of the service, so a different SerVAL Proposition emerges as a result.

Think how high street retail banks have sought to become more efficient by introducing call centres to replace customer service personnel at branches. This may be more efficient, but it has also created a totally new Service Experience for their customers – a different SerVAL Proposition.

Customers may or may not prefer this and be prepared to pay the same, more, or less for this experience.

A case can, therefore, be made for the view that true service efficiency produces the same Service Benefit and Service Experience by using fewer resources, i.e. eliminating waste in producing the same SerVAL Proposition.

This suggests **"lean thinking"** that involves reducing waste from existing systems and processes, rather than radical resourcing changes and process re-engineering, may be the route to efficiency in service organisations. This is least likely to change the SerVAL Proposition and should improve, rather than fundamentally change, the Employee Experience.

Changing the Service Delivery Mix, Service Delivery System and service creation process to produce the same Service Benefit at a lower cost, with a different Service Experience, and possibly a different price, is about creating an alternative SerVAL Proposition.

Seeking efficiency in service organisations can thus be a strategic decision, and not just an operational decision.

WHICH COSTS THE MOST TO PRODUCE, THE SERVICE BENEFIT OR THE SERVICE EXPERIENCE?

When considering the cost of serving a customer, the SerVAL Proposition suggests that the analysis should also consider which elements of the Proposition are the most costly to produce – the Service Benefit or the Service Experience?

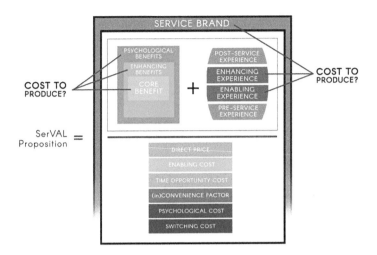

In the hairdressing example, below, the cost of cutting the hair (the time of the hairdresser, the cost of scissors and a basic chair, a mirror etc) proves to be relatively low compared to the cost of the Experience.

Let's say that the cost of employing an adequately skilled hairdresser, with basic hairdressing equipment, in a functional, accessible salon is £50 per hour. And the cost of employing a "name" hairdresser in a fashionably located salon, with a luxurious fit out with the latest magazines and top quality coffee and biscuits provided, is £100 per hour. The cost of the enhanced Service Experience is £50 per hour. 40% of this may be is generated by higher property costs, 40% by higher salary costs for the "name" hairdresser, and the balance by the coffee etc.

However, as identified earlier in this chapter, elements of the Service Deliver Mix can also influence the price paid, so the analysis also needs to consider the margin generated.

This means considering how much of the price in the SerVAL Proposition reflects the Service Benefit and how much the Service Experience.

In the example above, let's say the price for a "standard" haircut is £10 and that a "standard" hairdresser in a "standard" salon can perform 6 haircuts in an hour. The price is, thus, £60 per hour, generating a margin of £10 per hour. The price for a haircut in the "enhanced" salon is £30, and four can be achieved in an hour, thus generating an hourly rate of £120, and a margin of £20 per hour. The enhanced experience is thus generating £10 per hour higher margin, which represents a 25% return on the additional cost incurred through providing the enhanced experience. (£10/hour extra margin on £50 per hour extra cost).

Equally, such an analysis may indicate a high level of waste or value destruction in the SerVAL Proposition, and an opportunity to increase margin without reducing the value created for a customer in the SerVAL Proposition.

Let's assume that the price the hairdressing salon can obtain for an "enhanced" experience is £25, not £30. The additional costs of the experience then add no value to the service organisation, because the added value to the customer can only persuade them to pay a price that covers these extra costs.

The service organisation is wasting its money in offering this enhanced experience, as it is getting no return on it.

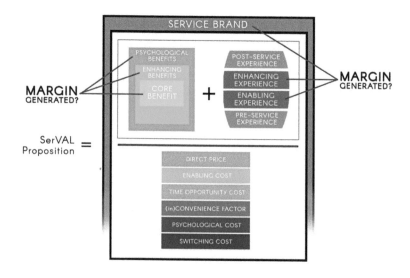

WHAT IS THE IMPACT OF FIXED AND VARIABLE COSTS/COSTS OF SALE & OVERHEAD BASED ANALYSIS ON COST MANAGEMENT IN SERVICE ORGANISATIONS?

Typically, the elements of the Service Delivery Mix would be considered as follows:

Element	Variable cost/semi-variable cost/Fixed cost	Comment
People	Variable	Most employees have short notice periods
Process	Not applicable	Processes not recognised as costs in budgets/P&L.
Tools & Equipment	Variable/ semi-variable	Depends on whether owned or leased, and terms of lease value.
Real Estate	Fixed/ semi-variable	Tend to be mostly on long-term leases. Can be semi-variable where leases are coming to an end or where the market is buoyant, so easy to dispose of.
ICT	Variable/ semi-variable	Depends on whether are owned or leased, terms of lease and value.
Brand	Variable/ semi-variable	Marketing expenditure on maintaining brand profile etc can be halted quickly, but some may involve longer-term sponsorship contracts etc.

The implications of the above are that when service businesses look to manage down costs, particularly if they need to do it quickly, their focus is likely to be on people and brand. These are the most variable costs, and then tools and equipment and ICT, which may, of course, be the elements that actually make them more efficient and effective.

Typically, this would be either through employing fewer people (which is only appropriate if there is excess capacity) or to replace expensive staff with lower cost employees. We discussed above the potential implications of that in terms of cost to serve customers. Another strategy is to replace people with ICT, but that can start to significantly change the SerVAL Proposition.

It may also lead to a reduction in marketing expenditure. This may reduce the effectiveness of the Brand, which may again also have an implication for the SerVAL Proposition.

It can be seen that the major elements of the Service Delivery Mix are typically considered as overheads.

Element	Cost of Sale/Overhead/Mixture of Both
People	Both
Process	Not applicable
Tools & Equipment	Either and mixture
Real Estate	Overhead
ICT	Overhead
Brand	Overhead

However, such an analytical approach for the costs of the Service Delivery Mix does not reflect their contribution to the organisation's SerVAL Proposition, and is not particularly helpful when looking at margin management in service organisations

WHAT CAN BE THE IMPACT OF COST SAVINGS ON THE SERVAL PROPOSITION?

A critical message from the commentary above is that it is vitally important not to forget the relationship of the cost drivers, the ingredients in the Service Delivery Mix and the Service Delivery Model, to the SerVAL Proposition.

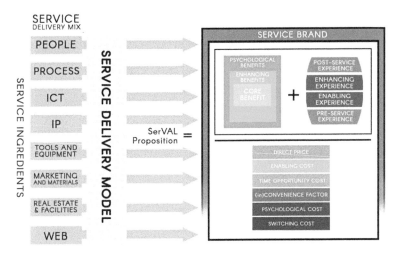

Developing the simple example at the beginning of this chapter – which involved people only in the Service Delivery Mix – moving from a high customer contact model to a low customer contact model, with less experienced people to reduce the cost to serve, will change the Service Experience due to a different level of customer contact and the customer dealing with a different type of person in the service organisation.

If dealing with experienced people and/or a high level of interpersonal contact is a key element of the Service Experience to the customer, then this may result in a fundamental change in the SerVAL Proposition.

It may lead to the customer only being willing to pay a lower price for the Service Benefit and Service Experience. The cost reduction may not lead to a margin increase, but a margin reduction.

SerVAL Proposition	Price	Cost to produce	Margin	Units bought per customer	Margin per customer
Alpha	12	9	3	2	6
Beta	8	4	4	3	12
Delta	6	4	2	4	8
Gamma	5	4	1	5	5

A further consideration is whether such changes, leading to the deliberate, or inadvertent, creation of a new SerVAL Proposition, may lead to a change in consumption patterns. For example, if a lower value/lower price SerVAL Proposition is created, with lower unit margins, will it encourage customers to buy more of it; thus increasing the overall margin per customer?

In view of the inherent link between the SerVAL Proposition and the cost to deliver the service, it can, therefore, be very misleading to consider the cost to serve customers in isolation from the price a customer is willing to pay. Service organisations must, therefore, understand whether cost saving initiatives will lead to increased margins, or to a material change in the SerVAL Proposition and a consequent potential downward change in Direct Price, which may actually reduce margins!

Therefore, an analysis of the cost of any and all resources in the Service Delivery Mix, and the costs of the Service Delivery Model, should be considered in terms of margin generation, rather than pure cost.

WHAT CAN BE THE IMPACT OF COST SAVINGS ON CUSTOMER RETENTION?

A further consideration that relates to changing the Service Delivery Mix and/or Service Delivery Model to reduce costs, even accepting a potential reduction in margins, is to consider the potential impact on customer retention. Will the deliberately new, or inadvertently new, SerVAL Proposition engender a similar, enhanced or reduced level of customer loyalty? Even if the margins are protected, or indeed enhanced, the customers' value to the organisation will reduce if they become less loyal.

SerVAL Proposition	Alpha	Beta	Gamma
Price/unit	£8	£5	£4
Cost/unit	£4	£3	£2
Margin/unit of service	£4	£2	£2
No of units bought per annum	2	3	4
No. of future years' loyalty	1	2	1
Total Customer Lifetime Value	£8	£12	£8

This could be because the first model is a high customer contact model that involves high prices, which due to market pressures are unsustainable. The service organisation amends its model to Beta model to retain a reasonable degree of customer contact, but changes the level of Benefits received, modifies the Experience and invests in Brand loyalty. This can attract a price of £5 and a degree of customer loyalty, plus some increase in the number of units bought, whilst still saving some of the customer's budget. It could have made a major change of its model, halving its costs and its prices, but the reduced investment in Brand and customer interaction leads to less loyalty, as its SerVAL Proposition is seen more as a commodity.

SUMMARY

The costs for a service organisation to serve a customer are driven by the raw costs of, and productivity of, the individual elements of the Service Delivery Mix. These are People, Process, Tools & Equipment, Real Estate, ICT and Internet, which in combination shape the basic unit costs of serving a customer.

The different elements of the Service Delivery Mix can, **in combination**, improve the productivity of each other; for example, ICT and tools improving the productivity of labour. These elements can also act as substitutes for each other, replacing a less productive element with a more productive element; for example, some equipment for labour to drive the cost of production lower.

Equally, the different ingredients of the Service Delivery Mix can reduce their combined productivity if they are in the wrong combination.

In particular, a balance needs to be sought between these ingredients because of the influence of the Service-Profit Chain and the potential negative impact of the rigid application of processes and ICT systems and working environments on human motivation and performance. This is the potential **Efficiency Trap.** Are the processes, ICT systems, tools and equipment there to serve the human element of the Service Delivery Mix, or vice versa?

This is likely to depend on which ingredients in the Service Delivery Mix, and which aspects of the Service Delivery Model, generate most value to customers.

It is also important to understand, as far as possible, how the service organisation' costs are driven by the creation of both the Service Benefit and the Service Experience for the customer, i.e. are most costs associated with generating the Benefit or the Experience?

It is then important to understand how highly the customer values the Benefit v. the Experience, and the trade-off they make, as discussed in Chapter 12. And also how much of the price is driven by each. In short, the service organisation needs to consider, as best it can, how much margin it does, or could, make from providing the Benefit and the Experience.

It is important to note that not only are the ingredients of the Service Delivery Mix and the Service Delivery Model, the principal cost drivers for the organisation, but they are also all key factors in shaping the SerVAL Proposition to the customer. Therefore, analysis of the two should not be separated.

When changing its Service Delivery Mix and/or Service Delivery Model in order to reduce costs, or to invest in providing greater Benefits or a different Experience, a service organisation needs to consider the impact of this on the margins it can earn, and the volumes of the service it can sell. The intimate association between the Service Delivery Mix & Service Delivery Model and the SerVAL Proposition means that changes designed to reduce costs can alter the SerVAL Proposition in a way that can lead to a change in the price that customers will pay for the Service Benefit and Service Experience, and hence not necessarily lead to margin improvement, and potentially further margin destruction.

It is crucial that any changes to the Service Delivery Mix and/or Service Delivery Model must be considered holistically in terms of the value created to the customer and the service organisation from the SerVAL Proposition. Failure to do so is likely to lead to value destruction.

Taking a holistic view of the SerVAL Proposition from both the customer and service provider's perspective is likely to protect them and grow value for both.

CHAPTER FOURTEEN:
WHAT FACTORS DRIVE THE COSTS TO SERVE A
CUSTOMER? KEY QUESTIONS TO CONSIDER

▸ Do you understand the true raw costs of serving generic and specific customers?

▸ Do you understand which elements of the Service Delivery Mix contribute most to the raw costs to serve a customer?

▸ How does your chosen Service Delivery Model impact the cost to serve the customer?

▸ How much do individual customers influence the cost to serve customers?

▸ Do you understand the experience curve of your employees and its impact on your cost to serve customers?

▸ Do you know how well motivated your employees are and the impact of this on your cost to serve customers?

▸ Do your employees have the most appropriate tools & equipment and ICT to be efficient?

▸ How does your real estate impact efficiency?

▸ How significant is your cost of employee churn to your cost to serve customers?

▸ Can you create a more efficient Service Delivery Mix without impacting the SerVAL Proposition?

▸ Can you create a more efficient Service Delivery Model without impacting the SerVAL Proposition?

▸ How are your costs to serve a customer allocated between producing the Service Benefit and the Service Experience?

▸ Are you inadvertently falling into the efficiency trap and changing your SerVAL Proposition to a lower margin one and/or one with lower customer loyalty?

▸ Do you take into account the impact on the SerVAL Proposition and Customer Lifetime Value when managing your costs?

WHAT FACTORS DRIVE CUSTOMER LOYALTY?

INTRODUCTION

In Chapter 13, we discussed the concept of Customer Lifetime Value, how this is a function of Customer profitability and the length of relationship with a customer. Then, in Chapter 14, we examined the factors driving the cost to produce a service. In this chapter, I am going to examine the factors that influence the length of relationships with customers, and how this might be predicted. This is commonly termed "customer loyalty".

KEY QUESTIONS

In order to provide some insight into customer loyalty, I will consider the following key questions:

▸ Does customer satisfaction lead to customer loyalty?

▸ Is choice important?

▸ Can loyalty be "agreed"?

▸ Can loyalty be "bought"?

▸ Are customers rational?

▸ Are brands important?

▸ Are interpersonal relationships important?

▸ What about habits?

▸ Are switching costs important?

▸ Are some forms of loyalty better than others?

▸ Are monogamous relationships with customers normal?

▸ How do you tell if customers are becoming more or less loyal?

▸ Are customers loyal because they are receiving too much value?

DOES CUSTOMER SATISFACTION LEAD TO CUSTOMER LOYALTY?

Never forget that we are all customers of many types of service organisations, as both private individuals and in our jobs. So stop and think why you remain loyal to some of your service suppliers.

I remain loyal to the refuse collector at my home because I have no choice. They are a monopoly provider to me. They have been procured and are managed and paid for by my local council, using money collected from me via national and local taxes. My local council is loyal to them, at least for a period, because they have a contract to provide the services to the council's residents for several years.

I remain loyal to the local shop in my village because it is convenient to buy bread and milk if I run out, and it sells my newspaper, and because I like the people who run it. I have built a relationship with them over a number of years, but I do go to other shops.

I have remained loyal to my bank for the past 30 years because I perceive it as being too much hassle to change, and I perceive the service I would get from most other banks would be pretty similar. I don't think I get a particularly good service, but it isn't terrible, and I do have accounts with a couple of other banks.

As you can see, I haven't mentioned customer satisfaction once! So are customers loyal because they are satisfied? Not necessarily, in my experience, both as a customer and provider of a service.

A number of research studies indicate that customer satisfaction does not have a simple "cause and effect" relationship with customer loyalty. Whilst this may seem surprising to some, going back to first principles, it shouldn't.

Firstly, a customer's demand for a service can vary as their Compelling Immediate Needs and Budget will change over time, i.e. people only buy a service when they need it and can also afford it, not just because they were satisfied in the past.

Secondly, Better Alternative Delivery Solutions may emerge that are more attractive to the customer, i.e. the competitive landscape may change. Therefore, in a situation of dynamic demand and supply, customer satisfaction by itself cannot be expected to lead to customer loyalty.

My family has two cars, made by two different manufacturers. My wife and I require them for different purposes. We use one to transport us to our differently located workplaces and a family car to transport the kids and dogs, who are often wet and muddy in the winter. Now both manufacturers make pretty similar cars that are suitable for both purposes, and we don't just choose two cars from the same manufacturer. I change the "non-family" car frequently, buying similar ones from various manufacturers, not because I am dissatisfied, and it is not usually economically advantageous to change either. This isn't rational consumer behaviour, but it isn't atypical consumer behaviour either.

However, research (Reicheld, 1993, and others) suggests that very satisfied customers tend to be much more loyal than satisfied customers, with a much greater propensity to buy additional goods and services, and a much higher propensity to act as a positive advocate or referrer of an organisation's services to third parties, i.e. to provide positive "word of mouth" ("PWOM").

It is absolutely fundamental to success to understand this point, because it means that service organisations need to aim for more than "just" customer satisfaction, and build their organisations accordingly; they need to aim for very satisfied customers, rather than just satisfied customers. They also need to understand the other factors influencing customer loyalty!

IS CHOICE IMPORTANT?

If an organisation has a monopoly position, then by definition its customers have no choice but to use it. Their customers are **not loyal,** they are **captives.**

Plenty has been written about the disbenefits to the customers of monopolies, how they lead to higher prices, lower levels of service, inefficiencies, excessive profits, etc, and that is why most countries have legislation relating to competition and anti-competitive behaviour.

On the other hand, a monopoly position provides considerable benefits to the service provider, as their customers have no choice but to use them. However, the source of this monopoly position is critical! Fundamentally, competitive strategy is about trying to create a monopoly position. Organisations are trying to eliminate competition by being clearly different from its competitors, in terms of Service Benefit, Service Experience and Total Cost to Customer, so that it is the only "obvious" choice for customers in that market or market segment. This enables the organisation to survive, thrive and earn higher profits. The sustainability of this competitive advantage will decide whether it has a temporary monopoly (to win a contract, say) or a longer lasting one. This might be considered an **"earned monopoly"**, i.e. the service organisation has earned it through offering a superior SerVAL Proposition. This involves **loyal customers.**

However, many service organisations benefit from an **"unearned monopoly"** position, particularly in public services and in-house support teams within organisations. For example, the finance team in most organisations has a monopoly position because they have no competition, and the business units are not allowed to use an alternative source of financial support. This involves **captive customers.**

CAN LOYALTY BE "AGREED"?

So customers can be captive because they have no choice. Can they also agree to become captives?

We explored the different types of arrangement between the service provider and customer in Chapter 9, when considering the different Service Delivery Models, and this highlighted that it is possible for an organisation's customers to "agree" and to be "loyal". In legal terms, this means agreeing a contract of some form. The customer agrees to buy a service (or goods) from an organisation for a period of time for a specified amount of money. In short, this is "contractual loyalty".

This agreement may or may not confer a monopoly position on the service organisation, i.e. the customer may agree that they won't buy the service from anyone else during the agreed period.

These contractually based loyalty arrangements don't just occur in the business-to-business service market, but also in the business –to-consumer market, albeit they are less common. Examples of "b2c" contracts are memberships of clubs, gyms, season tickets for public transport, season tickets for sporting events, etc. Such arrangements provide the service provider with a degree of certainty over customer retention and customer expenditure levels, and the service organisation knows it will receive a certain level of revenue for a certain period of time from that customer. This can make it much easier to plan resource requirements.

It should be recognised, however, that the contract holds the customer "captive", not "loyal".

I have spent significant amounts of time during my career as a customer, or advising customers how to extricate themselves from contracts with service providers who are not performing as required, or re-procuring with a different supplier at the end of the contract for the same reason.

There are some potential significant negatives for service organisations that can occur as a result of "contractual loyalty", and I explore these below under the heading, "Are some forms of loyalty better than others?"

CAN LOYALTY BE "BOUGHT"?

Some service organisations seek to "buy" loyalty. By this, I don't mean they offer a low price in their SerVAL Proposition, but offer additional rewards to customers who remain loyal.

This may take the form of discounts on future purchases, thus reducing the price in the future SerVAL Proposition, or through offering extra services or goods in future, thus increasing the Service Benefit or Service Experience element of a future SerVAL Proposition.

This approach tends to be much more prevalent in the b2c service market, with retailers, restaurants, credit card providers and airlines examples where such approaches are adopted.

It does occur in the b2b service market too, however. It is not unknown for law firms, for example, to provide price discounts in return for certain volumes of work being requested over a period of time.

In short, customer loyalty can be incentivised through extending the SerVAL Proposition over time, rather than seeing it as a discrete event. Loyalty is thus a reflection of greater, longer lasting value.

However, if the SerVAL Proposition is weaker than those of a competitor or alternative organisation then this will not lead to loyalty; although it may lead to captivity if it costs too much to switch, as discussed further below.

ARE CUSTOMERS RATIONAL?

The points above might also be considered the "rational economic and legal" view of customer loyalty. Of course, I am a rational economic person (except when it comes to cars), but I don't know about you...

When we consider our own decisions, the decisions of other people, observe how markets behave and read lots of research in the social sciences (particularly behavioural economics), we will see that customers aren't always rational (my research suggests only Mrs Manning is totally rational. She told me so herself).

The purpose of separating factors into "rational economic" and "irrational behavioural" factors, is not to spark a debate about what is/isn't rational, but to simplify our thinking in order to make a point and enable better questions to be asked!

So what "irrational" factors are at play? Some of the key "irrational" drivers of consumer behaviour include brands, personal relationships and habits.

ARE BRANDS IMPORTANT?

We care what other people think. The majority of us like to buy things, services and brands that people we perceive our peers would also buy. Another group will purchase "anti-establishment" things because they want to make a point that they are different from the majority. But they, in turn, are usually part of a minority group, rather than being a sole individual. Others will have specialised needs and belong to a smaller group and want to be seen as part of that group. Sometimes the minority group grows and becomes the majority group.

This suggests that people find some benefit in brands, whether they are mainstream or niche brands, including "anti-brands".

People are clearly seeking some psychological benefit when buying things. This might be considered in terms of Maslow's famous Hierarchy of Needs. And, yes, I realise this has gone in and out of fashion and been criticised by many, but it provides food for thought in terms of what "irrational benefit" may be tied up in the purchasing of a service. Buying a known brand, arguably meets the human need for "socialisation" and to feel a part of something.

Brands can also provide other psychological benefits, and this can be particularly important for services due to their intangible nature. At the most basic level, the fact that someone else has bought the service means there may be something worthwhile being delivered.

If that person is someone the customer knows, and/or respects or admires, then that makes the purchase decision easier. We think, if "So and so" bought this service, and he is no fool, so it must be quite good."

A brand may form part of a risk aversion need (remember, "Never get fired for buying IBM."). This can be very powerful in conservative markets, such as the purchase of services by the public sector, or high-risk areas/"bet the farm", decisions such as larger M&A projects for corporates.

On the other hand, a damaged brand, particularly in service organisations, can lead to significant losses of customer loyalty, sometimes very quickly.

The collapse of the accounting and advisory firm, Arthur Andersen, following the Enron scandal in 2002, is a startling example of how quickly and significantly brand damage can lead to the destruction of a service business – even one of the most respected, well-known and powerful in the world.

Customers, therefore, often form a loyal "relationship" with a brand that isn't necessarily economically rational, but is psychologically important. But what about "real" relationships?

DO EMPLOYEES INFLUENCE CUSTOMER RELATIONSHIPS?

Yes, they do, and their influence can be extremely important.

Firstly, employees will influence customer relationships, whether or not they deliver the expected Service Benefit and Service Experience. This will have an impact on customer satisfaction, which in turn influences customer loyalty.

Secondly, they will influence customer relationships by building relationships with customers, or not. Their ability to build relationships will be dependent on a number of factors, including the level and frequency of customer interaction.

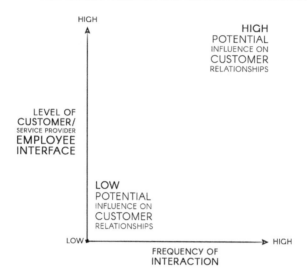

The ability to transform a high potential influence on customer relationships into a strong, positive, customer relationship will depend on the interpersonal skills of the employee and personal chemistry with the customer. This can be due to a range of factors, including personal or business interests, socioeconomic and/or cultural background, politics, age and sex.

ARE PERSONAL RELATIONSHIPS IMPORTANT?

Think, how do you select a service provider because there is an existing relationship with them? I suspect there are numerous examples that come to mind.

We have already considered how important empathy can be in the Service Experience, and a customer is more likely to get a higher level of empathy than from someone they know, just because they know more about them!

Customers may also be friends with the service provider. They like them and thus want to use them. They know their wife and children, brothers and sisters, and their parents, which can be very important in smaller communities. These relationships may also make it "difficult" not to use the service provider! There may also be some reciprocity. The customer buys something from the service provider because they buy something from the customer, creating a virtuous circle.

It is not just direct personal relationships that are important either. The customer may not have a relationship with the service provider, but their boss or business associate does. Or their partner, a relative, advisor, suppliers or other significant individual in their human network does. For example, they may have been recommended by someone the customer respects and/or whose approval they are seeking. And, of course, it can be really embarrassing and difficult for the customer to say "no" to someone that they know, who they are likely to come across a lot in the future. How poor does the service have to be, or how high the price needs to be before they choose not to use the service provider? Social pressure, eh!

Some of the leading thinkers on customer relationships describe various levels of relationship. Andrew Sobel, for instance, in his book, All for One, (Wiley, 2009) identifies 6 levels of relationship with a customer or potential customer. His framework is in the context of professional services, but I think it has wider applicability.

Level 1 : **Contact**

Level 2 : **Acquaintance**

Level 3 : **Expert/occasional supplier**

Level 4 : **Steady supplier**

Level 5 : **Trusted advisor**

Level 6 : **Trusted partner**

A key concept underpinning this is that the stronger the relationship, then the more loyalty the customer will show. To be a trusted advisor, the service provider really needs to understand the customer and have a high level of empathy.

What makes a personal relationship strong?

A number of factors make a personal relationship weak or strong in a service environment. We have discussed the level of empathy. It also involves the customer perceiving that their needs are being met over a period of time and over the delivery of a number of separate, individual SerVAL Propositions. For without the ongoing/repeat purchase of the service, the customer and the service provider are "just friends". A longer-term relationship, based on numerous transactions, means that the level of assurance the service organisation provides increases, the degree of reliability is seen as high and the customer trusts the service organisation's motives. This clearly takes time and effort.

In my experience, it also involves how frequently, recently and deeply the contact is. It is very difficult to build and sustain a strong relationship with someone you interact with infrequently and superficially for a short space of time.

It also reflects the nature of the way in which the customer and service provider interact. All things being equal, people tend to have stronger relationships with other people they meet face to face, compared to the people they interact with over the phone or solely on social media, or just exchange letters or emails with.

The service provider/customer relationship can involve a number of different relationships between a number of different members of the service provider's employees and the customer, and indeed with different customer stakeholders (as discussed in Chapter 10).

Service organisations can thus strengthen customer relationships through "customer entanglement" by having lots of relationships between their organisation and the customer.

In my experience, personal relationships can be a hugely important factor in customer loyalty, if not the most important factor. I would argue that they are more important in the provision of services than goods (although they are important there too) because service provision involves the interaction of service provider and service consumer.

Furthermore, the more bespoke the SerVAL Proposition, the stronger the potential relationship between the service provider and the customer is as it requires, by definition, a greater degree of intimacy and the sharing of information between the service provider and client.

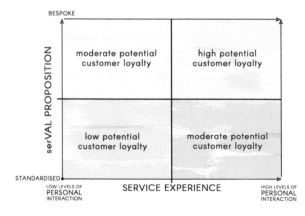

Are relationships important when the SerVAL relationship is not good?

In my experience, relationships also influence the customer's tolerance of "service failure" and whether the service provider is given the chance to put it right. We all tend to give people we have close relationships with multiple chances to get things right.

I recently went into a baker's shop whilst on holiday. The girl working behind the counter clearly hadn't been trained, and struggled to identify the products requested, the price of the products and how to operate the till. We were in a hurry and the delays were highly irritating. Whilst we had sympathy for her as an individual, we had none for the service organisation, and so would not choose to return there again quickly. (Although the products were very good, so there may be a trade-off between output and experience!)

A week or so later, I had a similar experience in our local shop at home. I know the people in there well and we usually have some banter. I was far more forgiving and could even joke about it with them. However, if it happened repeatedly, I would not appreciate the experience.

What about formal procurement processes?

But are relationships important in formal tenders and highly structured procurement processes? A lot of business-to-business service markets are heavily based on such an approach, and my experience is that they are still very important.

For example, it is not unusual in certain circumstances for the incumbent supplier to be asked to help prepare the service specification. How much easier is it to price a service and identify value adding bolt-on services, and for the customer to understand the service experience on offer, if the bidder is the incumbent? How much easier is it to make the service offering more tangible, if the service organisation is already providing the service? How will the procurer differentiate between two "close bids" – the devil they know or the devil they don't?

How objective and rational is even the most structured procurement process, as many of the factors other than price are intangible? How much of it comes down to trusting the individuals and/or their organisation to deliver the "value added" they promise? Who does the customer believe – the people they have known for years or people they only met a month before? How easy is it to reject, in a close bid, people they have worked with for years?

WHAT ABOUT HABIT?

Remember that when buying something intangible like a service, the devil they know is an easier decision for the customer than the devil they don't. This is because the previous SerVAL Proposition received makes the service a little more tangible than the one provided by a provider they have never used before. In short, service intangibility can work to the incumbent provider's advantage.

Furthermore, we are mostly creatures of habit (both good or bad!), and if we have used a service provider a number of times, we are more likely to keep doing so because it has become part of our routine.

Therefore, people may continue to use their "normal" service provider as a matter of habit, unless there is a good reason to change.

ARE SWITCHING COSTS IMPORTANT?

So, as we can see, customers are loyal for a combination of "rational" and "irrational" factors, but why else might customers remain loyal? Because the cost of switching – both actual and psychological – compared to the benefit of switching is too high. One strategic framework for "change management" I have seen is the following equation:

$C = A*B*D > X$

F. Robert Jacobs, Real Time Strategic Change pp 122-123 (in the Guru Guide)

Where C = probability of change being successful, A = dissatisfaction with status quo, B = clear statement of desired state after the change, D = Concrete first step towards the goal and X = cost of change.

Consider this in terms of customer loyalty, where:

C = probability of a customer switching to another provider

A = dissatisfaction with current service

B = robust understanding of benefits from alternative service provider

D = making proactive steps towards a replacement procurement

X = switching costs

It can be difficult to explain the benefits and service experience of an intangible service, so achieving "B" can be difficult to achieve for alternative suppliers. Switching costs – both actual and psychological – can be high, with the latter particularly the case where the degree of inseparability is high, the levels of empathy both high and important, and relationships are widespread and strong. This suggests that the level of dissatisfaction with the service in such cases must be pretty high for people to change. In the example below, very high levels of dissatisfaction are likely to be required for a customer to consider a change.

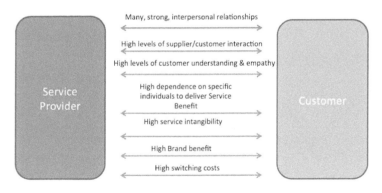

Where the equation for change is not clear-cut, e.g. in my bank example, then customer inertia occurs. The customer is not particularly satisfied, and may be dissatisfied with the current service, but doesn't believe that an alternative will be much better, particularly regarding both the effort that is required to start to change and the switching costs. But the customer remains loyal.

This means that a service providing high levels of Service Benefit, especially relative to competitors, is likely to create a stronger relationship between the supplier and customer than one providing lower levels of benefit.

This might be considered as follows:

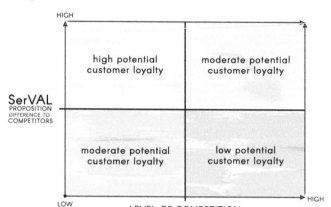

The Catch 22 of Switching Costs

The "Catch 22" in a service industry can be that whilst high switching costs in an industry may enable a service provider to hold on to its customers, it also makes it difficult to win new customers away from its competitors. The equation above also suggests that service providers may only need to be slightly better than their competitors to retain customers, but will need to be much better to win new customers. In a slow growth economy, where you have little competitive advantage, this can make it very slow and very expensive to grow customers organically!

All service organisations need to consider how they can create high switching costs for their services to protect their existing customers.

Clearly, the most powerful positive switching cost will be that the service organisation delivers far more value than its competitors. If this is combined with strong, in-depth personal relationships and a powerful positive brand, then the balance of the "switch or not" equation will be heavily weighted in favour of customer retention.

Service organisation can seek to create high actual switching costs, by having long contracts with punitive termination costs, through providing and retaining ownership of IT systems, or other equipment or assets, and/or through the provision, collation or the management of data and retaining ownership of that. They generally making it physically and commercially difficult to switch, as well as expensive. They are effectively holding their customer hostage. This is not necessarily a good achievement, as I will discuss below. Service organisations also need to consider how they overcome the switching costs that bind potential customers to existing service providers. Again, the best starting point is to offer significantly more value than their competitors.

One example I have come across of a service organisation that is seeking to overcome their switching costs is a document management and reprographics business that supplies printers and copiers to businesses. Where it is economically viable to do so, it buys its target customers out of their existing contracts with competitors.

ARE SOME FORMS OF LOYALTY BETTER THAN OTHERS?

We have discussed the concept of organisations providing positive customer retention by offering a significantly better SerVAL Proposition than their competitors. We have also identified the possibility of "tying customers in" with commercial arrangements, the potentially high switching costs and cases where there is no choice, which is often the case with in-house teams and public services. But what if the latter route is achieved without providing an acceptable SerVAL Proposition? In such cases, the service organisation has its customers held "hostage", as they are retained unwillingly. There is also the "middle ground" of customer inertia, which might be considered as "passive" loyalty. This creates a "Customer Retention Spectrum" as follows:

THE CUSTOMER RETENTION SPECTRUM

POSITIVE LOYALTY		CUSTOMER HELD "HOS-TAGE"
	"CUSTOMER INERTIA"	

Does the form of customer loyalty matter?

It might be argued that as long as a service provider retains its customer, then it doesn't matter. But think that through. They will become an unwilling, dissatisfied customer. Firstly, there can be significant financial consequences if someone is dissatisfied and doesn't want to remain a customer. They can demand a lot of attention, sucking in a lot of resources, and drive up the cost to serve them, as well as driving down the value. They can also delay and challenge payments, driving up costs again and tying up more working capital. They can be intolerant about minor performance breaches and seek damages or compensation, which can be particularly costly if the performance specifications are poorly drafted, or they involve a degree of subjectivity.

A whole advisory industry around making claims and counterclaims under Private Finance Initiative performance contracts has emerged in the UK. Where the relationship between the service provider and the customer is poor, this can lead to materially significant sums being at stake.

Construction contracts seem to generate payment/performance disputes anywhere in the world, whether they are for massive infrastructure or building projects, or the local contractor building a small wall.

One firm I know was looking to save costs and sought to end a contract for the provision of flowers and plants to one of their offices. Unfortunately, it proved to be an "unbreakable" (or "evergreen"!) contract, even though they had taken excellent legal advice.

However, the contract contained a clause that the plants must be well-maintained and kept in full leaf. The Facilities Manager thus decided to call out the service provider every time a leaf fell off the plant or it looked sick, which it did after the temperature was turned up. Eventually, the service provider decided the hassle of retaining the contract was more than it was worth and renegotiated. By then, of course, the relationship was terrible and an alternative supplier was chosen.

There are other potential consequences of customers being held "hostage" whilst dissatisfied with the SerVAL Proposition, such as negative word of mouth. If a customer is held "hostage", what do they typically do? They shout loudly to gain attention and tell as many people as they can about the poor service they are getting and how they can't get out of the contract. And the rise of social media means they can tell many more people, much faster, than ever before.

Equally, positive word of mouth is a benefit of providing an excellent service.

THE CUSTOMER WORD OF MOUTH SPECTRUM

**POSITIVE
WORD OF
MOUTH
"PWOM"**

"SILENCE"

**NEGATIVE
WORD OF
MOUTH
"NWOM"**

"Hostile" loyalty can also exist where there is no choice, i.e. the service provider is a monopoly.

Customer hostility can also have a significant negative impact on the morale of employees, who bear the brunt of this dissatisfaction in terms of (negative) personal interactions. They also have to use their time to deal with negative issues etc, rather than offering positive service to customers. In short, it can create a negative employee experience, as well as a negative customer experience. The importance of a positive employee experience to the success of a service organisation is covered in Chapter 6.

This suggests that customer retention might be considered in the following manner, in terms of the brand and word of mouth.

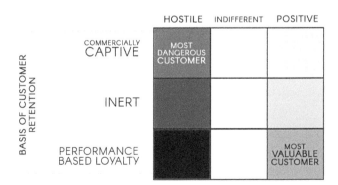

Whilst this is more prevalent in business-to-business service situations, because of the greater complexity of commercial arrangements, it also exists in business-to-consumer situations, such as with banks, insurance companies and car leasing.

I have been trapped in a car leasing contract where the vehicle was experiencing a lot of mechanical issues and the response of the dealer, the manufacturer and the manufacturer's financing arm was slow (unresponsive).

They provided little assurance they were knew what the problems were or that they could address them, and lacked any empathy with my situation (large financial outgoings, no car, disappointment with the product, which was inconsistent and unreliable in nature). Thus, they failed on most of the RATER scale, and I have told a lot of people about this.

Service organisations should, therefore, seek loyal, not captive customers. They need to be the service provider of choice for their customers and prospective customers.

ARE MONOGAMOUS RELATIONSHIPS WITH CUSTOMERS NORMAL?

Is it reasonable for a service organisation to expect to have a monogamous relationship with its customers? By this, I mean that customer won't be purchasing the service from a range of service providers over a given time period.

I have relationships with 3 banks, 2 credit card service providers and save with a number of different financial institutions. I use two or three different hairdressing outlets and visit a number of different restaurants, in a number of different price brackets.

I frequent several pretty similar retailers, including at least two supermarket chains, and use two or three petrol stations regularly. I engage a couple of different builders to work on my house and tend to use the garage where I bought my car to service it, but not always.

At work, we use several different recruitment consultancies and have relationships with several banks. We have one firm of auditors, but use different firms for other financial advice, including tax advice, and are contracted with different cleaning companies for different locations.

I could go on.

Monogamous and promiscuous relationships and SOW

My own experience in business-to-business and business-to-consumer markets indicates that many people don't have monogamous relationships with their service suppliers and that promiscuity is not unusual, and that is backed up by a range of research. Most people have relationships with several service providers for similar services. So a service organisation's loyal customers may also be loyal customers to one of its competitors.

This means that relationships with customers are often about obtaining, retaining and growing a share of their wallet, but not about having the whole of the relevant budget spent with the service provider's organisation. A low share of (relevant) wallet is often an indication of a lack of competitive advantage and/or weak customer relationships.

HOW DO YOU TELL IF A CUSTOMER IS BECOMING MORE OR LESS LOYAL?

A lot of studies have been undertaken in b2c industries, particularly catalogue retailing, to try and identify any clues as to whether customers are "alive" or "dead". This research indicates that the following elements can be good indicators of customer loyalty:

▶ The **Recency** of expenditure

This looks at the last time that a customer spent any money with the service organisation. The longer the gap, the less likely it is they have been retained as a customer. But how frequently they typically spend money with the organisation must be taken into account. If they make one purchase a year, then the fact they have not spent any money for 11 months may not be an indicator. But if they haven't spent any money for two years, then there may be an issue.

▶ The **Frequency** of expenditure

The more frequently a customer spends money with an organisation, the more loyal they are, as a customer doesn't spend money frequently with an organisation if there is an acceptable alternative.

▶ The **Monetary** value of the expenditure.

All things being equal, the greater the amount of money that a customer is spending, the more loyal they are likely to be.

However, this is relative to their whole budget and the actual cost of the item. In my experience, changes to monetary value demonstrate there are potential changes in a customer's loyalty and/or potential changes in their budget.

In simple terms, increasing levels of monetary value, maintained/increased frequencies of expenditure and the recency of the latest expenditure are good indicators of loyalty. These are tangible examples of the customers' purchasing behaviour, rather than relying on "what they say they are going to do".

Other research has claimed that the range and depth (number of items of the individual service) of services that a customer buys from a service organisation are another good indicator of customer loyalty. This is on the basis that a customer will not buy more of a service and more than one service from a service provider if they think it does not provide a good SerVAL Proposition.

Clearly, this is only applicable if the service organisation provides more than one service!

This research also indicates that the length of the relationship is a good indicator. Customers tend to have stronger relationships if this is the case and greater switching costs to service providers with whom they have had longer relationships.

But, of course, past satisfaction and past relationships don't necessarily indicate current or future satisfaction, It assumes that, for b2b service organisations, the length of the b2b relationship is an indication of long-term stable relationships with the individuals in an organisation. But personnel change roles within organisations and also move between organisations relatively frequently. So the "real" relationships may be very short.

Another element of actual spending behaviour is when they start to use competitors more, and the service provider's Share of Wallet declines, or if they start using the service provider more and the SOW increases.

Common sense indicates these are all good measures.

Other behavioural indicators outside actual spending include the behaviour of the customer themselves. If those people the service provider has a relationship with are not so keen to meet, return phone calls or emails, or tell the service provider what is going on in their organisation or their lives as much, then the chances are that the relationship is weakening and they are becoming less loyal. If the customer never tells the service provider these things, and the service provider finds out about key matters relating to the customer that are relevant to them from external sources, then they probably haven't got a very strong relationship.

Service organisations can use "relationship assessment tools" to categorise relationships in a manner that is similar to the Sobel list above.

Other measures of potentially changing customer loyalty include changes to:

▶ Customer satisfaction levels

▶ The number and nature of complaints

It is possible to estimate the degree of, and changing nature of, customer loyalty of customers. Proactively doing so enables service organisations to anticipate and respond to growing and declining customer loyalty.

IS THE SERVICE PROVIDER DELIVERING TOO MUCH VALUE?

Of course, one reason why customers may be loyal is that the service organisation is delivering far more value than its competitors, and far more value than it receives in return. The latter either means it is charging too low a price, or if the market wouldn't support a higher price, then it is spending too much in delivering a higher Service Benefit and/or a better Service Experience, and thus reducing its margin.

"Any fool can give good customer service" if (the right) resources are thrown at providing a service.

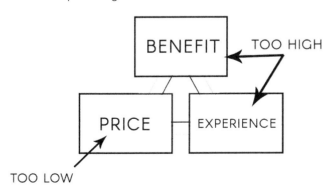

SUMMARY

Customer loyalty is far more complex than just being based on customer satisfaction, albeit customer satisfaction is a core aspect of customer loyalty. In particular, there are significant psychological elements involved with customer loyalty that are closely related to the number and strengths of the relationships between the customer, the supplier and the supplier's brand. This can make the level and nature of customer/service provider interaction in services particularly important, and service providers need to consider very carefully the benefits of reducing such interface to achieve other objectives, such as efficiency.

Positive **"customer loyalty equation"** can be considered as being a function of a range of factors and is represented as follows:

Positive Customer loyalty = f (CSAT, PDIFF, SBL, SPR)

Where

▸   CSAT = customer satisfaction with current and ongoing SerVAL Proposition

▸   PDIFF = clear positive differential between service provider's SerVAL Proposition and alternative suppliers and solutions

▸   SBL = strong brand loyalty

▸   SPR = strong personal relationships

The probable level of customer loyalty and the likelihood of customer retention can be measured by using a range of tools, including behavioural ones.

The behavioural tools include assessing the levels and patterns of historic expenditure levels, including the **R**ecency, **F**requency and **M**onetary value of expenditure, and the **R**ange, **B**readth and **D**epth (volume) of the service purchased. It should also include the **Length** of the relationship. They can also include "relationship assessment" tools that address key questions around the strength and depth of interpersonal relationships between the customer and the service provider. Measures of customer satisfaction, such as the **Net Promoter Score,** are covered in Chapter 12.

Performance measures can also include customer "churn" statistics, i.e. the number of customers being gained and retained.

It is important to recognise, however, that customer retention is not the same as customer loyalty.

Customer retention can be a reflection of the cost/benefits of switching, habit and the ability to switch. It is quite possible to retain customers that are not loyal because they are commercially "tied in" to a service organisation and/or they have no choice and/or the switching costs of moving are too high, relative to the benefits. However, retaining a customer that doesn't want to be retained can be costly and damaging to the organisation, generating negative word of mouth, damaging the brand and damaging employee morale.

However, whilst customer retention can be achieved by creating high switching costs, this is a tactic that, at best, should be used to delay the switching of dissatisfied customers or previously inert customers, as the service organisation seeks to rectify service failures or to re-establish relationships and/or competitive advantage. Unhappy customers who are long-term "hostages" can be very damaging.

The damage wrought by unhappy hostage customers include long-term damage due to Negative Word of Mouth and hence brand damage, negatively impacting employee morale and increasing the costs to service the customer and, thus, reducing short-term margins.

Customer retention may not be due to either providing an excellent SerVAL Proposition or by tying the customer to the service organisation. Customer inertia can also be a major source of retention, particularly where the benefits of change are unclear and the switching costs are high. The intangible nature of many services can make the benefits of such a change vague and can support customer inertia in service businesses.

It is also important to recognise that there is a "Catch 22" of customer loyalty. In industries where customers are naturally loyal or inert, a significant competitive advantage or great performance isn't required to retain customers. However, a significant advantage is required to win new customers. This may mean that the service provider needs to offer a much better SerVAL Proposition than is required to retain customers in order to win new customers. The cost and benefits of this needs to be considered. It can also make organic growth very slow.

Fundamentally, it must be recognised that, over the long-term, customer loyalty is based on both performance and the strong positive relationships that exist between people and people and brands.

CHAPTER FIFTEEN:
KEY QUESTIONS THAT SERVICE ORGANISATIONS SHOULD ASK THEMSELVES ABOUT THEIR CUSTOMERS' LOYALTY TO THEM

▶ How many customers do you have?

▶ How long have they been customers?

▶ Which of your competitors do your customers also have relationships with?

▶ What is your customer retention rate?

▶ Which customers are you losing?

▶ Why, and to whom, are you losing them?

▶ What is the rate of customer gain?

▶ Why are you winning them and from whom?

▶ How much choice do your customers have?

▶ How clear is your competitive advantage to your customers?

▶ How many of your clients are positively loyal/ retained through inertia/held captive?

▶ What are the consequences of this?

▶ How important is your brand to customer retention?

▶ How strong is the relationship your customers have with your brand?

▶ Can you increase the effectiveness of your brand in achieving customer loyalty?

▶ How important are interpersonal relationships to customer retention?

▶ How many of your employees, on average, have a relationship with each customer?

▶ How strong are the personal relationships with your customers?

▶ How can you strengthen these relationships?

▶ How satisfied are your customers?

▶ Is this changing?

▶ Are your customers' spending patterns with your organisation changing?

▶ Is your customers' relationship with your employees changing?

▶ Is your customers' relationship with your brand changing?

▶ How much of a share of wallet of your customers' wallets do you get?

▶ Is that changing?

▶ Are you delivering too much value to some of your customers in order to retain them?

▶ Are customer retention and customer loyalty increasing or decreasing?

▶ What are you going to do about it?

HOW DO YOU INCREASE THE VALUE OF A CUSTOMER?

INTRODUCTION

In Chapters 13 through to 15, we have reviewed the factors that impact the value of a customer. In this chapter, I will explore what a service organisation can do to protect or increase the value of that customer.

KEY QUESTIONS

As the value of a customer is based on the profits that are generated from the revenues received from them, and the length of the period these profits are received, plus the positive word of mouth obtained from the customer, this chapter is going to address the following questions.

▶ Is there a customer revenue cycle?

▶ How can we increase revenue from a customer?

▶ How can we increase margin from a customer?

▶ How can the length of a relationship with a customer be extended?

▶ Is extra margin more valuable than extending the length of a relationship?

▶ How can we increase positive word of mouth from a customer?

▶ How do you manage customer value?

IS THERE A CUSTOMER REVENUE CYCLE?

It is normal for the revenues that are received from a customer to vary over time. This is because the needs of individuals and organisations typically change, and can become more or less compelling over time, as their circumstances change. Furthermore, customer's budgets can also be expected to change over time, as their circumstances change. Consequently, a customer's willingness and ability to pay for a service – their demand for the service – can be expected to change across periods of time.

In addition, the duration of the Service Benefits received by the customer also vary, as Service Benefits have a life, in the same way that goods, such as washing machines do. For example, the benefits of a financial audit last for a year, a haircut for a few weeks.

The duration of a Service Benefit, therefore, creates a mini "demand cycle". The length of this cycle also depends on how discretionary and deferrable the services are – the haircut cycle might be extended from a month to two months, or to four months if longer hair becomes fashions.

The combination of changing levels of demand over time and the demand cycle can, therefore, be expected to create a variable revenue stream from a customer.

A "typical" customer revenue stream may look as follows:

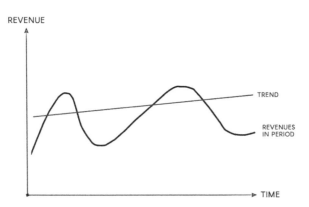

It is important to recognise that the customer revenue cycle means that any "snapshot" taken of revenue received from a customer in a particular period may not be representative in the long run, and a customer may appear more or less profitable in the short run, than they are over the long term.

It is also important to understand the drivers of these cycles, and whether they are interdependent or independent for groups of customers, as this will indicate whether the aggregate revenue for the organisation is likely to move in peaks and troughs, and/or whether it can be smoothed.

Furthermore, it is important to remember that revenues are driven by two elements, namely price and volume, when considering customer revenue streams. An assessment of customer revenue streams, therefore, requires an understanding of what is driving trends in both elements.

Between 2000 and 2007, the largest 100 law firms in the UK, increased their prices by 6% per annum, on average representing more than a 50% increase in revenues over the period driven, just by price increases. Volumes also grew, largely in parallel with GDP growth.

Such analysis will assist with forecasting, budgeting and managing organisational capacity.

HOW TO INCREASE REVENUES FROM A CUSTOMER?

The revenue from a customer can be increased in only two ways; either by increasing the price for the service (which is likely to change the SerVAL Proposition, unless additional Service Benefit or Experience is provided, or Total Cost to Customer remains the same or lower) and/or the volume of services purchased. Sometimes, can only one can be achieved at the expense of the other, so be careful and have particular regard to the impact on margin, as shown below. We have discussed pricing in Chapter 11. So, when and why will a customer buy more volume from a service organisation?

There are two ways of increasing the volume of services purchased by a customer – either by selling the customer more of the same service, and/or selling them some other service provided.

Selling more of the same service

A customer will only buy more of the same service from an organisation if:

▶   It needs more of the service; and/or

▶   It chooses to spend more of its current budget for the service with that service provider.

The first occurs when it has a CINBBADSS. In short, it needs more of the service and it can afford to buy it. This will be because the customer's circumstances have changed and/or the benefit of buying more of the service is perceived to be higher.

All things being equal, a growing business customer might be expected to have an increased demand for many of the services it purchases, and vice versa. Similarly, if we look at those services driven by "change" activities, then the businesses that are changing are likely to have an increased demand for such services, compared to those that are "stable".

The demand for the service can also increase because the service organisation has better demonstrated the benefit it will provide.

For example, if a law firm's Employment Law team can demonstrate to their clients that earlier and more frequent use of their services and better training will lead to fewer and/or less costly disputes with employees, then the demand for their services may increase.

There are additional, alternative ways to grow revenues from a customer for the same service if it decides to spend more of its existing budget on a service with a particular service organisation, instead of another one. As a result, the service organisation will increase its share of a customer's expenditure. often called the Share of Wallet, for that service.

So why does a customer start buying more from one service organisation and less from their other supplier(s)?

This occurs because:

▸ They are satisfied with the service that the increasingly favoured service organisation are already providing them with

▸ They have been buying that service from the increasingly favoured service provider for a sufficient period of time to be convinced that they will be consistently satisfied with that service

▸ They have built a relationship with the increasingly favoured service organisation and trust it.

Equally importantly:

▶ They have grown dissatisfied and/or less loyal to their other service provider(s)

▶ The benefits of switching to the favoured service organisation outweigh the costs

▶ They are psychologically prepared to change their purchasing patterns.

In short, there are push and pull factors.

THE **PUSH** AND **PULL** FACTORS OF
INCREASING SHARE OF WALLET

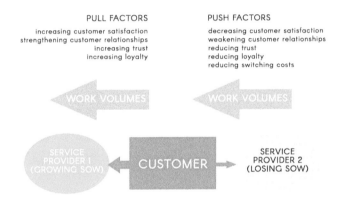

PULL FACTORS

increasing customer satisfaction
strengthening customer relationships
increasing trust
increasing loyalty

PUSH FACTORS

decreasing customer satisfaction
weakening customer relationships
reducing trust
reducing loyalty
reducing switching costs

WORK VOLUMES   WORK VOLUMES

SERVICE PROVIDER 1 (GROWING SOW)   CUSTOMER   SERVICE PROVIDER 2 (LOSING SOW)

A "force field" analysis can be done, comparing push and pull with other suppliers. Increased SOW requires a change in the balance of force. Trust is particularly important in services because of the factors that we have explored already, such as perishability, intangibility, the customer/service operative interface etc. Changing service providers is always a leap of faith from the "devil you know" who is more tangible – because of service memories – than the "devil you don't".

The time it takes to build trust will depend on a range of factors, including:

▶ The importance of the service and, hence, how much risk they are taking

▶ The tangibility of the output and the experience

▶ The frequency of use

▶ The level of customer/service operator interface;

▸ The strength of relationships

▸ The brand ("trust me, I am a doctor!)

> For example, if you get your haircut once a month, you will have a reasonable idea of how consistently good your hairdresser is after 6 months. If you use a lawyer once every year, it may take 3 or 4 years to gain an understanding of how consistent they are.
>
> If you get a bad haircut, it isn't the end of the world and may last a couple of weeks. If your house purchase or divorce is badly handled, then there can be major, long-lasting and expensive issues.

A study by Xerox Research, which I was told about at Cranfield University in 2003, indicated that very satisfied customers have a propensity six times higher than merely satisfied customers to purchase additional things from their suppliers. This reflects a much higher degree of trust. Of course, it may not be the case that this applies to all customers for all services and products, but it clearly makes a point!

Increasing the share of wallet from a customer can take time and requires a change in two relationships – between the service organisation and the customer, and the customer and another provider – as well as a psychological adjustment in spending behaviour by a customer, to put "more eggs in one basket". We have already seen that "promiscuity" is a normal purchasing behaviour for many customers.

If a customer trusts and are very satisfied with the provider they have a long-standing relationship with, but still likes to use several suppliers, are they likely to switch to one of these other service suppliers, particularly if the benefits are intangible? Service organisations, therefore, need to understand the dynamics of their customers' relationships with other suppliers, as well as their own, and make the benefits of switching very clear.

Upselling

A service organisation might also increase customer expenditure if its service has, or could have, a range of service levels, such as a bronze, silver or gold service, and then persuade a customer to move to a higher service level.

The different forms of vehicle recovery offered by roadside recovery organisations, such as the AA and RAC in the UK, are good examples of this. The basic service might just involve towing your vehicle to the nearest garage if you break down. The next level of service might also give you a lift home, and the higher level of service might include a "home start" if your vehicle won't start at home.

Banks also adopt a similar approach. They start with basic accounts and then offer higher service accounts, such as including a "built-in" overdraft facility, and a premium one that includes a personal relationship manager, and add-ons, such as free holiday insurance.

Another way to increase revenues from a customer is to expand the scope of the core Service Benefit.

For example, from having the outside of your car washed to having the inside valeted too. In our hairdressers, the customer may move from a simple cut to having their hair coloured. In the facilities services business, they may move from buying your office cleaning services to also include your window cleaning services.

From your legal practice, they may increase the scope of your property advice from rent reviews to including lease acquisitions and disposals.

Or it may include adding a supporting Service Benefit.

A good example is when a maintenance business I led added a water testing service that to its core central heating maintenance services.

For £20 the condition of the hot water system could be checked (which had a big influence on heating efficiency). This represented only a 5% increase in price on the basic maintenance service, and could be sold cheaply because the maintenance operative was already on site and working on the system.

To make money as a stand-alone service, it would need to cost several times that amount, and would not generate sufficient value to be purchased by a customer.

"Upselling", as such approaches are termed, fundamentally involves persuading the customer to purchase a different SerVAL Proposition. The new SerVAL Proposition may involve significant or marginal differences to the incumbent SerVAL Proposition. In order to achieve an "upsell" service, organisations need to consider whether:

▶ They are able to offer various "levels of service"

▶ Whether or not they can supplement their core service with "bolt on" services

▶ Whether their customers would be willing and able to buy different levels of service and pay different prices for them.

Customers will only buy the upsell if they have a need and a budget, are satisfied with the service they are getting from you, and trust your capabilities and motivation to deliver a wider service.

The ability to upsell is, therefore, a function of the following factors:

Upsell= f (CINBBADSS, delivery capabilities, CSAT, Trust,)

Upselling strategies should, therefore focus, on established customers where levels of satisfaction are high and relationships and trust are strong, and where the add-on service can generate a noticeable benefit.

Cross-selling

The second way to increase the volumes of a service purchased by a customer is if the service organisation can provide a wider range of services and it can persuade its customer to buy an additional, different service from it. This is typically termed "cross-selling".

At the hairdressers, they may also decide to try the nail manicure service and facial services. At the FM company, customers may buy building maintenance services, as well as cleaning services. At the law firm, they may expand from buying real estate services to starting to buy construction contract advice and employment law advice too.

Cross-selling will only occur, however, if the customer has a CINBBADSS for these extra services. Furthermore, it requires that they either have no current provider for these services or decide to change from an incumbent service provider to a new service provider.

And, finally, they also need to trust the alternative service organisation and perceive it to be equally capable of providing this other service as their incumbent provider and other competitors.

The conditions for a successful cross-sell can, thus, be considered as follows:

Cross-sell = f (CINBBADSS, delivery capabilities, CSAT existing service provider, relationship with existing service provider, trust, competitor strength, benefits of switching > costs of switching)

It can, therefore, be seen why cross-selling may take time to achieve, or not be achieved at all. It takes time for a customer to become very satisfied with what they are receiving from that service provider and be sure they provide a consistent level of performance; to build trust with a service provider; to be confident that they are equally capable of providing the additional service; for there to be clear benefits from switching suppliers; and being happy and prepared to switch.

In 2003, I did an informal study of organisations that were claiming cross-selling was a key element of their growth strategy. I looked at Facilities Management companies and banks, amongst others. Of those who publicly commented on how much of their business involved cross-sales, the level of achievement was around 15% of the revenues being achieved from cross-sales.

All things being equal, it is easier to sell an expanded scope of an existing service (an "upsell") compared to a "cross-sell", because the level of trust/"leap of faith" that is required is lower, and is less likely to require a switch from an incumbent service provider.

This explains why, in some markets, cross-selling can be slow for some services and is a long-term growth strategy, which can be particularly difficult where relationships are strong, such as in Professional services.

This, in part, explains why a lot of professional service firms seek to "poach" relationship holders from competitors to win new clients and/or to cross-sell more of their own services into that client.

HOW DO WE INCREASE MARGIN?

Again, this is a simple concept in principle, but it needs thought in practice. Margins will be increased if the gap between revenues and costs increases. This can be achieved either by increasing the price per "unit" of service sold; for example, raising the price of a haircut from £10 to £11, or by reducing the cost of producing the haircut. We discussed costs and efficiency in Chapter 12.

So, how can a service organisation reduce the cost of producing the haircut? This cost is fundamentally a function of how long it takes to cut the hair, the cost of the person cutting the hair, and the cost of the hair salon premises etc. So they can cut the hair quicker, and/or use a cheaper person to cut the hair, or cut the hair in less expensive premises. But what does this do to the Service Benefit and the Service Experience? It can be seen that cost reduction strategies may lead to a change in the SerVAL Proposition.

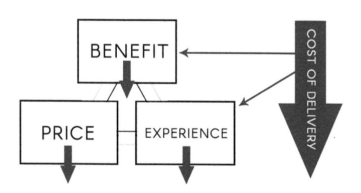

There is, therefore, a danger that cost reduction strategies also drive down prices, and hence margins, because of changes to the SerVAL Proposition.

Cost	Price	Margin	Margin %
£8	£10	£2	20%
£6	£7	£1	14.3%

Indeed, it might be that an investment in the Service Ingredients in the Service Delivery Mix leads to a SerVAL Proposition that attracts a premium price and increases margin, which is the example above in reverse.

The examples above assume a fixed price. However, some service businesses don't operate on a fixed price basis, but on a time-based/volume-based charging rate. If you use less time to undertake a service, you will receive less revenue and less margin in monetary terms.

And for some service businesses the price and cost vary, depending on the experience of the person doing the work, but not in a fixed way. In many professional service businesses, the difference between price and cost is highest for middle-ranking professionals. For example:

Grade	Fee per hour	Cost per hour *	Gross margin/hour
"Partner"	£100	£80	£20
"Associate"	£80	£50	£30
Consultant	£60	£40	£20
Trainee	£40	£25	£20

Do you want to move the work from an Associate to a Consultant?

This can also extend to where the work is performed.

It is not unusual for fee rates for professionals to be higher in some locations than others; for example, in London compared to Bristol in England. In fact, the employment cost of professionals can vary by 20% to 30% between these locations. Real estate and other overhead costs can also be much less.

But will a client continue paying "London fee rates" if the work is carried out by professionals in the firm's Bristol office? Will higher margins be earned if it is done in Bristol at Bristol fee rates, or London at London rates? Or will the client choose a competitor who will do it in Bristol anyway because they charge the Bristol rate? And what if it is moved to the Mumbai office?

There is also a potential trade between margin in % terms and volumes. It is not unusual to find in many businesses that the organisation's largest customers by volume don't generate the highest percentage margins, although they do generate the highest margins in monetary terms. This is often because they have negotiated discounts for volume, or the service organisation has been less assertive in pricing with these customers because they need the volumes to support their overheads. Be careful that you don't trade margin % for monetary margin and impact the overall viability of the organisation.

Service providers, thus need to understand how and where they generate their margins. They also need to understand there may be a margin/volume trade-off, and it can be dangerous to consider improvements for a particular customer without considering the impact on the whole organisation.

HOW DO WE INCREASE THE LENGTH OF A RELATIONSHIP?

The other way to increase Customer Lifetime Value is to extend the life of the customer relationship.

We have examined customer loyalty in Chapter Thirteen, where the key to positive customer loyalty was summarised as follows:

Positive Customer loyalty = f (CSAT, PDIFF, SBL, SPR)

Where:

▶ CSAT = satisfaction with current and ongoing SerVAL Proposition

▶ PDIFF = clear differential between the service provider and alternative suppliers and solutions

▶ SBL = strong brand loyalty

▶ SPR = strong personal relationships

Therefore, the way to increase the length of the customer relationship is to:

▶ Increase customer satisfaction

▶ Ensure the customer perceives a clear difference between the service provider's SerVAL Proposition and those of its competitors

▶ To build strong brand loyalty

▶ To build strong personal relationships between the customer and the service provider's employees

These are all driven by the Service Delivery Mix, the Service Delivery Model, the selected SerVAL Proposition, its VITAL characteristics, the effects of the Service Profit Chain and the customer perceiving that the SerVAL Proposition was delivered as they expected.

IS EXTRA MARGIN MORE VALUABLE THAN EXTENDING THE LENGTH OF A RELATIONSHIP?

Customer Lifetime Value is a product of profit margin earned in a period, and the number of periods over which it is earned. In order to increase CLV, is extra margin more valuable than a longer relationship? This is a question of mathematics, as demonstrated below.

Customer	Current situation	Increase margin by 50%	Increase relationship length by 50%
Year 1	20	20	20
Year 2	20	30	20
Year 3			20
Year 4			
Year 5			
CLV	40	50	60

Customer	Current situation	Increase margin by 50%	Increase relationship length by 50%
Year 1	20	20	20
Year 2	20	30	20
Year 3	20	30	20
Year 4	20	30	20
Year 5	20	30	20
Year 6			20
Year 7			20
Year 8			10
CLV	100	140	150

Customer	Current situation	Increase margin by 50%	Increase relationship length by 50%
NPV at 10%	£75.82	£104.63	£101.57
Year 1	20	20	20
Year 2	20	30	20
Year 3	20	30	20
Year 4	20	30	20
Year 5	20	30	20
Year 6			20
Year 7			10
Year 8			20
CLV	100	140	150

It can be seen that in the first situation – where a reasonable expectation of the length of the relationship is two years – that another year's contribution increases CLV more than just getting a higher margin in year two does. However, obtaining the higher margin in year one would make it equal.

In the second example, assuming that there is a five-year contract and the alternative is increasing margin or extending from two and a half years, then the extension is again preferable, assuming that margin increase takes place in year two. However, once the cash flows are discounted, it becomes preferable to increase the margin. Now, in the real world, is it likely that margins can be increased by high percentages?

Well, that depends! If they are very low, possibly. If the margins are reasonably competitive, then it is less likely, unless the organisation is very inefficient. This means in practice that an extra years' relationship is likely to create more value.

Clearly, what a combination of higher margin and a longer relationship is better. However, this is a somewhat academic exercise because it is extremely rare for there to be a binary situation of "increasing margin" or "increasing length of relationship".

The analysis is more useful to demonstrate that a short-term push for profits, if it jeopardises customer relationships, is likely to destroy value. Conversely, assuming there is a reasonable financial contribution from a customer, then developing long-term relationships with customers creates value.

HOW CAN YOU INCREASE THE POSITIVE WORD OF MOUTH FROM A CUSTOMER?

In Chapter 13, we identified that "positive word of mouth" from customers is an additional source of value to the organisation. This is because it may directly lead to other customers to choose the organisation as its service provider. In addition, it will generally build and/or reinforce the firm's reputation and brand, which as we discussed in Chapter 2, are important parts of the Service Experience and the psychological benefit delivered to customers.

So how does a service provider increase the "PWOM" that it receives from its customers? Again, this is relatively simple:

▶   It increases the number of its customers whose satisfaction and loyalty to the organisation is high and

▶   It encourages more of these customers to provide PWOM.

It can start this latter process by asking customers for references, quotes and whether the service provider can use their brand on its marketing literature etc. It can assist them to do this, as many customers are busy and cannot or will not spend a lot of time doing this. It can also think how new media can assist with this, such as short videos, tweets, Facebook page, etc. This might be considered a relatively "passive" advocacy of the service organisation by the customer.

The service organisation can make this advocacy more proactive by inviting customers to speak at industry seminars etc, where the audience might include other customers and potential customers, and other members of the service organisation's and customer's own human networks. It can take this further by having "customer clubs" and "customer conferences".

It might also consider rewarding them for introductions to new customers. A lot of business-to- consumer service organisations do this – ranging from large corporations, such as satellite TV firms, to local businesses, such as hair salons.

It is much more likely that a customer will allow themselves to be referenced and generate PWOM to their human network, and through social media, after the service provider has supplied them for some time, and they trust that the service provider is reliable and consistent in its delivery of the SerVAL Proposition, and are thus confident in allowing their name to endorse the service.

This isn't rocket science. It is about recognising that loyal customers are an asset and this asset can be utilised proactively.

HOW DO YOU MANAGE CUSTOMER VALUE?

In order to effectively manage and increase customer value, a service organisation thus needs to have a good understanding of the following matters:

- ▶ The customer's needs and budgets for the service(s) they can provide, and how these are changing
- ▶ How much share of customer wallet they have, and how much their competitors' have
- ▶ How satisfied the customer is with their service and their competitors' services
- ▶ The degree of loyalty and trust the customer has with them, and with their competitors
- ▶ The customer's preferred and evolving buying behaviours
- ▶ The level of financial contribution that the customer is making to the service organisation
- ▶ The key drivers of this financial contribution
- ▶ The ability to increase prices, increase volumes and/or manage costs, and the implications for customer margin and potential length of relationship with the customer
- ▶ The overall contribution the customer makes to the financial performance and value of the service organisation – that is the context of the customer to the organisation
- ▶ How best to obtain and use PWOM from this customer.

Service organisations, therefore, need to research, investigate, analyse and understand their customers, plan how to respond to their findings and act upon them.

In short, they need to proactively manage the customer as a key asset of the organisation.

SUMMARY

The value of a customer can be expected to fluctuate across different time periods, reflecting changing needs and budgets, and the service lifecycle. So any given snapshot of customer value is unlikely to be representative of long-term value. Customer value analysis should, therefore, be undertaken, looking at longer-term trends.

The lifetime value of a customer can be grown through:

▶ Increasing revenues relative to those currently forecast by:

    o Selling more volume:

       • Of the same service

       • Of an "upgraded" service

       • Of "add-on" services

       • Of different services

    o Increasing prices

    o A combination of the two

▶ Increasing margins:

    o Increasing prices

    o Reducing cost relative to the price

    o Gaining volumes to spread overheads further

▶ Proactively obtaining and using Positive Word of Mouth

▶ Developing long-term customer loyalty and extending relationships.

It should be noted that price increases, if not accompanied by reductions in the Total Cost to Customer, will result in a different SerVAL Proposition.

Most of the revenue increasing options, other than selling more volume of the same service, involve selling a different SerVAL Proposition to the customer.

This revenue growth, whether through offering more of the same SerVAL Proposition or different SerVAL Propositions, can only occur:

▶ When the customer's needs and budget increase and/or

▶ Through winning additional share of the customer's wallet and/or

▶ Potentially, making the benefits of the service more apparent, so that the customer switches expenditure from elsewhere to buy more of this service.

It should also be noted that when reducing costs the service organisation must be mindful that this may materially change the Service Benefit and/or the Service Experience, which may, in turn, lead to a reduction in price and thereby decrease margins. Again, the result may be a different lower margin SerVAL Proposition.

All of this requires the service provider to have:

▶ In-depth knowledge of the customer and their other suppliers (the service organisation's competitors)

▶ A clear differential of its services from those of the competitors

▶ Clearly demonstrable, pertinent, benefits that are obtained from using the service

▶ Customer satisfaction and loyalty

▶ An understanding of the drivers of margin in the market and within the service organisation.

Or good fortune in a rising market.

CHAPTER SIXTEEN:
KEY QUESTIONS THAT SERVICE ORGANISATIONS
SHOULD ASK THEMSELVES ABOUT HOW TO INCREASE
THE VALUE OF THEIR CUSTOMERS

▶ Do you know the current expected client time value of
your customers?

▶ Can you measure revenues by the service type and
individual item for each customer?

▶ Do you know the expenditure cycles of your customers?

▶ Do you know your customers' budget for your services?

▶ Do you know what is going to happen to that budget
over the coming time periods?

▶ Do you know how much of that budget is spent with
your organisation?

▶ Do you know how much of that budget is spent with
competitor organisations and who they are?

▶ Do you have the opportunity to offer "different levels"
of service to your customers?

▶ If so, how many of your customers are receiving and
paying for each level?

▶ Which of your customers may benefit from receiving a
different level of service?

▶ Can you add "bolt-on" services to your core service
to deliver more value to your customers and create
more margin, and greater differentiation for your
organisation?

▶ Have you other services that you do offer, or could
offer, that your customer may want to buy, where you
can offer a compelling value proposition?

▶ Do you know the financial contribution (margin) that
each customer makes to your organisation?

▶ Have you identified well thought through margin
growth strategies for your customers (that include
price, volumes and costs)?

- Do you understand how cost reduction might impact the price that customers will pay for your service?

- Do you know how satisfied each of your customers is with your services?

- Do you know how satisfied each of your customers is with your competitors services?

- Do you know how much your customers trust you and how loyal they are?

- Do you know how much your customers trust your competing suppliers and how loyal they are to them?

- Do you know your customers' purchasing behaviours and preferences regarding the number of suppliers they want to use?

CHAPTER 17

A BETTER UNDERSTANDING OF SERVICE SUCCESS

INTRODUCTION

I started this book with the stated objective of trying to develop for myself, and provide others with, a basic practical framework for gaining a better understanding of how to make service organisations more successful.

In doing so, I wanted also to identify how best to avoid the pitfalls that many, including myself, appear to have made along their journey to service success or failure.

To achieve this, I have drawn upon my own very broad experience of leading, managing, advising, serving and observing service organisations.

I have also applied the knowledge and insight that I have gained from studying leading models of service theory and (like all of us) from my experience as a customer of many types of service organisation.

Chapter by chapter, I have built this framework and explored the detail behind it. I have approached this through highlighting and addressing the questions which I consider to be key to the issues covered in that chapter, although no doubt I have missed a few questions too!

This final chapter provides an overview of the key concepts covered, so far and concludes with a diagrammatic framework showing how they all link inextricably together – which is the core message!

I believe that failure to consider services and planned, or

unplanned, changes to services in a holistic manner is likely to cause, and indeed has caused, significant issues for service organisations.

I would go as far to say that all these concepts are so closely interlinked that they are, in reality, inseparable.

KEY QUESTIONS

I am going to summarise the framework by considering the following key questions:

▶   What is a service?

▶   Why do people buy a service (or not)?

▶   Who is the customer?

▶   How to create a service?

▶   How do customers assess a service?

▶   How much does it cost to produce a service?

▶   What is a customer worth?

▶   How to measure customer performance?

▶   How much more successful can your service organisation be?

WHAT IS A SERVICE?

The starting point of the analysis was to define what is meant by a "service", because the rest of the understanding follows from there. I believe that a good way to define a service is as follows:

▶   *A service is an activity performed by an individual or an organisation ("the service provider") for an individual or an organisation ("the customer") that provides that customer with some form of benefit and an experience, typically for a price.*

▶   *The generation of the Service Benefit and Service Experience usually involves a combination of ingredients, including people, processes & systems, marketing and other communication materials, ICT and internet, knowledge and intellectual property, tools & equipment, and real estate. This is the Service Delivery Mix, which is bound together through a Service Delivery Model.*

▶ *Creation of the service is often simultaneous with its consumption, and, compared to manufacturing of goods, typically involves relatively high levels of interaction between the service provider and the customer.*

▶ *Services tend to have a number of characteristics that differentiate them from "goods", including relative intangibility and perishability, and they tend to demonstrate relatively high levels of unplanned variability.*

▶ *The Benefits received by the customer of a service can be thought of as potentially comprising three parts. Firstly, a "core" Benefit, i.e. the reason they actually want the service. Secondly, "enhancing" or "extra" benefit(s). And thirdly, a psychological benefit. In some cases, the psychological benefit is the same as the core benefit. Often the psychological benefit is derived from the service organisation's brand. The psychological benefit is also often closely related to elements of the Service Experience. The brand might be seen as a "wrapper" for the service.*

The Service Experience received by the customer can also be broken down into several parts. There is the basic experience that arises from the core activities that are required to deliver the Service Benefit. I have termed this the "Enabling" Experience. Then there are those experiences provided to make the overall Service Experience better for customers. For example, providing a cup of coffee at a car dealer or at a hairdresser. I call these the "Enhancing" Experience(s).

Service organisations also need to consider that there are elements of their Service Experience that they don't directly provide or control. These are the experiences that the customer has in order to procure the service, and those that follow receipt of the service. I call these the pre- and post-service experiences.

A simple example is the experience of being stuck in traffic and trying to find a parking space when going to and from a retail outlet. An internet-based retail experience doesn't involve this, and these experiences can be the key reason for choosing, or not choosing, to buy the service from that service organisation.

I have also concluded that it is not sufficient to end the definition of a service as something that provides a Service Benefit and Service Experience, because this ignores the reality of how customers judge whether a service is good, bad or indifferent, or even if they want it in the first place. The price that they pay for the service provides a key context for the Service Benefit and Service Experience. This is the "value for money" part of the relationship. A relationship that can be termed the "Service Value Equation".

This equation doesn't just involve a trade-off between Service Benefit and Service Experience versus Price. In practice, customers also accept a degree of trade-off between the Service Benefit and the Service Experience they require.

However, whilst a reasonable Benefit with a poor Experience may be tolerated – depending on the price paid and the competitors' offerings – a reasonable Experience with a poor Benefit will not be!

The Direct Price that a customer is willing to pay for the Service Benefit and Service Experience will depend on five factors:

▶ The level of Benefit and the Experience received.

▶ The price that other service providers will charge for providing the same, or similar Benefit and/or Experience.

▶ The cost of alternative service solutions, such as doing it themselves.

▶ The costs of switching to and from suppliers.

▶ Their available budget.

In short, demand and supply.

As with the Service Benefit and Service Experience, a detailed consideration of the price paid by a customer for a service, as well as examples provided to me by others, indicate that the actual price paid by customers for a service is greater and more complex than just the "Direct" price they pay to the service organisation.

Just as there are pre and post-service Experiences, there are also costs of procuring the service, such as travel costs in the example above. There are also the non-monetary costs of this, which I have termed the "convenience factor". Again the travel and parking example above illustrate that well.

As well as the psychological benefit received from a service there can also be a psychological cost for using one. For example, switching from one service provider a customer has used a lot to a new one, who they know only by reputation. There may also be actual switching costs associated with moving from one service provider to another.

And finally, like all activities, there is the opportunity cost of the activity. One striking example of the importance of the opportunity cost was given to me by a social care organisation. It involved the father who wouldn't bring his child to therapy, because he would rather be doing something else.

The retail example above is another good example. The opportunity cost of the time spent travelling and walking between shops when the alternative was shopping at home over the internet, whilst watching sport or a soap on TV!

Altogether, these might be considered the "price bundle", or what I have termed the Total Cost to Customer.

The individual Service Value Equation provided by a service organisation can be considered, as its chosen (deliberately or otherwise!) value proposition to its (targeted or otherwise!) customers. I have termed this its SerVAL Proposition, which can be represented thus:

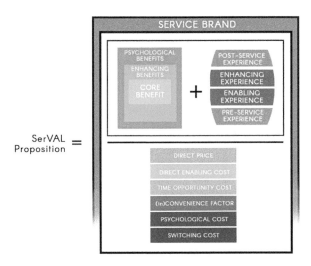

WHY DO PEOPLE BUY A SERVICE (OR NOT)?

Customers buy services and goods because they have a need. That may be a need they derive themselves, or a need that is created for them by a third party, such as lawmakers and regulators, or a need that the service provider "creates" for them. Needs might be considered as comprising basic needs, such as food and shelter, distress needs, such as the need for a broken heating system to be mended quickly in the winter, and discretionary needs, i.e. the "nice to haves".

For a customer to seek to satisfy their need, it must be a compelling need, relative to all their other needs. For example, who needs their nails glossed when they haven't got any food? And they need to have a budget to pay for it. Hence, basic needs get addressed before discretionary needs.

For service providers, this means that meeting the need must be affordable for the customer, both in absolute terms, i.e. have they got to have enough money to pay for it. And in relative terms, i.e. they prefer to afford it, compared to something else. No one has a limitless budget, so all expenditure involves a degree of choice. Every sale is competing for a share of someone's wallet.

That need also needs to be immediate, and the budget immediate or else the purchase can be, or needs to be, deferred. In summary, for someone to buy a service, they must have a Compelling, Immediate, Need and a Budget. The service provider's solution must also be preferred by the customer to alternative means of obtaining the benefit ("substitutes"). For example, the customer may decide to "do it themselves". It must also be preferable to the SerVAL Proposition provided by the service organisation's competitors. In summary, a service provider's SerVAL Proposition must be Better than Alternative Delivery Solutions, and consider Switching costs.

It is thus key for service organisations, when seeking to assess the potential volume, frequency and value of demand for its SerVAL Proposition, to think CINBBADSS the seller (sic!).

WHO IS THE CUSTOMER?

There are three parts to this question.

Firstly, and obviously, it is necessary to understand who might buy the service and who the service organisation are trying to sell it to. That derives from the customer's need, the benefit it provides and their ability to pay. The CINBBADSS discussed above.

Secondly, it comes from segmenting the market to understand who is willing and able to purchase the particular combination of Service Benefit, Service Experience and Price that the service organisation is offering, i.e. the customers for that particular SerVAL Proposition.

And thirdly, it involves understanding that in many cases there is not a single customer for each particular SerVAL Proposition delivered. For example, the person or organisation paying for the service may be different from the person(s) experiencing it or gaining the benefit from it. Whilst this tends to be the rule for business-to-business services, it is also typically the case for public services, and is often the case for business-to-consumer services. A simple example of the latter would be the parent paying for a service for their child. A group of "customer stakeholders" is, therefore, not unusual.

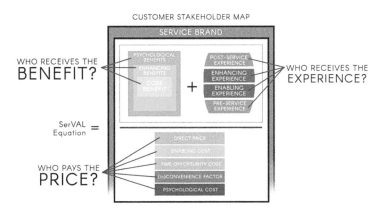

HOW TO CREATE A SERVICE?

All services are created from a common range of ingredients, which are People, Processes & Systems, Real Estate, Tools & Equipment, Communication materials, Intellectual Property & Knowledge, ICT and the Internet, and Brand. These ingredients can be mixed together in a wide range of permutations, which I have termed the Service Delivery Mix. The chosen mix is one potential source of differentiation and thus a competitive advantage.

Each of these ingredients has an impact, both individually and combined together, on the Service Benefit and Service Experience, as well as on the cost of service delivery. The latter is a reflection of the raw costs of the individual ingredients, and also how the combination of them influences their productivity and, hence, the unit costs of service delivery.

The chosen Service Delivery Mix is deployed using a service delivery system, of which there are a number of types, which can be termed the Service Delivery Model. These tend to be categorised based around the following characteristics.

▶ Degree of customer contact.

▶ Nature of relationship with customers:

  • Continuous delivery of service

  • Discrete transactions

  • Formal relationship (membership, contracts)

  • Informal relationships (public transport, mail, radio)

▶ Where the service is delivered:

  • A customer comes to service deliverer

  • Service deliverer comes to the customer

  • Arm's length delivery (e.g. through the web)

▶ The nature of demand compared to supply.

▶ Level of customisation.

▶ Level of labour intensity.

▶ The level of judgment exercised by, and operational flexibility given to, the service deliverer.

The improvement and developments in ICT and the internet over the past few years have provided the biggest change in the potential ingredients in a service for many decades, and have enabled better or new Service Delivery Models.

The Service Delivery Model selected by the service organisation (inadvertently or otherwise!) will have a major influence on the Service Delivery Mix required. For example, if the model requires high levels of interpersonal contact, then that will require a certain type and number of people in the Mix. The selected model will also have a major influence on the nature of the Service Benefit and Service Experience produced.

A key consideration in any service is how important people are indirectly creating the Service Benefit and Service Experience. The more important they are in the Service Delivery Model and Service Delivery Mix, the more important, their Performance, behaviours, Productivity and Loyalty are for the customer and to the service organisation.

The nature of this relationship is set out in the Service-Profit chain model. My modified version of this is set out below.

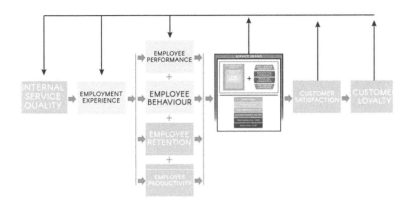

The typical characteristics of a service, namely intangibility, variability, perishability, simultaneous production/consumption, and close involvement of the customer with the service provider, reflect a combination of the Service Delivery Mix, Service Delivery Model, the effects of the Service-Profit chain, and also the nature of the Service Benefit and Service Experience being provided.

The importance of these characteristics is that they impact how easy it is to sell the service, as it is generally harder to sell more intangible services. The SerVAL Proposition is weaker because the CINBBADS are less clear.

These characteristics also affect how customers assess the service they perceive they have received, with customers generally disliking unplanned variability and perishability making it hard to demonstrate that the service has been received and/or difficult for the customer to remember what it was like.

The importance of these characteristics of a service means that they might, therefore, be considered the VITAL characteristics of a Service.

▶   **V** ariability of the service

▶   **I** nvolvement of customer with production of the service

▶   **T** angibility of the service

▶   **A** ttainment of the service benefit, experience or price

▶   **L** asting service benefit or experience or price?

HOW DO CUSTOMERS ASSESS A SERVICE?

Customers will assess the SerVAL Proposition that they perceive they have received compared to the one they expected to receive. A key measure of customer success is a positive Net Promoter score. This basically means that they would be willing to recommend the service and service provider to friends, family, colleagues and other third parties.

The SerVAL Proposition that customers expect to receive will depend on their memory of what they have received before from the service organisation (their "service memory") and from what other people have explicitly or implicitly told them they will receive from the service organisation ("word of mouth"). It will also come from their experience of receiving a similar service from other service organisations, and from what those other service organisations explicitly or implicitly say they will deliver. And, of course, from what the service organisation itself has explicitly or implicitly told them that they will receive.

As part of their evaluation, customers will try to assess what Service Benefit they have received. This can be difficult when the Benefit is intangible, perishable, deferred or preventative, or are part of a "moveable feast". For example, services providing energy cost savings for buildings are dependent on a range of factors outside the service provider's control, such as the way the building is used, the weather, the price of energy, the way that the heating systems are maintained, who uses the temperature control etc.

They will also assess the Service Experience they have received, and sometimes this is easier to assess, and therefore has greater focus, than the Service Benefit. Typically, customers will consider the Reliability, Assurance, Tangible, Empathy, and Responsiveness of a service organisation, with these performance metrics varying in importance for different services and different customer groups. Customers will also consider whether they trust the motives of the service provider in providing them with the service. The large number of "mis-selling" issues in financial services provide good examples of where customer trust has been abused and lost. Customers will assess price in terms of what they actually paid against what they had budgeted to pay, and this includes all elements of the Total Cost to Customer. For example, I never expected to spend 3 hours in the traffic to get to the retail outlet, only 30 minutes. I didn't realise it would be that difficult to park and got lost, as I am much more comfortable driving to where I usually shop.

Finally, customers also like to consider whether they get a "good" "deal" on the Direct Price. And, remember, there are often a number of different customer stakeholders receiving and/or paying for the SerVAL Proposition, not a single person, so how well is it meeting the needs of all of them?

The key outcome of service delivery is to win and retain the loyalty of profitable customers.

HOW MUCH DOES IT COST TO PRODUCE THE SERVICE?

In order to understand how profitable a customer is, it is necessary to understand how much it costs to produce a service. The cost of production for services is a function of the raw costs of the service ingredients in the Service Delivery Mix, and their productivity, which shapes the unit costs of production. The raw costs of production are fundamentally a reflection of supply and demand for that ingredient, and hence local markets/geographic location can have a major influence on the cost of the ingredient. By way of example, a reason for a lot of outsourcing and "offshoring" by service organisations in the USA and Western Europe has been to access lower labour costs in countries, such as India.

The productivity of the service ingredients, and in particular the people involved, is in part, a reflection of the Service Delivery Mix, and how each ingredient can enhance or restrict the productivity of another. For example, having the right tools and equipment can assist labour productivity. Or more productive equipment can replace labour. The other key drivers of productivity, as far as people are concerned, are having the right skills, experience and motivation to perform.

The right skills come from recruiting people who already have those skills and/or their ongoing learning and development within the organisation. Furthermore, all things being equal, the more experience that the person has, then the more productive they will be, up to a point. That point will vary, depending on the experience curve for individual services. Employee motivation is also key to employee productivity, as well as employee behaviours. Motivation is thus the key to overall service performance. It is quite possible for a very skilled, experienced employee with all the right tools and equipment to deliver poor performance or behave in an inappropriate manner. Hence, the importance of the Service-Profit chain concept.

The Service/Profit chain effect can also lead to an "efficiency trap", where service organisations who are seeking greater efficiency and less variability through the use of standardised processes in the Service Delivery Mix can de-motivate employees. Any such de-motivation can be expected to have a knock-on effect on performance and behaviour. This, in turn, impacts the Service Experience and possibly the Service Benefit, and thus can create a different SerVAL Proposition. This, in turn, may attract a lower direct price for the service, and hence may eliminate any desired increase in margin being sought through the efficiency initiative. It may also lead to a loss of customers. The productivity of service ingredients is also a reflection of the Service Delivery Model, and in particular, whether bespoke or standardised services are being produced. The bespoke production of anything – goods or services – can be expected to be less efficient than mass production. The Service Delivery Model also impacts productivity in another way. That is the level of customer, or other third party, involvement in the service delivery process. Generally, the greater the level of customer/third party involvement in the service delivery process, other than in "self service" models, the lower the relative productivity of the Service Delivery Mix, as customers "interfere" with the processes and cause delays; just think about the person in front of you (it is never you!) in the Post Office queue!

Finally, when considering the costs producing and delivering the SerVAL Proposition, it is also important to seek to understand, as far as possible, the levels of cost associated with producing the Service Benefit and those associated with producing the Service Experience, as well as how these two elements impact the Direct Price. In short, where and how does the service organisation add the most value and make most margin? Service Benefit or Service Experience?

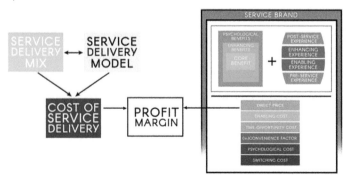

WHAT IS A CUSTOMER WORTH?

Having gained an understanding of how much it costs to deliver a given SerVAL Proposition, it is also important to evaluate whether, in fact, it is economically sustainable, and otherwise attractive, for the service provider to deliver such. This involves assessing what a customer is worth – that is the value it brings to a service organisation.

Fundamentally, a customer brings two sources of value to a service organisation – cash flow and reputation enhancement.

The former represents a combination of the periodic positive cash margin generated from the customer, and the number of periods over which this cash margin is delivered. This is often termed Customer Lifetime Value.

Customer	Current situation	Increase margin by 50%	Increase relationship length by 50%
NPV at 10%	£75.82	£104.63	£101.57
Year 1	20	20	20
Year 2	20	30	20
Year 3	20	30	20
Year 4	20	30	20
Year 5	20	30	20
Year 6			20
Year 7			10
Year 8			20
CLV	100	140	150

In simple terms, the cash margin is generally the direct price, less the cost of producing the service when paid.

The direct price a customer will pay for the service will reflect the level of Service Benefit and quality of Service Experience being delivered and the customer's CINBBADSS. In short, supply and demand.

It should be noted that for in-house service organisations, not-for-profit organisations or public services, the cash margin may be nil. This is sustainable. Where it becomes negative, then it is not sustainable. That is one of the challenges being faced by public services in many western European economies, where the organisations are being run at a deficit, funded through government borrowing.

Customer Lifetime Value is best increased through increasing Customer Loyalty and, thus, extending the number of periods over which the cash margin is received. That is largely a reflection of mathematics. The exception can be where a service organisation is earning exceptionally low margins from a customer with significant opportunity to increase them, and/or where very short-term customer relationships are the norm.

Reputational value is the value that a customer creates in terms of the positive word of mouth. They proactively spread in the market about the service organisation, or which the service organisation spreads on their behalf, by referencing them in marketing communications. This leads to positive brand development and enforcement, which in turn reduces some of the intangibility of the service and the service provider. It can also lead to direct referral of new customers. Equally, negative word of mouth from customers can destroy organisational value.

HOW TO MEASURE CUSTOMER PERFORMANCE?

Many service organisations claim to put customers at the centre of their organisation. Even assuming that this is true, is that the right thing to do? In simple terms, any service organisation, given unlimited budgets and resources, should be able to deliver excellent customer service. But that isn't the real world. It isn't sustainable.

Such a service organisation is providing too much value to the customer.

Equally, in the short term, any service organisation can maximise its margins/minimise its budgets to deliver a service by reducing the quantity and/or quality of resources in its Service Delivery Mix, and/or by not totally meeting customer's expectations. But that will lead to customers leaving, telling others about the poor quality service they have received, damaging the Brand, asking for their money back and/or not paying, litigation etc. So that isn't sustainable either.

Such a service organisation is extracting too much value from the customer.

A sustainable service organisation, therefore, needs to deliver, and be perceived to deliver, the SerVAL Proposition that its customers need, expect, can afford and will choose ahead of alternative delivery solutions/competitors' offerings, and which, in turn, provides an appropriate level of value to the service organisation's providers of capital, without running out of cash.

In short, there needs to be a balanced exchange of value between the service provider and service customer.

Service organisations, therefore, need to put Customer Value at the centre of their organisation, not customers. By which I mean achieving a sustainable balance between the value created for customers and the value created from customers.

HOW MUCH MORE SUCCESSFUL CAN YOUR SERVICE ORGANISATION BE?

To be (even) more successful your service organisation needs to deliver more value and extract more value, in a balanced way to, and from, its current and potential customers.

It also needs to clearly communicate and demonstrate to the customer the superior value it is creating for them, relative to that created by its competitors and relative to the alternative service delivery solutions available to the customer.

The answers to how it can achieve this will come from:

▶   The organisation itself

▶   Its current and potential customers

▶   Its competitors

The questions that can help to generate these answers include many, if not all, of those raised in this book. No doubt you will raise others too.

But remember that the success, or otherwise, of the service organisation will be based on considering the demand for the service, the service creation and delivery process in an integrated, holistic manner, as shown below.

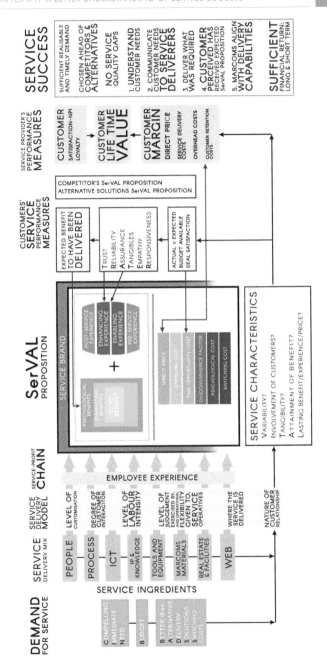

CONTACTING THE AUTHOR

The author can be contacted at
andrewmanning@professionalservicemanagement.com

Website addresses:
http://www.servalproposition.com